David Merron was born in London's East End and evacuated as a wartime child to the countryside. After National Service, he spent fifteen years as a member of a kibbutz in Israel, during which time he began to write short stories and anecdotal accounts of kibbutz life. He continued to write on his return to England, including short stories and articles for magazines. Having participated in an MA writing programme and in several writers' groups, he has written and self-published two novels and a short-story collection. He holds a master's degree from UCL and lives in North London. For more information visit www.davidmerron.com.

D1114326

www.**transworldbooks**.co.uk

Goodbye East End

AN EVACUEE'S STORY

DAVID MERRON

CORGI BOOKS

TRANSWORLD PUBLISHERS
61–63 Uxbridge Road, London W5 5SA
www.transworldbooks.co.uk

Transworld is part of the Penguin Random House group of companies
whose addresses can be found at global.penguinrandomhouse.com

Penguin
Random House
UK

First published in Great Britain in 2015 by Corgi Books
an imprint of Transworld Publishers

A CIP catalogue record for this book
is available from the British Library.

ISBN
9780552171472

Typeset in 11/14pt AGaramond by Falcon Oast Graphic Art Ltd.
Printed and bound by Clays Ltd, Elcograf S.p.A

Penguin Random House is committed to a sustainable
future for our business, our readers and our planet. This book is made from Forest
Stewardship Council® certified paper.

MIX
Paper from
responsible sources
FSC® C018179

5 7 9 10 8 6 4

Contents

With thanks to all those people who, during the Second World War, opened their homes and shared their family life with strange and sometimes awkward children from the cities.

Prologue

The all-clear sounded at daylight. In the shelter it was dark when Mum woke me. Rubbing sleep from my eyes, and still shaken from our midnight flight through the bombs and flames, I clutched her hand tightly as we climbed the metal stairs and emerged into an acrid smell of charred wood and burning oil and rubber.

Splintered glass and white ash carpeted Commercial Street. Trolleybus wires dangled loose across the road. Smoke hung everywhere in the air, while steam rose from doused, smouldering shops. At Gardiner's Corner sodden suits, shirts and underwear, blasted out from the Fifty Shilling Tailors where Dad had bought his suit, lay strewn across the pavement. I cringed as we passed: they looked like crumpled bodies.

By Aldgate East station we stopped for a moment. Mum glanced down at me, her face grey, eyes bloodshot and hair tied up in Uncle Barney's maroon silk scarf.

'We're going straight back to the country, David,' she quavered. 'We'll just go to the old house first. Some of your clothes are still there and you can change. You can't go back looking like that!' My jacket and short trousers were creased and soot-streaked.

At the corner of Great Alie Street, firemen directed their hoses onto a pile of smoking rubble. A chrome and black counter-top stuck up like a crumpled aeroplane wing. That was all that remained of old Max's fish-and-chip shop, where we used to buy a ha'porth of chips and a penny gherkin. One of the men wiped his smoke-blackened face and nodded at Mum.

'Don't think they'll be fryin' tonight, Missus,' he quipped, with a faint smile.

Walking down St Mark's Street, I wondered whether our house was still safe. Although it was near the docks, it had escaped damage so far. But as we turned the corner, I saw that our luck had run out. Only the first two houses on our road had escaped. Our own outside walls were intact but through the empty doorway I could see the wet, charred remains of floorboards, ceiling laths and roof timbers.

At the far corner of the street, three firemen were rolling up canvas hoses. One took off his helmet and looked at Mum, his bald head glistening with sweat.

'Sorry, love. No chance. Caught a bread basket, this lot did.' The 'bread basket' was a parachuted pannier of incendiary bombs that spilled out close to the ground to concentrate them. He glanced down at the hoses. 'And we ran dry. Everyone did. Didn't have a chance, luv,' he said again.

As well as ours, the Rowsteins' corner house had gone and Shirley's next door was burned out, too. She had been my playmate for as long as I could remember – Shirley with

her long, fair ringlets, singing 'On the good ship *Lollipop* ...'
Now she would have to move away as well.

I looked up at Mum. She stood with one hand to her
cheek, staring in through our open doorway. Everything that
wasn't burned was soaked or covered with soot. A corner
of a *Film Fun* comic was stuck to the passage skirting-board.
At least I had a new home – and a billet in the country. We
were lucky. If Dad hadn't got that van last week and brought
the rest of our furniture ...

Mum was crying silently. 'Come. There's nothing for us
here, David,' she murmured, casting one last look at what
had been her family home since the end of the First World
War. She tugged at my hand. 'Let's get to the station. I'm
taking you straight back to the village.'

As we turned and walked back up the street I began to
feel better. Going back. To Mrs Baker and Frank and the long
garden. Back to the country ...

Chapter 1

September 1939

Evacuation. It was a new word. One I had had to learn quickly. At eight years old I vaguely understood that it meant being sent away somewhere with my school but without my family. What I could not anticipate, though, were the changes it would bring to me personally – and, no doubt, to anyone else who went through the experience.

Before September 1939, my world was bounded by the four Tenter Streets that formed a tight, dense corner of London's East End. They were probably named after a medieval 'tenter field', where weavers spread their washed cloth to dry and bleach. The area was a square of three-up, two-down and backyard-loo Victorian terraces, of smoke-blackened brick and grey slate roofs. The abrupt plunge into a vividly green early-autumn countryside and wide blue skies made an indelible impression that persists to this day and shaped much of my life.

My childhood until then was that of the East End Jewish community, of first- and second-generation immigrants who had fled the pogroms and persecutions of Tsarist Russia from the end of the nineteenth century until the First World War. It ranged from deeply traditional grandparents, who spoke only Yiddish, to those born in London and already almost indistinguishable from the general population. For me and my friends, our parents worked mainly in tailoring, cabinet-making and shopkeeping, or had stalls down Petticoat Lane – the famous clothing market – the younger ones branching out into offices and commerce, still understanding Yiddish yet speaking only English.

My dad, Jack Malina, was a ladies' tailor, not very tall but well built and with a blue chin despite frequent shaving. Born in a *shtetl* – a Russian village with a mostly Jewish population – his worldview remained somewhere between Brest Litovsk and Whitechapel. He was only fourteen when his father died and had made his own way across Europe, a boat ticket from Bremen to London sewn into the lining of his coat, to join his older brother. He arrived a couple of years before the First World War began, and in 1917 was conscripted into the army. He spent almost two traumatic years in Flanders.

Dad was more familiar with Yiddish than English and that language permeated our everyday life. When I was first evacuated, I hesitated to ask my foster-parents for a bowl as I knew it only as a *shissel*.

Shortly after his release from the army he had married my mother – quite a beauty from their wedding photographs. One of a large family, Mum had been born in the East End and had had a good schooling. She was an avid reader, getting through many of the latest novels, borrowed from the Whitechapel Library. As she bustled around the kitchen, she sang 'We'll Gather Lilacs' and other songs from thirties musicals. Now, like most working-class women in the East End, she had a lined face and hennaed her greying hair.

Jewish immigrants had brought over their religious tradition and practice and, of course, the synagogue. We spent Friday nights and Saturday mornings in prayer, and celebrated all the festivals and holy days. At the end of each service a stream of chattering worshippers flowed down Alie Street and St Mark's Street and into the small houses for supper or lunch while, on the way, news of deaths, marriages and births – in that order – was relayed and commented upon. Everyone had an opinion.

Meanwhile, we youngsters would pull at our parents' hands, just wanting to get home and eat. We'd waited all through the long service to get out to play or go home for a meal. Of course, Friday nights meant a smashing supper but Friday also meant no lights, no wireless, no writing or drawing, and the endless Sabbath ennui.

For me, there were only two bright spots in our religious practice. The first was the few minutes on Friday night in the synagogue when all the young children gathered on the rostrum under a huge prayer shawl to take a sip of the sweet red *kosher* wine from Palestine. As the silver goblet was passed round, we all tried to hold it longer against our lips to drink more, but the *shamash* – the beadle – was up to our tricks: he would snatch it away and move it on to the next. The second bright spot came during the annual Celebration of the Law, when the women, who occupied a balcony above the main hall, would throw down sugared almonds for the kids to scramble about and pick up. Sadly, neither made up for the tedious synagogue hours.

Unlike my older brother and sister, Arnold and Rita, I resented being shut away in a stuffy hall to mumble prayers I didn't understand, while my friends from less devout families played outside.

Mum was a great cook and our Friday-night meal would usually consist of her fried fish and chicken soup with matzo balls. Saturday lunch was often *choulent* – a special stew. We weren't allowed to cook on the Sabbath so on Friday afternoons my brother and I often took a large blue saucepan of *choulent*, tied at the top with a clean white tea-towel, to the baker's. Mr Cohen didn't bake on the Sabbath but his oven remained hot, so many families in the neighbourhood brought their *choulent* pot, paid a few pennies and left it to cook overnight.

On Saturday, after morning synagogue, Rita and I would go to collect it; girls and children were allowed to carry on the Sabbath. All the way home, my mouth watered at the smell. I couldn't wait to get my teeth into the meat and the chewy dumplings. One of the first things that struck me when I arrived at my country billet was the unfamiliar smells coming from the kitchen – especially that of bacon frying.

Every so often after Friday-night synagogue, our whole family would have supper at my grandparents' house. Grandma, whom we called Booba, and Granddad, or Ziyder, were Mum's aged parents. We sat silently around the laden white tablecloth, Booba covering her head with a shawl, then circling her hands over the candles as she recited the blessing. Ziyder would break the soft white *khollah* bread and distribute a piece to each of us. I was fond of my grandfather with his tiny white goatee beard. He and Booba had come over from Poland in the 1880s and had had a small shop in Middlesex Street, until they retired. The old man was also a cobbler and sometimes I would watch him repairing shoes on his last, which he held tight between his skinny knees.

* * *

Dad's tailoring trade was notorious for stopping and starting, according to the season's fashions. Whenever neighbours or uncles came round, the talk, in a mixture of English and Yiddish, was often about 'lay-offs' or, conversely, the *bren*: working all hours and Sundays to complete an order for Simpsons or Selfridges. Otherwise conversation focused on the *ferdlekh* – horseracing.

'Barney had two winners yesterday, Missus,' Dad might say, when he came home. He always addressed her as Missus; Mum called him Jack.

'Doesn't let you know about all his losers, though,' Mum would comment disparagingly.

Barney, Dad's elder brother, was slightly shorter than Dad but both had deep cleft chins and bushy eyebrows. 'Like two peas in a pod,' Mum would say. I sometimes wondered whether Dad placed bets with the bookie's runner who came down the street drumming up business, a short, skinny man in a large flat cap. If he did, they wouldn't have been for much – Mum wouldn't have been slow to put him right.

All through the summer of 1939, the talk had been of 'The Crisis', Cousin Alf and Uncle Barney arguing about whether there would be a war or not.

'Hitler wouldn't dare invade the Polish Corridor.' Alf, tall with dark, Brylcreemed hair, was adamant. I had no idea what he meant. 'We have a treaty with the Poles.'

Dad's heavy brow knotted. All summer he had fretted about his married sisters and their families in Poland – he would put money aside to post food and clothing parcels to them. I still have his last Post Office confirmation slip, dated June 1939. After the war, Uncle Sam went to Poland but found they had all perished along with the whole community.

I usually ate in what Mum called the scullery – our small, dark back kitchen. The dining room was mostly used on Friday night. We rarely sat in the front room, with its sofa and armchairs, and I first sensed that there was trouble in Europe when Mum rented it to a refugee a year or two before the war started.

Myer was a young man from Vienna. He spoke broken English and we became quite friendly. One day he agreed to take me to a staged circus at the Rivoli cinema if I promised to stay for the film afterwards. When the black and white gangster film got going, I became so scared that I badgered him to take me home, which, after a short while, he did. 'It's the last time I take him,' he muttered to Mum, annoyed. 'Too late to go back now!'

'Shouldn't have made him do that,' said Mum afterwards. 'He's an orphan and a refugee as well.' When war broke out Myer volunteered for the army and I don't know if he survived – I still feel guilty about that film show.

I often wondered what a 'crisis' was but, as it seemed that I was the only one who didn't know, hesitated to admit it. The year before, following Hitler's annexation of Czechoslovakia, there had been a 'crisis', written in large black letters on the front page of my father's preferred paper, the *News Chronicle*, but nothing had happened. So, despite the headlines and adults' talk, as long as it remained a 'crisis', I supposed there wasn't going to be a war.

For we kids of the Tenter Streets that year's holiday time carried on much as before: playing knock-down ginger on the doors in the surrounding streets and occasionally getting a cuff round the ear if anyone caught us. Sometimes we'd gallop round to Aldgate High Street in pairs with string harnesses or play rounders with a tennis ball. The only traffic danger came from plodding horses with carts heading for the Co-op depot at the end of our street.

One highlight of that cool summer before the outbreak of war was an old, turbaned man coming round with a large wooden box, ringing a small bell and calling, 'Indian toffee! Indian toffee!' With our ha'pennies we would buy newspaper twists of the sticky sweet and sit on our mums' scrubbed door-steps trying to make them last.

During most summer holidays, we spent a week or two in Southend or Westcliff, on the Essex coast, at a *kosher* boarding house. Mum was always moaning at the prices they charged and the poor service, Jewish landladies being like any others – but more so. She would have settled for a week at a non-*kosher*, cheaper place but Dad wouldn't consider it.

Evacuation and the war came suddenly – in that order. Until the end of August 1939, the school summer holidays were like any other. Then, a few days before we were due back for the new term, Mum started taking me to school. We left home very early in the morning. I'd just turned eight and until then I'd known only one five o'clock, the one that signalled teatime. Now I realized there was another, which happened long before I was ready to get up. After a snatched early breakfast, my mother hurried me through the grey, almost silent backstreets of the East End.

'What's being evacuated?' I asked, not for the first time and trying to keep up with her while playing my habitual game of avoiding the cracks in the pavement – treading on them brought bad luck.

'Going away somewhere in the country.' She sighed, her face drawn. She had already told me that, if war came, the school would be sent to the countryside, but otherwise she seemed to know little more than I did.

If she did know more, she wasn't letting on and probably for good reason. My parents had been through the First World War, Dad with the Labour Corps in the hell of Ypres, Mum dodging the Zeppelin bombs falling on the East End and the docks. Everyone said it would be much worse if it happened again.

In the late 1930s, as Hitler occupied Czechoslovakia and threatened more, and Britain appeased, the screening of the 1936 H. G. Wells film *The Shape of Things to Come* – which predicted a catastrophic second war in Europe – heightened fears. I wasn't allowed to see it and, despite my mother's insistence of 'not in front of the children', the horrific impression it had created soon percolated down to us kids through the adults' comments and worried faces.

My classmate, Gerald, had seen the film, sneaking into the Troxy Picture Palace in Mile End Road with his elder brother. He enjoyed scaring the rest of us stiff with half-remembered scenes of massed flights of bombers, heaps of smoking rubble and poison gas. Lanky Sid Harris, one of my best friends – sharp nose with a shock of fair hair – said that Gerald was exaggerating to make an impression. But within a year I had experienced the first two and was living in constant fear of the third.

Evacuation. It had taken some months for its significance to sink in: that my schoolmates and I would be sent away from our parents, and that it would be quite some time before we came back. Meanwhile, we and our teachers would be a tiny island in the midst of a sea of country folk, many of whom had never met a Londoner – and certainly not a Jewish one.

Inside the tall, grey-brick building of Buckle Street Infants' School off Leman Street, instead of the usual lessons in sums and writing, or painting, or singing with our teacher at the piano we read, drew or played Snakes and Ladders and Ludo. During those days in school at the end of August, while we waited for a decision from the local education authorities, the teachers made sure we were quiet and occupied, or left to doze, and that we were attached to our luggage, coats, gas-mask boxes and food parcels, ready to move off at a moment's notice.

Miss Alice Pizer, our headmistress, was a short, compact woman, with white hair neatly tied back in a bun and tortoiseshell glasses hung about her neck. She was the epitome of organized calm in the face of potential chaos. She would come in and talk quietly to my class teacher, her younger sister, Esther, their foreheads furrowed. Esther Pizer was taller than her sister with a lovely calm face, wavy brown hair and soft dark eyes. The Pizers were of that generation of women who, with their prospective husbands under the mud of Flanders or seriously disabled, had little chance of marriage or family and became the nurses, teachers and welfare workers who held society together between the wars.

For two long mornings we sat doing little, and each afternoon we trooped home again. On the morning of Saturday,

2 September, I felt sure that, after a few hours of hanging about, I would soon be home again. That day, however, was different. On Friday, 1 September 1939, Hitler invaded Poland. Britain and France gave him an ultimatum to withdraw. And that changed everything.

On that third day at school – a Saturday, no less – the first sign that something was brewing came when we were labelled. One by one we were called over to the teacher's desk to have a sealed brown envelope bearing our name and initials tied to our jacket or coat lapel. The teachers each had one, too, and small groups of curious children – mainly girls – ran from one to the other trying to find out their first names. Neither let on: the informality of war had yet to surface.

It must have been around midday when the signal came. Like many other children, I'd fallen asleep on the polished woodblock floor of the classroom. When the younger Miss Pizer woke me, my first thought was that we were being sent home again. 'Come,' she said softly, as she leaned over me. 'We're really going away now.'

'You mean we're not going back home like yesterday, Miss?'

'No,' murmured Miss Pizer, 'not this time. Come.'

My stomach turned. Suddenly I was anxious. How would Mum know we had gone? Who would tell her? When I didn't come home that afternoon, like I had on the previous days, she'd think I'd been knocked down by one of the lorries rumbling down to Wapping Docks. Mum was always worried about my crossing Leman Street. And we were going to travel on a Saturday as well – *Shobbos*! What would Dad say about travelling on the Sabbath?

The classroom grew noisier and noisier, with everyone

shuffling and chattering. I stood up, put on my jacket, rain-coat and cap, then reached up to the window ledge for Mum's bright blue sugar-paper bag of food packed for the journey that no one had really expected would take place. Long barley-sugar twists stuck out of the top, glowing like gold in the sunshine coming through the wired-glass windows.

Then everyone was moving and I was swept along in the crush, through the double doors and down the wide stone staircase – a noisy, chattering river carrying me with it.

'Looks like we're really off this time, Ronnie.' I grinned at my best friend as we bumped against one another on the stairs.

''Bout blinkin' time an' all,' said Ronnie, his ginger hair sticking out in all directions.

'Know where we're going?' I asked.

Ronnie shrugged. 'A long way out in the country, my dad says.'

Immediately I pictured thatched cottages, milkmaids and cows in the fields, like in my storybooks.

Down in the playground, the whole school was assembling, everyone shouting and being hustled into lines by the teachers. I'd never experienced anything like it and just let myself be pushed into place. I felt a hand grip my arm.

'Here!' It was Rita, four years older than me and at a different school. 'Come here. Get in line with me.' What was she doing here? Having a bossy sister around was the last thing I wanted, especially as none of my friends was saddled with one.

In a long column, four abreast, we wound out of the school gates between the tall, smoke-grimed warehouse walls of Buckle Street and into bustling Leman Street, the teachers scurrying back and forth, trying to keep us in line. Since Rita was the eldest she was put at the front and I had to be with her, my classmates taking the mickey, giggling and pointing.

Rita was lugging our huge brown suitcase with one hand and holding the school banner with the other. I had a rucksack on my back and clutched the paper food parcel tightly to my chest, the string of the gas-mask box cutting into my shoulder. A week or two previously we'd had gas-mask drill in class, giggling at the farting noise the air made as it pushed past the side rubbers when we breathed out, never imagining it might be something we'd need to know for real.

As we neared Aldgate High Street several mothers, alerted by the East End bush-telegraph, began to arrive and run alongside us. Some were calling out, others crying. Anxiously I looked for Mum but couldn't see her. Suddenly Ronnie's mother appeared and pushed a small brown-paper package into his coat pocket.

'I've got enough food already, Mum,' he protested.

Mrs Marks pinched his cheek. 'You can never have enough,' she replied. Then, patting his head and mine, she drew back and was lost in the crowd. I was relieved that she had seen me: Dad and Mr Marks worked in the same tailor's shop. At least he would let Mum know I had gone.

Near Aldgate East station, shoppers and shopkeepers stood in doorways, and people leaned out of upstairs windows, all gawping at our long, chattering crocodile. At the front strode our headmistress with her umbrella and bulging leather brief-case – a Pied Piper leading the children out of the city.

'Say goodbye,' a voice called from a window above a shop, laughing. 'You may never see them again!'

* * *

At Gardiner's Corner – the busy junction with Aldgate High Street and Commercial Street – we stopped at the kerb. It was where, playing the devil at a quiet moment in the traffic, we used to run out to place a ha'penny on the tram tracks. After a tram had rattled past, we'd dash to pick up the same coin, now hot and squashed. Today, at nearly midday, heavy traffic was thundering by in both directions: would we ever get across?

A policeman appeared alongside the headmistress and spoke briefly to her. Then he strode into the road, his helmet barely visible amid the cars and lorries. Thrusting a white-gloved hand into the air, he blew on his whistle and – like Moses stretching his rod over the Red Sea – everything came to a halt.

Lorries, cars and buses backed up in a gigantic traffic jam. Bus drivers leaned out from their cabs, grinning and waving, as we hurried across the highway, stepping over the tram lines. We were like the Children of Israel crossing the Red Sea, this time fleeing from the armoured chariots of the modern Pharaoh with his black moustache and red armband, who threatened to come over the English Channel, along the Thames and up Cable Street. I was sure he would come up Cable Street because that was where Mosley's Blackshirts had tried to march.

One Sunday afternoon a few years previously, Dad and my brother Arnold had marched off at lunchtime 'to stop the Fascists'. Mum cautioned me to stay at home and, to make sure I did, she told me to sit on the front step and forbade me to move.

Opposite our house was the rear yard to the Co-op depot in and out of which, every weekday, shaggy-fetlocked horses drew heavily laden carts. Unusually, that Sunday the gates were wide open and inside there were lots of mounted police and a few

Black Marias. With growing curiosity I had sat and watched the coming and going all that lunchtime.

When I went out again later, I was amazed to see ambulances and police vans unloading dishevelled officers, many with bloodstained white bandages round their heads and arms in slings. Who would dare to attack a policeman?

That evening, Dad and Arnold had returned with a few neighbours, all cock-a-hoop, telling us how the dockers had joined the Jews in fighting the police, who were protecting Oswald Mosley's Blackshirt marchers. It went down in history as 'The Battle of Cable Street'.

Arnold was eight years older than me, with a square face and wavy brown hair. By the age of fifteen, he had already left school and was working at the Houndsditch Warehouse. Pre-war, it was tough for a working-class lad to continue studying. He had a good head for figures, and had he been a bit younger, the 1944 Education Act would have given him the opportunity to go to grammar school. Arnold was a champion swimmer. He spent the last part of the war in the Royal Navy, the only Jewish matelot on his ship, and astonished that at least half of the crew couldn't swim.

Now as we crossed the high street, it seemed ages before we reached the far side where, standing under the blue canopy of Aldgate Station, I turned to look back. The policeman's white glove had disappeared and the traffic was moving again.

By the time we all trooped into the station booking hall, scores of parents had arrived to say goodbye. I looked back to see if Mum had come but the barriers were closed. All I could see was a mass of puffy red tear-stained faces pressed against the gates, through which came a chorus of names, with 'Goodbye' and 'God bless'.

As if fearful that the barriers would give way, ticket collectors and police had linked arms to push back against the weight of the crowds, the forest of arms, hands and fluttering handkerchiefs. It was a sight I would never forget. I just hoped Mum wasn't caught up in the crush.

Rita took my hand and hurried me down the steps to the Metropolitan Line platform where a train was already waiting – a special train, just for us.

Chapter 2

The Village Hall

After much pushing and shoving, I found myself in the train's restaurant car, which seemed really posh. A whistle blew and, as we drew away, I wondered again where we were going. We rumbled through Baker Street, emerged from the underground tunnel into the daylight and sped past Wembley Park, where rich Uncle Sam lived. At Harrow on the Hill we all had to get off and wait on the platform to change trains. I have a strong memory that the new one was a steam train and, as it pulled in to the platform, there was another mad rush. Again, I was jostled amid the noisy crush of children – everyone wanting to grab a window seat.

I wondered how long the train journey would be. The furthest I'd ever been was to Southend and never without Mum. I stared out of the smoke-grimed window at the sunlit green countryside, passing through stations with strange names, like Moor Park, Sandy Lodge, Chorleywood and Chalfont St Latimer, then a deep white chalk cutting in the hills. At that point, lulled by the gentle rocking of the train, I fell asleep.

I remember dreaming of a long, dark tunnel at the end of

which was a brilliant blue light. I asked Mum why the light never came any nearer and, as she leaned forward to reply, the train jolted to a halt and I woke up. 'Come on, sleepy,' Rita said. 'We're here.'

I rubbed my eyes and yawned. 'Where?'

Rita dumped the rucksack on my skinny knees, then pulled our case from the overhead rack. 'Don't know. We've arrived, that's all.'

I couldn't understand why she was being so ratty. Rita was a few inches taller than me and her straight brown hair was usually cut in a bob with a fringe; she wore a coloured slide on one side. She had long black eyelashes and always looked determined. Later, as a teenager, she never lacked for boyfriends. While I was generally in rumpled shorts and jacket, she was always neatly dressed – that day in a pleated skirt, navy-blue jumper and white socks.

Through the window, I saw a black asphalt platform and, on the wall, a railway poster. No station nameplate. Two older boys rushed through the carriage, treading on my feet. I glared after them.

'Watch out, you lot!' I yelled.

One turned. 'Get a move on, dozy, or you'll be goin' back again.' It was Sammy Rosen, short and podgy, the class bully. It wouldn't be the last time we clashed.

I yanked my cardboard gas-mask box out from under the seat and hitched the rucksack onto my shoulders. Then I glanced up at the luggage rack. The blue paper bag had gone!

'Here.' Rita held it out to me. 'Hang on to it this time.' Clutching it to my chest, I peered inside, checking that the magic barley-sugar sticks I'd almost left behind at Harrow were still there. Mum had said they'd give me special energy for the journey.

Out on the platform, I was still wondering where we were. At the far end, the engine puffed, sending steam into the narrow strip of blue sky between the station canopy and the carriages. The guard – a short, burly man in blue serge – strode down the edge of the platform, flicking the heavy varnished doors closed with his wrist. The brass handle jumped as it latched with a sharp clunk.

The engine whistled, there was a hiss of steam, and shouts echoed along the platform. 'Stand back! Stand back!'

The carriages jerked forward and began to slip past with ever-increasing speed. Finally, the guard's van flashed by, the guard staring wide-eyed at the jumble of children and luggage spread across the platform.

With the train gone, the station seemed strangely quiet, but before the hubbub could renew, the headmistress spoke:

'Now, then.' A pause. 'Listen carefully!' Another pause. No one moved or spoke; it paid to keep quiet when the headmistress was speaking. She was hidden by the crowd but I could picture her as if she was right in front of me: brown tailored costume, beige stockings, hair swept to a bun at the back of her head and those tortoiseshell glasses.

'Take all your luggage,' she continued, 'and make sure you don't leave anything behind. No pushing when we move off. There is ample time!'

We set off and I was carried along willy-nilly up the steps and across a bridge. The rucksack pulled at my shoulders. The gas-mask box dug into my ribs. And, by the time we lined up again on the far platform, my raincoat was rucked up on one side, socks were round my ankles and I was sweating.

Once more, Rita was chosen to lead the column and carry the school banner. I had to line up with her, my friends teasing and giggling. Rotten old Sammy and his cronies jeered.

At that moment, across the tracks, I saw, at last, a large blue and white nameplate: Aylesbury. In the days before dual carriageways and motorways, Aylesbury was remote and unfamiliar to an East End kid. It could have been anywhere. 'Aylesbury ducks! Aylesbury ducks!' I heard someone chuckle, but I had no idea what they were talking about.

Out in the cobbled station yard, three red-faced men, with fair hair and broad leather belts pulled tight under bulging bellies, were heaving sacks of coal onto a cart. They straightened up and stared as we filed past, reminding me of the carters outside the Co-op depot in South Tenter Street, even though the latter were short and dark-haired, in frayed jackets and peaked caps.

Across the road, there were large houses with driveways. I glanced up at my sister. 'I thought we were going to the country.'

Rita sighed. 'How should I know?' She took my hand again. 'Must be the nearest railway station, I suppose.'

Our long crocodile wound along the street as local people stood in small groups and stared. Rita was holding our white oilcloth banner. Painted on it, in red and black, was 'Buckle Street Jews' Infants' School. London. E.1.'

Everything around me was so different from our grey-black houses at home – wider roads, tiled roofs, red-brick houses, trees and garden hedges. The people looked different, too. Taller and ruddy-cheeked. Still, I consoled myself, we were from London, the world's biggest and best city, capital of the British Empire, which coloured half the countries in my school atlas red. London was the centre of the world. Not like this out-of-the-way place.

A sleek brown pony trotted past, pulling a two-wheeled trap. I thought again of the Co-op delivery drays parked in our street, with their huge shaggy-maned carthorses, each leg bigger than my whole body. As they munched from their jute nosebags, we would dare one another to dash under their huge, sagging bellies. Once a horse had turned and taken a nip at my hair, sending me tearing through our front door to cry in my mother's lap, and wonder why Arnold couldn't stop laughing.

Even though he was eight years older, Arnold and I generally got on well, apart from one time when I had been looking through his stamp collection. I must have been about seven. Admiring the colours of some of the stamps, I'd stuck them on the windowpane to see the light through them. How Mum stopped him beating the life out of me I'll never know.

Soon we approached the centre of the town. The traffic noise increased – it was almost as loud as in London – and we came to a large square. It was crammed with red, green and orange buses, some standing, others entering or leaving, and everywhere there were crowds of children with harassed teachers.

While we waited to cross, two old ladies in long coats and black hats looked us up and down. 'Deary me,' muttered one. 'Such poor little mites and so far from their mams.'

'Yes,' tutted the other. 'There's a sad thing, tha's for sure.'

I didn't hear any more – I didn't want to. As we crossed the road, the brown envelope tied to my lapel blew up into my face and my eyes misted. No longer did I feel the proud Londoner, come to show them all what was what. I was just another little nipper, on my own in a strange town full of funny people. My mum and dad were a long way away, far beyond the hills we'd passed through in the train just before I'd fallen asleep.

Feeling lost, I gripped Rita's hand tighter and my mind spun back to the anxieties of the past months, Dad and my uncles talking of war, 'crisis', air raids and Hitler. I glanced up at the sky, wondering whether the war had started while we were on the train. Would the Germans bomb London on the first day? Where would Mum and Dad take shelter? And what about Granddad Ziyder? He was very old and wouldn't be able to run to the shelters.

As I pictured his white beard and soft grey eyes, I remembered the penny I'd borrowed, the penny that had caused such a fuss. I never had gone round to apologize, like Dad said I should – there'd been no time before we were told to wait in the school every day, packed and ready to go. Now I wouldn't be able to for a long time. What would Ziyder think of me? Dad had been angry but Ziyder hadn't seemed to care. I'd have to wait till the war was over to give it back – and how long did a war last?

Rita's sharp tug at my hand brought me back to the present. We'd crossed the road and were standing on one side of the square. At the end there was a tall, rectangular church tower, and along the other two sides, rows of red-roofed houses and shops. It was as crowded as Petticoat Lane on a Sunday morning.

Lines of schoolchildren stood everywhere, some in smart blazers with blue and white stripes, or grey with red piping and caps to match. Most were just like us in navy-blue raincoats or grey jackets, carrying suitcases, rucksacks and cardboard gas-mask boxes – and all with a brown envelope tied to their lapels.

Tall men in grey suits, holding manila files, hurried between the different groups, leading them this way or that and urging them onto buses. As soon as one bus left, a new one eased into its place and another school started to get on. And the noise! Adults calling, children shouting, engines roaring and belching smoke – today we'd call it 'organized chaos'. It was all part of the huge effort to move tens of thousands of schoolchildren out of the cities and into the countryside.

I was so busy watching everything that I didn't notice that our school, too, had started to board. Someone tapped my shoulder. It was my teacher, Esther Pizer. 'Up you go,' she smiled, 'with the others.'

I jumped onto the rear platform and ran up the steps to the top deck. The ginger mop of Ronnie Marks poked up from the front seat. He turned and grinned, buck teeth like headlamps.

'Wotcher, David. Here. Saved a space for you.' I dumped my rucksack under the seat and sat down with a thump. We bounced up and down together, giggling and waiting for our pals, for all the gang to be together.

'Seen Sid and Alfie yet?' I asked.

Ronnie shook his head. 'No. Not since the station.'

I looked back towards the stairs. 'Hope they get on our bus.' We bounced up and down again.

The top deck filled, but Sid and Alfie still hadn't come. Suddenly Ronnie jumped up and pointed.

'Look. There they are!' Down below, most of our classmates were getting on the bus in front. 'And Sandra's with them,' he shouted. 'With Miss DeWinter. All of 'em!'

Seeing Sid and Sandra together made me think for a moment of the previous year. Sid and I had been wondering what girls had between their legs where our 'things' were. So we devised a plan to take little Sandra for a walk behind the old garage. We'd ask her to show us hers if we showed her ours – and each give her a penny as well. Which seemed only fair.

Sid did the negotiating and she agreed to come behind the small garage near Prescott Street. All went well, until at the last moment she changed her mind and said no. Laughing, Sid snatched up her dress but she jumped back then ran away, crying her eyes out.

'Can't trust girls to keep a promise,' Sid moaned. I agreed. And we went to buy sherbet fountains instead. So we never did find out – at least not until our teens. However, Sandra told her mum and Sid was called into the headmistress's office the next day for a dressing-down. Somehow, I got away with it, which Sid felt was unfair. It dented our friendship for a while.

Ronnie jumped to his feet. 'Look. They're leaving first!'

I pressed my nose to the window as their bus drew away. 'What a cheek! Rotten luck.'

'Not fair. Not fair,' sang Ronnie. 'They'll beat us to it!' We thumped on the front window but no one turned to look back as the bus accelerated, swung out of the square, and was gone.

I stared through the side window. Below, the headmistress was waving her arms and arguing with one of the tall men. He held up a thick sheaf of papers and was shaking his head. I nudged Ronnie.

'Cor,' he said. 'Ain't never seen Miss Pizer so cross, have you?'

'Not like that.' Reaching down, I pulled up my knee-length socks. 'Wonder what it's about.'

A moment later the man turned and strode away. The teachers looked at each other and then, frowning, slowly boarded our bus. At that the driver, who'd been standing to one side, hopped into his cab, started the engine and we moved out.

Outside the town, the road divided and we took the left-hand fork. Ronnie and I hunched forward, urging the bus to go faster – we wanted to catch up with the others.

'Can't see 'em,' said Ronnie eventually, sitting back.

'Me neither,' I murmured. I picked up my blue bag, broke off two pieces of barley sugar and gave one to Ronnie. As we crunched and scanned the empty road ahead, I wondered what had become of the other bus with our friends on it. It was one of the many separations from familiar people and places that would dog me throughout the war years. One after another, the people and things I had once taken for granted would disappear, leaving me feeling abandoned and having to fend for myself.

On the top deck the two of us sat silently, gazing out over the late-summer scene. The bus brushed against the hedgerows of the narrow, winding road beyond which a patchwork of small orchards and fields stretched away to the horizon. Rows of brown corn-stooks arranged like tiny tents stood across yellow stubble.

As we stared, a cloud crossed the sun, bringing a long black shadow that crept like a giant caterpillar across the landscape. Was there really a war? Everything still seemed so peaceful.

I leaned close to Ronnie. 'D'you think the war's started yet?' I whispered, not wanting the two older girls behind us to hear and think I was ignorant.

'Nah. Course not!' Ronnie never whispered.

'How d'you know for sure?' I asked, rubbing my nose.

'Cos they'll blow sireens, my dad says.'

'What d'they sound like?' I persisted.

'Well. Er . . .' Ronnie circled his hands in the air. 'Summat like a hooter. A big car hooter.' He didn't seem very sure.

'P'r'aps like a ship's foghorn,' I said, remembering the Eagle Line steamers on the Thames as they hooted for Tower Bridge to be raised, their huge red paddles thrashing the water to foam and their yellow funnels belching smoke. We often stood by the Tower of London – our playground – watching the ships taking East Enders on trips to the seaside at Southend and Margate and reading out their names on the bows. Just a year later those ships took part in the Dunkirk evacuation when the *Laguna Belle*, a ship much loved by our parents, was sunk.

Soon, tiled roofs showed through the trees and, gears grating, the bus slowed and turned into a narrow lane. A low branch skidded along the roof and we ducked. It was probably the first double-decker that had ever come that way. After more twists and turns, it braked to a halt. Abruptly, the noisy chatter ceased and everyone pressed their noses to the windows. Had we arrived? And where were we?

Esther Pizer's voice floated up the stairwell. 'Now, then. Come down slowly. And remember to bring everything with you.'

Joining the crush of blue raincoats, suitcases and gas-mask boxes, Ronnie and I clomped down the stairs and out onto the tree-lined roadway, gathering by a wide gateway that led into a large, gravelled courtyard. At the back stood a single-storey, pebble-dashed building with a steep, tiled roof.

The bus drew away and we spread across the road. I looked up: the sky was the bluest I had ever seen it. No aeroplanes; not even vapour trails. Nothing. There couldn't be a war. Yet when we'd left London that morning, workers had been filling sandbags outside Leman Street police station.

By the wooden gatepost stood a large black notice-board. Painted on it was a white cross and beneath it: 'St Mary's Church Hall'. The words and the cross made me hesitate: what would my father say? Despite everyone pushing past me through the gateway, my legs wouldn't budge and I stood stock still, hands clenched. Dad was not only strictly religious but his dislike of anything Christian – probably stemming from his childhood in Tsarist Russia – must have been instilled in me.

I suppose I would have been stuck there all day had not my sister grabbed me by the arm and hustled me across the court-yard, buffeted on all sides by chattering children. I shook her off and we squeezed through a double doorway.

Inside, rows of low benches, like we used for PE, stretched across the rear half of the hall. After settling ourselves along them, I noticed two women in dark green uniforms sitting behind a trestle table piled high with papers. On their shoulders were the letters 'WVS'. Did the 'W' stand for war? My teacher, Esther Pizer, stood to one side of them and our headmistress on the other. She was talking to a tall, red-faced man with a white moustache. Next to him stood a balding man in a black jacket and white clerical collar – I tried hard not to look at him. In the far corner by the door a large group of women, some in coats, others in aprons and dark dresses, were staring at us and muttering to each other.

I sat between my sister and Ronnie. 'Are they the ones who are going to look after us?' I asked.

'Dunno,' said Ronnie. 'Don't much fancy that one with the sharp conk, do you?'

'Looks strict,' I agreed. 'Not like our mums, are they?'

Ronnie was about to reply when the headmistress stepped forward and the hall fell silent.

Holding up a file of papers, she called, 'Max Phillips!' and pointed to the table.

Max, face bright red, picked up his case and stumbled out to the front. Every pair of eyes turned to watch as one of the women in green snipped the envelope from his lapel, opened it and took out a sheet of paper. Looking down at her files, then turning to the women in the corner, she called, 'Mrs Reed!'

A short, grey-haired woman in a brown coat came forward, smiled at Max and took his case, then turned towards the door. Head bent, Max followed her out of the hall. We watched him go as if we might never see him again.

One by one, my schoolmates were called, went to the table and away through the door with one of the women. Then it was Ronnie's turn. Poor old Ronnie, he got the one with the sharp nose. After a while, I looked around the hall. Sid, Alfie and all my friends on the other bus still hadn't arrived. And they'd left first! Without Ronnie, I felt alone and weary. The wooden parquet floor was dusty and the heavy oak beams in the ceiling seemed to press down on me. I clutched the blue bag. It was now crumpled and torn, the long sticks of Mum's barley sugar broken into small pieces. My eyes misted and I wished she could be there now to take me home.

Chapter 3

The Vicarage

A sudden movement of Rita's arm woke me – I had dozed off, leaning against her. We were the only ones left in the hall. No more women waited and the teachers and WVS women around the table were talking quietly among themselves, glancing at the two of us.

Rita was biting her lip, knuckles white. By now, through overhearing her talking to some of the older girls, I knew that she wasn't upset with me. The year before she had won a scholarship to the Central School and was very proud of her black velour hat with the red band. She was supposed to have gone away with her school but instead, to keep the family together – and perhaps to keep an eye on me – Mum had made her come away with my school. In the weeks leading up to our evacuation, in the evenings after I'd gone to bed, she'd had furious arguments with Mum. Now, as we sat here like dummies, I knew she'd be even angrier. As for me, I already had tears in my eyes.

My teacher looked across the hall and smiled, then walked over and crouched beside me. I looked up, wiping my cheeks with the back of my hand.

'No one wants us, do they, Miss?' I murmured.

She took out a small white handkerchief to mop my face. 'No. It's not that at all.' Her other hand lay on my knee. 'Your billet lady is late for some reason. But Mrs Black, that lady there,' she nodded to one of the women in green, 'will take you round in her car.' She glanced at Rita, then back to me. 'There. Going in style. Just you two!'

She gave me the handkerchief and I blew my nose. 'Thank you, Miss. Thanks.'

The teacher stood up. 'Come. Take your things with you.'

We shuffled forward to the table and I stared at the woman as she snipped the envelope from my lapel and opened out the sheet of paper. Earlier that morning, I'd burned with curiosity to know what was inside. Now, at last, I could see: my name, address, Mum and Dad's names and, in a small square at the side, the capital letter 'J'. I supposed that meant 'Jewish'.

The headmistress took my rucksack and gas-mask case and Esther Pizer helped me into the car. I clutched the blue bag to me and felt excited when the engine began to purr and we drew away from the church hall. I'd only ever been in a car once before; this one smelt of warm leather. Turning to look back at Miss Pizer, I saw the sun shining through her hair, making it glow like gold, and I remembered when I'd first joined the school. Every afternoon, we infants had to rest on canvas beds for an hour or two but I'd never wanted to sleep: I preferred to chatter to the kid next to me.

'Now you must rest, David.' Miss Pizer's soft voice had soothed me. 'It will make you grow big and strong.' As my eyes closed, her hair had shone gold from the sunlight streaming through the high windows – just like it was now.

I was very fond of Esther Pizer. I learned later that it wasn't unusual for small boys to have a crush on their teacher but, at the time, I felt I was special to her because of the way she smiled at me and laughed at my jokes. Little did I guess then how much I would come to rely on her – especially during my second year away from home.

Rita clambered into the car beside me, the door slammed, the engine started and we were on our way to our new home. I wondered what the woman there would be like. Better than Ronnie's, I hoped. Glancing back through the small rear window, I saw my teacher still standing there. Her smile stayed with me long after she was out of sight.

The car drew up by a row of new brick houses and, while Rita and I waited a few paces back, Mrs Black walked up the path and knocked. A curtain twitched at the side window and she knocked again. The front door opened slightly and a pair of eyes peered out. Then, abruptly, it was flung wide and a small, dark-haired woman in a flowery blue apron and pink slippers stood on the mat. She looked flushed and tousled, like Mum when she'd just got out of bed.

'My goodness me,' she gasped. 'I'm so sorry, Mrs Black. Must ha' fallen asleep waitin' for Mr Clark to get home. What's th' time, then?'

I strained to listen. She had a country voice, but not the one the comics used on the wireless. Did all the people here speak like that? And why did she call him 'Mr Clark'? Mum would have said: 'My husband'.

Mrs Black glanced at her watch. 'I make it half past three,' she said, sounding like the nit nurse who regularly came to our school, 'but I could be a little fast.'

The woman frowned. 'Not like him bein' late.' She leaned forward and lowered her voice. 'Must ha' been kept back at the aerodrome. You know, with all what's goin' on now.'

I wondered what she meant by 'going on'. If Mr Clark was a soldier, it would be really exciting to live here. I could learn how to fire a gun in case the Germans came. I couldn't wait to tell Ronnie.

'Well, then,' smiled the woman at the door, standing aside and beckoning to Rita, 'you'd best come in, m'dear.' My sister picked up our large brown suitcase and stepped into the hall. I shouldered my rucksack and followed her. The banisters were painted white and the hall and staircase had red runners. Much posher than the old brown lino that covered our hall at home – and I'd always thought country people were poor.

Suddenly I felt the woman's hand on my shoulder. 'Er, Mrs Black?' she said. Mrs Black had started to walk away. She stopped and turned. 'I did tell the vicar one, you know. An' a girl.' She lowered her voice again. 'Specially with what the doctor says an' all tha'.'

Balancing on the wooden threshold, I stared down at the fluffy pink slippers on the mat. Her hand was still heavy on my shoulder and twisting my body from side to side, the gas-mask box swinging around me, I wondered what the doctor had said and why she didn't want me. No one seemed to want me. All I wanted to do was go back home to Mum.

Mrs Black walked back to the door. 'Oh dear. I thought it was all arranged?' She glanced down at me, then up at the woman's face. 'I'm only the chauffeur, as you might say.'

'Well. We've only the one spare bed. An' there's the linen an' all tha'.'

Mrs Black took my hand. 'Oh dear,' she said again. 'I suppose I'll have to run him back to the hall. The vicar is still there, I know.'

At that Rita sprang forward. 'No! My brother has to stay with me. I promised my mother!'

'Please.' Mrs Black raised a hand. 'At least you're settled. Your brother will be well looked after, you can be assured.' She tugged at my hand again. 'Come, young man. We'll soon have you sorted out.'

Rita bit her lip, then shrugged. She'd promised Mum we'd stay together but what could she do? 'How will I know where he is?' she asked.

'Your teachers will tell you, I'm sure,' said the woman. 'Don't worry, please.' Holding my hand, she led me back to the car.

Back at the church hall, I slid from the car seat and stood by the gatepost, kicking stones across the road, as my teacher came out.

'Hello, David,' she said. 'Didn't think we'd be seeing you so soon.'

I didn't smile. 'They ain't got no place for me, have they, Miss?'

'Yes, they have. You're with the Clarks.'

'But she ain't got no room, Miss. An' no bed. I heard.'

'Don't worry.' She crouched beside me. 'You won't be left to sleep with the cows in the field. The vicar is in charge of billets. He'll sort it out.'

Billets, I thought. So that's what the word meant – village houses!

I looked across the road to the hedgerow. Orange rosehips glowed in the sunlight; a gentle breeze swayed the treetops and somewhere, high up, a rook cawed. My teacher noticed me looking.

'Very lovely here, isn't it, David?' she said softly.

'Yes, Miss. Like that picture in the nature book at school. Sort of not real, like, Miss.'

One day in school we'd been looking at pictures of rivers: a mountain torrent, with white, thrashing waters, and a placid river-meadow scene. I said I liked the green meadow best. 'But that's beautiful, too,' she'd said, pointing to the torrent, 'in a different way.' She didn't make me feel that her opinion was more valid than mine and that was why I liked her. She made me feel that my ideas were as good as hers, even when I'd once painted a picture with a whole sky a dirty white, because that was how it looked over London. She was a bit cross that I'd used up half a tin of powder paint, though.

At that moment, the bald man in the white collar came out of the hall with the headmistress. He leaned down towards me. 'So this is the young man, eh?' He was tall, with grey eyes that twinkled behind steel-rimmed spectacles. I thought of Dad again and felt awkward – even guilty – for standing so close to a Christian priest. 'Well,' the man continued, 'no room at the inn, eh?' He smiled. 'We'll just have to lodge you in our manger for the time being.'

I stared at my teachers, puzzled, because they, too, were smiling. What was so funny? Would I have to sleep on straw with the horses? And how did you address a vicar? Sir? Mister? Vicar? The white collar and grey shirt front scared me. He might have a gold cross under that shirt, like the big one they carried in procession to the tall church down Prescott Street every year.

The teacher noticed my discomfort. 'The vicar means that you can stay in the vicarage for now. That will be nice, won't it?' Again, I feared what my father would say but there was no way I could refuse to go with them. I consoled myself that the teachers would explain everything to him.

We walked together a short distance up the lane before turning in through a large, red-brick gateway and up a gravel drive. Miss Pizer took my hand, led me through a tall white door and up a dark wooden staircase.

In a small room, she sat me on a bed.

'You should have a rest now,' she said. 'I'll wake you for tea later.'

I kicked off my shoes and glanced down at the blue bag. Not wanting to see what remained of the barley sugars, I stuffed it into my rucksack. Poor Mum. She'd packed everything so nicely that morning. Fruit, sandwiches and the barley sugar. I hadn't even said goodbye properly. When I'd last seen her, Mum had looked so worried, deep lines in her face. I could still feel the spot where she had kissed me. Now all her barley sugars were broken. And she was so far away.

I lay down, and as my teacher covered me with a blanket, her fingers brushed my cheek, just like when I used to sleep in my infants' class in the afternoons. Perhaps I could stay with her in this billet. I began to like the idea of being on my own, without Rita telling me what to do.

Miss Pizer went out, leaving the door ajar, but I couldn't doze. How long had we been travelling? Did Mum know where I was? Would I have to go back to Mrs Clark? And if they couldn't find a billet, would I have to go back to London alone? Soon the weariness took over and I fell asleep.

It must have been mid-afternoon when a tap at the door woke me. A faint grey light filtered through the ivy that hung outside the small window. I sat up as my teacher came in then slipped on my shoes. Smiling, she flattened my hair and straightened my shirt. She took me into the bathroom where I rinsed my face then led me down the dark wooden stairs to a wide, stone-paved hall.

Dark oil paintings in heavy frames hung on the pale-green walls. The only time I'd ever seen huge pictures like those was when my brother had taken me through Whitechapel Art Gallery on his way to the library, never in an ordinary house, not even at rich Uncle Sam's in Wembley. Most of the paintings were of old men with long grey beards. Some had gold circles around their heads.

Beside the French windows to the garden there was another picture, this time of a bearded man in flowing robes, like an Arab's, and a Star of David on his turban. That puzzled me: what was the Jewish star doing in a vicar's house? What made me really uneasy, though, was a black wooden cross with a half-naked man hanging from it on the wall above the fire-place. I knew very little about Christianity and the Crucifixion, but I did know that that figure must be Jesus Christ and that I mustn't look at it. George, my classmate who was half Jewish, said the Jews had killed Christ, and that was why my older brother and his friends had street fights with the *goyim* from Chamber Street.

Even though I later rejected Jewish religious observance,

the family distaste for those symbols of Christianity remained deeply imbued in me, accentuated at the end of the war when the newspapers were full of reports of the horrendous anti-Semitism of the Holocaust.

I turned my head away and stared into the nearest corner at a picture of an old man leaning on a stick. 'St Francis,' said the label at the bottom of the gilt frame. His soft, wide eyes – just like Granddad Ziyder's – looked straight at me and, again, I thought anxiously of that penny.

But a magnet seemed to pull my eyes towards that black wooden cross and I had to force myself to look away. Dad had warned me that it was a sin even to look at Yoysel. 'That was how they converted Jewish children into Christians,' he'd said. That was what they did in the green and white house on the corner in Spitalfields. 'Mission to the Jews,' it said over the doorway. Dad always made a spitting sound as we passed by: 'For a bowl of soup and a *shtikel* bread,' he would mutter, 'pah, pah, pah!' Later I learned that some destitute Jews, arriving in the East End, went to the Mission to take advantage of the free meals.

I always sprinted past that corner on the way to my aunt's blouse workshop in Fournier Street, fearful that a hand would reach out to pull me inside. I often wondered what they did to 'convert' you. I imagined being strapped under a huge machine, like the ones I'd seen at Mum's hairdresser's, and dressed in a long white smock, like the boys in the Catholic procession in Prescott Street, while in a dark room at the back, someone like Black Demon, the arch-villain of my comics, would be pulling a lever and sparks would shoot out.

The doorbell rang. Miss Pizer went to answer it, then called me out.

'Mrs Black is here, David. She'll take you back to the Clarks now in her car.' I ran to get my jacket and rucksack from the hall, disappointed: I'd been hoping to stay billeted with my teacher. I was fed up of being tossed backwards and forwards, like a shuttlecock.

The vicar and the WVS ladies must have cleared up the misunderstanding and provided extra bedding: when the car pulled up, the blue front door swung open and Mrs Clark stood there, her straight brown hair neatly combed with a hair-clip on one side.

'Come on in then, little 'un.' She smiled down at me. 'Your sister's waitin' for you.' She called up the stairs, 'Rita. Your brother's here. Come down and have some tea.' The front door closed, Rita appeared, and we all went along to the kitchen. Through the glass panes in the rear door I saw a long garden and, beyond, a low wooden fence, a green field and tall trees.

At the time I puzzled over the woman's change of heart, and wondered whether the vicar had some magic power over the villagers. However, the foster-parents received the then princely sum of ten shillings for each child and, of course, there was the 'wartime spirit'. Apart from some isolated cases of money-grabbing, though, I still admire the way the village people opened their homes to strange and often awkward children.

The kitchen table was covered with a checked red cloth on which stood a tin of biscuits (soon to become scarce with sugar rationing), a green teapot and a white jug of milk, covered with a muslin cloth fringed with beads. At home we poured milk straight from the Co-op bottles – they had wide necks and cardboard tops, with a fingerhole in the middle, which we used to make table mats by winding scraps of wool round them then joining them together. I couldn't see any milk bottle and thought perhaps she had got it straight from a cow. As she poured tea, I wondered if she used the old leaves to clean the carpets, like Mum did.

The woman glanced across the table at me as I nibbled a biscuit. 'My,' she said, half smiling. 'We need to get some colour in them cheeks, tha's for sure.' She turned to Rita and, as they started talking about laundry and clothes, my mind drifted. I was in a strange house, having tea with a strange woman I'd only just met – and I'd be sleeping there, too, for how long I didn't know. Already it felt quite natural, as though we'd always been there.

Chapter 4

Pork Sausages

As I was sitting in Mrs Clark's kitchen a short while later, the front door clicked and a man's voice called, 'Sorry I'm late, love. Another ruddy parade.' Mrs Clark got up and went into the hall. 'Fire-fighting drill again,' the deep voice went on. 'Demolition squads . . .' I strained to catch their conversation, wondering if it was about us or 'the crisis', as footsteps came towards the kitchen.

'So,' he smiled, as he came in, 'these the new lodgers, then?' He was a tall, sandy-haired man with a bushy moustache and the bluest eyes I'd ever seen. He wore an air-force uniform with three stripes on the sleeve. A real RAF sergeant! I couldn't wait to tell Ronnie.

Taking off his jacket, he sat down and looked straight at me. 'What's your name, then?'

'David,' I whispered.

'Hey!' He grinned. 'Bet you can shout louder'n that!' He turned and smiled at my sister. 'And your name is . . . ?'

'Rita,' she said, blushing.

Then he saw the tin of biscuits. 'We should have visitors every day!' He winked at me and immediately I took to him.

After tea, Rita took me up to our room. It had two beds and blue flowered curtains. Beside the fireplace there was a red-painted chest of drawers. My sister took me into the bathroom for a wash. I protested that I'd had one at the vicarage, considering that to be sufficient for one day, but it didn't help. The bathroom had a large white tub, basin and gleaming toilet with a seat that lifted up.

'Cor. Right posh,' I whispered to Rita. At home, we washed in an enamel bowl in the stone kitchen sink and our toilet was out in the backyard. The bath was made of galvanized tin, which Mum filled from kettles and pots heated on the coal range. In winter, she lit the range so it would be warm in the kitchen, and when I was in the bath she sat on a chair against the door – I didn't want my sister or her friends barging in.

Back in the bedroom I lay on the bed and started to read my copy of the *Wizard* until, dog-tired from the early morning, the journey, then being shuttled to and from the vicarage, I dozed off.

The sun was low through the window when Rita shook me. 'Come on,' she said, glancing at her wristwatch. 'It's half past seven and they've called us for supper.' She straightened my shirt and tried to brush my hair to one side. It fell forward again and she gave up.

After the mix-up of the morning, the Clarks were obviously doing their best to make us feel at home. In the front room, a wooden table covered with a light green tablecloth stood end-on against the side wall. I sat by the wall with Rita beside me and Mr Clark – 'Call me Malcolm' – opposite. His wife was in the kitchen.

'We've got bangers for tea.' Malcolm smiled. 'Bet you like sausages, eh, young 'un?' My mouth watered at the smell of frying that wafted in from the kitchen. The table was neatly laid, just like it would be for our Friday-night meal at home, except that there was butter on the bread. At home, there would never be milk products with a meat dish – our dietary rules forbade it.

While Mr Clark dished out baked potatoes and cabbage, his wife came in and forked three sausages onto his plate, then two for Rita, two for me and one for herself. As she sat down and took a potato, she nodded at me. 'And if you're good,' she said, 'we've got something nice for afters.'

She started to eat. So did Malcolm. I didn't. I was looking at the sausages. They weren't at all like the ones we had at home. These were fat, pale and shiny – like the little pink pigs in my storybook. I was sure they were pork and glanced at Rita. She was eating a potato and hadn't touched them either. The smell was making my mouth water – and I was hungry.

Scared of offending the Clarks, I decided to try one but wanted some brown sauce – like I always did with sausages. I picked up the bottle of OK sauce and shook it and in my anxiety, started to shake it harder and harder. Suddenly the top flew off. Sauce shot out of the bottle, splattered onto the wall beside me, then dribbled down the light yellow wallpaper. I gasped and tried to say sorry but my throat had dried. I wished that the floor would open up and swallow me.

It was Rita who broke the silence. She had just cut a tiny piece of sausage and was now staring, open-mouthed, at the wall. With a sharp clatter she dropped her fork onto her plate, then burst into tears. 'I'm sorry . . . I can't . . . I promised my father I wouldn't eat *treifa* . . . I didn't want . . .' She sobbed. 'I didn't want to say no. I'm so sorry, Mrs Clark. I'm sorry for the sauce. David . . . he didn't mean it . . .'

On and on, sobbing and trying to catch her breath, tears streaming down her cheeks as the sauce continued to trickle down the wall. Suddenly, she pushed back her chair, thrust the plate away and buried her head in her arms, her dark hair spilling onto the tablecloth as she cried and cried.

The two grown-ups looked from me to Rita, then to the wall, their faces drawn and bewildered. Mrs Clark's face reddened. 'That's what comes of doing the vicar a good turn,' she cried. 'That's the thanks I get.' Taking a handkerchief from her apron pocket, she held it to her eyes. 'As if I know what they can and can't eat. As if we haven't got troubles enough of our own, like.'

I sat frozen, feeling absolutely wretched. We'd only just arrived and already we'd insulted their food, I'd ruined their wallpaper and they were angry. They wouldn't let us stay here now. We'd be sent back home.

I burst out crying too, whining that I wanted to go home, wanted my mum and I was sorry about the sauce, my sobs mingling with my sister's.

Malcolm got up and came round the table. Gently laying two large hands on my shoulders, he leaned down and half whispered in my ear, 'There, lad. Was only an accident. Could have happened to anyone.' I continued crying. 'Come,' he said. 'We'll leave the girls to it, shall we?' He eased me out of the chair and, as we climbed to the bedroom, I wiped my eyes with the back of my hand, trying to stop crying and mumbling, 'Sorry, Mr Clark, sorry, sorry,' all the way.

'Here.' He smiled as he sat me on the bed, his blue eyes twinkling. 'Brought any games with you?'

'Just my cards.' Sniffing back the tears, I pulled the worn pack out of my rucksack.

'Huh. Gambler, eh? What can you play?'

'Rummy.' I sniffled, as I slipped off the rubber band.

'Okay. You deal.'

We played and, gradually, I began to feel better, releasing the tension that had built up over the last few weeks of false alarms, rumours, then leaving home.

Downstairs, Rita continued to cry, but increasingly softly, and from time to time I heard Mrs Clark's voice. Eventually, just their two voices drifted up the stairs as we played in the late sunlight with the smells of the countryside filtering through the open window.

The cawing of rooks settling in the elms across the field broke the silence. As Malcolm dealt the cards and we started to play again, I glanced out of the window. Beyond the garden was the field I'd seen at teatime and at the far end a hedgerow bathed in gold from the setting sun, everything so green and wide open, so different from the poky grey streets at home.

That may have been the moment when my love affair with the English countryside began.

'Seven of clubs. Trumps!' Malcolm's voice cut into my thoughts. 'Just look at that, then! Caught you dreaming, didn't I?'

I shrugged and smiled. 'S'pose you did.'

I slept late the next morning – and might have slept even later, but through the stillness of the village Sunday morning, church bells pealed into my dreams and woke me. It was 3 September 1939. They were the last bells to ring before they were silenced for 'the duration' – the dreary term used to mark the indefinite length of the conflict – except as a warning of enemy parachutists or an invasion.

I sat up, disoriented at first, then recognized the Clarks' spare bedroom. Kneeling on the bed, I pulled aside the curtains. The back garden and the meadow beyond were suffused in hazy sunlight. I was dying to run down and explore but Rita woke up, jumped out of bed and hurried to the bathroom. I was bursting and ran to rap on the door, almost peeing on the landing before she eventually came out.

'Are y' ready for breakfast, then?' Mrs Clark called up.

Rita poked her head round the bedroom door. 'Coming, Mrs Clark. Just a minute.'

There was thick porridge and boiled eggs. I sprinkled three large spoonfuls of sugar on my porridge and watched it turn to syrup. I wondered whether they had Force flakes here, my favourite cereal, with the funny man on the box – he had a white spoon growing out of the back of his neck.

'Lovely day,' called Mrs Clark from the sink as we ate.

'Yes,' said Rita, 'so sunny.' She paused. 'Perhaps we could go for a walk around the village, Mrs Clark.'

'Well, you jus' do that. Reckon it'll be a bit small after your London, so you won't be gettin' lost.'

Outside the air was still and warm, smelling fresh. Pollen tickled my nostrils and a brown and orange butterfly flexed its wings on a purple thistle. I brushed my hand along the high grass and tiny seeds fell away like rain. A bumble bee hummed past, its bright orange rump zigzagging along the verge and I ducked my head, fearful of its sting. This was the real country!

Then I became aware of shrill birdsong high above me. It went on and on without stopping, like when we tried to whistle by sucking in a breath. Try as I might, I couldn't see its source anywhere in the sky. But it was my first meeting with the skylark – and that tiny bird became the symbol of my time in the countryside and my lasting love of it.

We walked on towards the village hall, trying to remember the way we had come in the car, and seemed to be the only ones about. Just as I was wondering where all the villagers were, a voice called, 'Rita!' Two children were standing at a junction. It was Barry, from the oldest class, with Stephen, my classmate Gerald's older brother. At last, someone else from our school! We waved and ran towards each other, meeting beside a white wooden signpost. 'Church,' said one arm. 'Aylesbury,' said the other.

'Where's Gerald?' I asked.

'We've had to split,' said Stephen. 'He's in another billet.'

Our small group walked on, talking about our billets – and still we were the only ones on the road, no villagers and none of our other friends. Everyone seemed to be indoors. Was it always like that here? Opposite the vicarage, I glanced up the driveway. Perhaps my teacher would be there and might see me but no one came out.

Barry was telling Rita about the older boy in his billet, who attended the village school. 'Says the headmaster is real strict. Uses the cane an' all.' For a moment I cringed, then consoled myself that in our school it was never used. Miss Pizer said we would always be in our own classes and that was why the village had given us the hall.

Further along the lane, Stephen stopped. 'What time is it?'

Rita glanced down at the wristwatch Auntie Cissie had bought for her thirteenth birthday, then stamped her foot, annoyed. With the trauma of the night before, she'd forgotten to wind it so it had stopped. 'Why?' she asked.

Stephen clapped his hands together. 'Cos at eleven o'clock war's being declared.'

'How do you know?' said Rita, turning pale.

'We heard it on the wireless yesterday,' said Stephen. 'That's why there's nobody around. Bet everyone's stuck to their sets.'

While Barry and Stephen continued arguing about the time, Rita walked along the hedgerow, flicking her hand over the leaves. Suddenly a small terrier scampered round a bend in the road, jumping up and barking at us. It was followed by an old man holding a knobbly walking-stick.

Stephen ran up to him. 'Er. Morning, Mister. Can you tell us the time, please?'

'Huh. Time you're wantin', then?' he muttered, with a toothless smile, as he looked us up and down, ''Vacuees y'are, eh?'

'Yes, Mister,' said Rita. 'We came yesterday.'

'Oh, I know that. Couldn't ha' missed all that rumpus, could I?' He dug into a brown waistcoat pocket and pulled out a silver pocket watch on a long chain. 'Five past eleven, give or take a minute,' he said, and snapped the cover shut. 'Never more'n a minute out.' He slipped it back into the pocket. 'Not in thirty year.' He bent down, picked up a stick and threw it down the road. The terrier scampered off to retrieve it and the old man followed.

'Thank you, Mister,' called Barry. The man waved.

'There you are,' snapped Stephen. 'Told you so. We must be at war already.'

My stomach felt funny. I didn't want to be 'at war'. 'Still needn't be,' I said. 'There ain't no planes and bombs and things like that.' Then I added, feeling grown-up: 'Could just be a crisis.'

'There don't 'ave to be planes and stuff, Titch,' said Stephen, leering down.

'Well, there'd be maroons, then.' Mum had said they'd let off maroons when the Zeppelins came over to bomb in the First World War. I imagined them to sound like very loud hooters.

'Stupid clot,' snapped Stephen. 'They got sireens this time.' That was the way Ronnie had said it.

'Well, there ain't none of them either, is there?'

Rita stepped between us to stop the argument just as a clear voice floated to us from behind a hedge. We all stopped dead in the road, listening. I pulled aside the twigs and leaves and peeped through the branches. A window in a white-walled cottage was open and, inside, a man and a woman stood facing one another as a wireless announcer declared, 'Ladies and gentlemen. The Right Honourable Mr Neville Chamberlain.'

The woman raised a hand to her forehead as a thin, sombre voice came from the wireless.

'I am speaking to you from the Cabinet Room at 10 Downing Street . . .' and droned on, until I heard, 'Consequently, this country is at war with Germany.'

The woman rested her head on the man's chest and he wrapped his arms around her. She started to cry. The man stepped back and the wireless clicked off, leaving only the sound of quiet sobbing.

I wondered why the woman was crying. Maybe the man was a soldier and would have to go and fight. I straightened up and walked back across the road to sit on a grassy bank.

Above, huge oak boughs arched across the lane. Through them I saw clear blue skies and all around us was the quiet village Sunday. Could it really be war? A few days before, when Dad was listening to the wireless news, I'd heard a report about Warsaw being bombed.

Now Stephen and Barry began to outdo one another with vivid accounts of the H. G. Wells film.

'An' the skies are full of planes. Millions of 'em,' said Barry.

'Yeah, an' the anti-aircraft guns ain't no good and they all get blown to bits.' Stephen threw up his arms to indicate explosions. 'Then there's gas and everyone chokes – even down the Underground!' I imagined our house burning and Mum running through blazing streets to fetch Ziyder to the shelter. I felt scared and must have looked it because Rita stepped in.

'Stop it, you two,' she snapped. 'Shut up!' Chastened, they fell silent. And as we walked back down the lane, I wondered again how long a war lasted. Dad said the last one had gone on for four years. Four years! I'd be as old as Rita when it finished.

At the junction, we parted. I was sorry to see the others go. For a brief moment it had been like old times. Now Rita and I were on our own again.

When we went into the house, Mr Clark was listening to the wireless. He said there'd been an air-raid alert in London, but it was probably a false alarm. Reassured, I went up to my bedroom where I covered the drawing pad Auntie Esther had given me just the week before with tiny aeroplanes spitting bullets at each other – the product of my active imagination. If there was a war, we were going to win, weren't we?

At that moment the wonderful smell of baking wafted up the stairs and I realized I was hungry. Must have been from the country fresh air. The smell reminded me of Mum's *choulent* stew. And when Mrs Clark called, 'Dinner's ready!' I ran down, ravenous.

We started with a huge piece of Yorkshire pudding in thick brown gravy. I'd never had it before and wondered why it was called that – we weren't in Yorkshire. Then we had roast chicken, potatoes and long green beans – 'runner beans', said Malcolm. I'd never had those before either and they crunched between my teeth. As Rita helped to clear up, Mrs Clark said we could do what we liked that afternoon – 'As long as you're quiet!' I was too full to think of doing anything other than lying on the bed reading my comics.

In our bedroom, Rita was writing a letter and I supposed Mum and Dad were probably visiting family, like they did every Sunday afternoon. Really boring that always was, and I was glad to be out of it. Inevitably it involved a long walk to one of our numerous relatives, which was no fun either. Dad seemed to know the whole East End and we would have to stop every few yards along Whitechapel Road so he could shake hands with practically everyone we passed while I shifted from one leg to the other, tugging at his hand. Later we'd sit in a stuffy room with nothing to do except wait for a piece of cake and a cup of tea, and all the time the adults would talk, talk, talk of family, of children, of new babies.

Often, the conversation broke into Yiddish, which I couldn't understand, and despite their respect for learning, few of the families we visited had any books. Our house was the same. It was probably because books cost money, were regarded as a luxury and anyway could be borrowed from the public library.

That afternoon, a light breeze ruffled the curtains as I lay back and stared up at the changing patterns of light on the ceiling. Tomorrow we'd start school. I couldn't wait to see Ronnie – and to tell my teacher all that had happened. Perhaps it wouldn't be so bad being evacuated after all.

I woke early on Monday morning, knelt on the bed and pulled aside the curtain to look out. It was cloudier than the day before but still bright. Excited, I dressed quickly, eager to finish breakfast and get out to meet my friends. Alfie and Sid must have arrived by now and there would be so much to tell one another.

Malcolm Clark had already left by the time we came down for breakfast. We had porridge, then fried egg on toast, which tasted much the same as it did at home but a strange smell hung in the air. When Rita went up to get her satchel, I peeped into the sink. A blackened frying pan lay there with what looked like bits of pink cord floating in the soapy water. Later I learned they were bacon rinds. Then Rita called, 'Hurry up, David, or we'll be late!'

Ronnie's ginger mop stood out in the crowd hanging around the gateway to the church hall. I ran up and grabbed his arm. Ronnie spun round. 'Wotcher, David!' he shouted. 'Harold said you were left till last.'

'Yes. Our billet lady fell asleep or something. Still,' I grinned, 'we got taken round in a car.'

'Lucky blighter. We had to walk to the other side of the village. Miles it was. Honest.'

The village was probably less than a mile across, but in the East End, we didn't walk long distances. The school, the synagogue and the local shops were all within half a mile, and a trudge up the Mile End Road to relatives' houses was the only 'long-distance' trek we made. For anything further we took a penny bus ride.

'The man in my billet is in the air force,' I boasted. 'A sergeant! You got the one with the sharp conk, didn't you, Ronnie?'

'Oh, she's not bad – and, blimey, you should've seen the Sunday dinner.' He shaped a huge, round belly with his hands. 'I couldn't move all day!'

We continued chatting about the billets, the different food: parsnips, Yorkshire pudding, suet pudding – 'An' when it's got raisings in it,' Ronnie giggled, 'it's called spotted dick!'

We looked around for the rest of our friends. Only Gerald was there. No Alfie. No Sid Harris. No Shirley from next door, with whom I used to play doctors and nurses, or any other of our regular gang. We were puzzled: nearly half the class seemed to be missing. We remained puzzled until the headmistress rang the bell and made us line up silently around three sides of the square courtyard.

'Now then,' she began. 'Through a shortage of billets, half of the school has been sent to another village.' She couldn't say when or whether we would all be together again.

I looked around the dusty yard, grasping now what she had been arguing about at the bus station. It seemed that all my friends who had been on the other bus had gone somewhere else – and even Ronnie lived on the far side of the village. Why hadn't Sammy Rosen been on the other bus? Suddenly all the expectations of the early morning vanished.

Now, as I looked around the courtyard, searching for a friendly face other than Ronnie's, the headmistress raised her hand again and we fell silent.

'Now, listen carefully,' she continued. 'As Miss Pizer and I are the only teachers here, you will be divided into just two classes.' She paused. 'And the oldest class will be going to the village school.'

A low murmur ran around the courtyard. Rita was staring at the ground, scooping out a small hollow as she twisted her toe in the dust. Clearly she was recalling Barry's remarks about the headmaster.

As the older ones gathered by the gateway, the rest of us trooped into the church hall, which had now been partitioned into two. Across the floor, on our side, there were four rows of tables and chairs. At the front was a large table for the teacher and, by the wall, two battered wooden cupboards. After our homely classrooms in London, everything seemed so bleak and bare – but this would be my school for the next two years.

Ronnie and I made for the back row.

'Just a minute,' came Esther Pizer's voice. 'I will tell each of you where to sit.' She placed Ronnie at one end of the front row and me in the centre of the second. When we were all seated, she came round with books, exercise books and pencils, and told us to write about our billets. 'Quietly,' she added.

The reputation of the village headmaster must have reached our headmistress, because once we were all settled and working, she came round from the far side and spoke to my teacher.

'If you could keep an eye on both classes, I'll take the older ones to the village school,' she whispered. 'The children seem quite apprehensive.' I felt sorry for Rita, first for having had to leave her friends to come with me and now having to go to a completely strange school – where they used the cane.

Later we were given loose paper and crayons and told to draw something from the village. I drew a stile I'd seen in the hedgerow down the lane, its step poking through the fence.

Esther Pizer paused as she passed behind me and I looked up. 'Could do better if we had paints, Miss,' I said.

'I'm sure you could.'

Above the shadowy green hedge and black wooden fence, I'd coloured a cobalt sky with a blazing yellow sun. 'At least your sky isn't all white this time,' she added.

'Well, it is blue here, isn't it, Miss?'

'Yes, it is,' she nodded, 'and that's very nice.' As she carried on I wondered whether she meant the picture or the village. Picking up the yellow crayon, I made the sun even brighter.

Chapter 5

School Time

The headmistress returned from delivering the older children to the village school just in time to announce the mid-morning break, adding, 'As soon as you hear this handbell, you stand still. On the spot. At the second ring, you come in. Quietly!' Even though we were just two classes, she had no intention of letting up on discipline.

Out in the courtyard at playtime, Ronnie and I soon collected a bunch of others to play tag. At the rear there was a low wooden fence to the churchyard. A new girl, who had joined the class just before we came away, was hunched over it, staring at the gravestones. I called to her to come and join our game but her shoulders were heaving. She was crying.

At that moment Gerald grabbed my arm. 'Gotcha!' he yelled.

'Wait,' I said. 'Fainites.' This was our accepted word for dropping out. 'I'll come back in the next game.' Gerald looked surprised. But fainites was fainites and he ran off.

I knew that the girl's name was Marion and called her again. She shook her head and buried her face in her arms on the fence rail. I went over and asked if she wanted the teacher and again she shook her head. All I could see was a tousle of unruly fair hair. No one else seemed to care and I felt really sorry for her.

Just then Sammy, who must have been watching from the gateway, came running across with two of his cronies. He'd been carving notches in the gatepost with a red penknife.

'Cry-baby. Cry-baby, Marion.' He grinned at his friends. 'Anybody got a big 'andkerchief for the cry-baby?'

'Leave her alone,' I snapped. 'She's upset.' Rita had mentioned that her mother was in hospital.

Sammy leered around at the gathering crowd of children then pointed at me. 'Cor. Jus' 'ark at Titch.'

'Her mum's very ill,' I shouted, even more annoyed. 'You just leave her alone!'

Sammy continued to sneer. 'G'arn, Mr Knowall. She told you special, did she? Fancy 'er, do you?' He ran over to the gatepost, shouting, 'David loves Marion! David loves Marion! Let's carve it on the post, eh? Then everyone'll know. Ha ha ha.'

I saw red. I flew across the courtyard and flung myself at him, my arms flailing like windmill sails. Sammy quickly recovered, dropped the knife and fought back. Ronnie ran over to take my side and Sammy's cronies joined in. Soon, a tangled mass of arms and legs and flying jackets was raising a cloud of dust, with excited children egging us on.

Hearing the commotion, my teacher came out, ran across the yard and pulled back two of the onlookers. 'Stop it!' She raised her voice: 'Stop this at once!' Then, almost screaming: '*At once*. Do you hear me?'

No had ever heard her shout like that. Everyone froze. Slowly, silently we stood still, heads hanging, hands limp.

'He started it, Miss,' growled Sammy.

'Liar! You did,' I shouted.

'Quiet, all of you,' she barked. 'I don't care who started it!' She was breathing heavily, her face flushed. 'Now, listen. I will not have fighting in the school. Or anywhere, for that matter.' Her voice quivered. 'There will soon be enough fighting in the world . . .' she paused and looked at all of us, from one to another '. . . and I will not tolerate fighting here. Do you all understand?'

A low chorus answered her. 'Yes, Miss Pizer.' I'd never thought she could be so angry.

Suddenly she spotted the freshly notched gatepost, then the knife on the ground.

'Who did this?' She glanced around the huddle. 'Own up the boy whose knife did this!' Silence. It would have been my chance to pay back the bully but snitching to a teacher was against our code.

Faced by the common silence, she took to asking each boy in turn. Sammy baulked at telling an outright lie – it was bound to leak out anyway – so he owned up. And that was the last he saw of his knife. I glanced at Ronnie and we smiled. At that moment, the headmistress rang the bell once, then again, and we trooped back into the classroom. The lesson hit home. We were only half of the school but the same discipline indeed still applied.

At the end of school, Miss Pizer called me back. 'I know from the other girls that you were trying to help Marion.'

'But that bully had to start on her, Miss.'

'Fighting doesn't help, though, David. And with all of us away from home, we have to stick together, don't we?'

68

'Yes, Miss,' I muttered sheepishly.

'Remember, next time come and see me instead.' She smiled and ruffled my hair. 'And that goes for you, too. If you need help, you will come and see me, won't you?'

'Yes, Miss. Thank you, Miss.'

When I got outside, everyone else had gone. I ran up the lane until I came to the stile and swung myself into the hayfield beyond. There, I lay on my back, gazing up into the sky. From high above came the song of the invisible bird I'd heard the day before but now it was growing louder. At last I saw it – a tiny bird fluttering its wings and hovering for a few seconds before dropping down then hovering again and repeating all that and all the time singing, before it it vanished into the next field. I'd seen my first skylark.

I could have lain there all day, but as a breeze sighed through the tall elm trees along the lane, my stomach rumbled. At home I never seemed hungry and Mum always had trouble making me eat. Here, though, after just a few days in the country air, I'd acquired a hearty appetite.

Young minds adapt quickly and my new routine soon took hold. I grew used to the narrow bed and the stiff white sheets boiled in the copper in the kitchen. Dirty clothes disappeared from my room and were replaced with clean ones. As I lay in bed at night, without the traffic noise I was used to at home, it seemed so quiet – just the breeze through the trees or an owl hooting.

Mrs Clark had her house rules and told me off if I lost a sock or jumped up from the table before the end of a meal. She reminded me to wash behind my ears, just like Mum, but she was never nasty. The time passed without my noticing and Tenter Street slipped further and further from my consciousness.

Rainy weekends, though, could be really boring. In London, the houses were so close that rainy days didn't seem to matter – there was always someone nearby to play with. Here, in pouring rain, there was no way we could face walking along the open roads or through muddy fields to meet up with our friends.

To pass the time, Rita and I played cards or Ludo, or listened to the wireless. Otherwise I read and reread the comics I'd brought with me, and the few from the parcels that Mum sent. In the *Dandy*, Desperate Dan was still eating cow-pies but there was no war in Texas. Korky the Cat, disgusted at being rejected by the army, was mobilizing all the cats in his street into a private force. The older boys' paper, the *Wizard*, began to run war stories.

Mrs Clark allowed Rita to stay up later than me and upstairs, after reading my comics, I often knelt on the bed to look out of the window as it grew dark and silent. Then, remembering the blackout and the warden in Arthur Askey's radio show *Band Waggon*, shouting, 'Put those ruddy lights out!' I would jump down, switch off the light and go back to staring out into the darkness. It was so peaceful that, apart from odd news snippets on the wireless, the war still seemed very far away.

Then, about a month after we arrived, the headmistress announced that our parents were coming to visit at the weekend. I was excited at the prospect of seeing Mum but had mixed feelings about Dad's arrival.

Even before the evacuation, I had always found Dad's religious strictures and the synagogue oppressive, so evacuation had been something of a relief.

I took no pleasure at all from attending the stuffy synagogue in Great Alie Street every Friday night and Saturday morning, with long services in a language I couldn't understand. Each prayer was recited at least twice, once by the *khozen*, the cantor, slowly trilling his notes up and down, then again by the congregation repeating it line for line. Sometimes it would be three times. 'As if God couldn't hear the first time,' I always moaned. And if one of my friends sat nearby and we whispered, Dad would snap, '*Sha*! *Sha*!' and point to the prayer book.

Then there were all sorts of silly rules at home, like not being able to switch on the lights or wireless after the Sabbath came in on Friday night until it went out on Saturday night. In the winter, we had to read or play board games or cards by the light of the *Shobbos* candles. When they flickered and went out, we had to go to bed.

On Saturdays, we couldn't go to the pictures or buy ice-cream because you weren't allowed to carry money; we couldn't take a tram or a bus because we would be making the driver and conductor work. But if the *goyim* weren't allowed to work either, why did we have a *shobbos-goy* come to light our fires in the winter on Saturday? Kids are very quick to pick up inconsistencies. And if the Sabbath was for joy, as the Bible said, why was it so miserable?

Rita didn't seem to mind and diligently followed what Dad said but, then, as a girl she had fewer obligations. My brother Arnold also seemed unbothered by the rules and long synagogue services. Like Dad, he took it as part of life and we never talked about it, even when I was older. Later I admired him for 'rescuing' an abandoned prayer shawl from a Chinese shop in Singapore while he was serving in the navy.

Granddad Ziyder was just as observant but that never bothered me. Perhaps I forgave him because he was part of the old, foreign-born generation, though often I wondered if he really enjoyed the dismal *Shobbos*.

I still don't know why I, the youngest, should have reacted differently from my older brother and sister to all this, but evacuation served to heighten those feelings. Dad was sure to ask about my prayers and what I did on *Shobbos*. More than that, I was anxious he would find out about the bacon.

One Sunday morning a week or two previously, I had woken early while Rita was still asleep. I washed, dressed and ran downstairs to the back garden. I was beginning to love that garden. As I went through the kitchen, Malcolm Clark was having breakfast and, as on most mornings, there was that tantalizing smell. After our first night's traumatic meal, however, Mrs Clark had been taking no chances and his breakfast things were usually cleared away by the time we came down.

'Hello, lad.' He smiled, surprised. 'Thrown you out of bed, have they?'

'Sorry, Mr Clark,' I said. 'I didn't know the time and it's sunny so I thought I'd go in the garden.'

Alongside his eggs and fried bread lay long, thin strips of a pinkish-coloured meat I'd never seen before. It smelt really appetizing.

At that moment Mrs Clark came in and saw me staring at the plate.

'You're not supposed to eat that, are you?' she said, more as a statement than a question. 'Though if them rationin's are goin' to be what they say,' she added, 'there won't be much meat at all, apart from pork an' bacon.' She went over to her electric stove, which looked much posher than our blackened gas one at home. 'Anyway, sit you down and have your porridge.'

As I sat opposite Malcolm he winked at me. 'Here, boy. Want a nibble?' He offered me a tiny scrap on the end of his fork.

'Stop that, Malcolm,' snapped Mrs Clark, 'we don't need more trouble.'

'Well. A tiny bit wouldn't hurt, would it?'

I remembered then that the headmistress had told us a few days earlier that the chief rabbi had given permission for young children in evacuation to eat whatever they were given. It was a bowing to the inevitable for, as Mrs Clark had predicted, rationing would soon bite deeper into food stocks.

I knew little about the chief rabbi, except that at Passover our *kosher* food had little labels attached: 'By permission of the Court of the Chief Rabbi'. I used to wonder what kind of court it was. Did they wear wigs, like judges, and if so, how did they keep their hats on over the wigs? Either way, if *he* said so, I supposed we could also eat bacon now.

After a few spoonfuls of porridge, I looked at Mrs Clark as she stood by the sink. 'Well, our teacher says we can eat anything cos it's wartime, Mrs Clark. *Children* can, anyway, the headmistress said.'

'You sure?' Her eyes narrowed. 'You're not just saying that, are you?'

'No. Course not, Mrs Clark. You can ask Miss Pizer. Honest.'

'There y'are.' Malcolm held out his fork again.

I was just about to take the nibble when Rita came into the kitchen.

'Morning, Mrs Clark. Sorry I'm late.' She must have come down the staircase quietly and I was sure she'd been listening.

'Oh, you're not late,' said Malcolm. 'Just that your brother was up at the crack of dawn.'

Rita was looking at Malcolm's outstretched fork, her face taut. Mrs Clark noticed. 'Your brother says he's allowed to eat anything now. Is that so? Because it would make it much easier for the rations, y'know.'

Rita didn't answer at once and I stared into my porridge, knowing that she was annoyed.

'Well, er . . . yes, the teachers did say that it wouldn't be wrong for the younger children. But I'd still like to ask my parents first, really.'

Malcolm shrugged and withdrew his offering, and I bent over my breakfast, furious, my neck growing hot. Why did Rita have to interfere? At that moment I hated her. I'd got away from Dad's rules and now she was replacing him. Only last week she'd fasted on Yom Kippur, the holy Day of Atonement, even though young girls didn't have to. Perhaps Rita felt some sense of security in keeping to the way things had been at home.

The next morning a light mist hung in the air as we walked to school. Still annoyed and silent, I deliberately kept to the other side of the road from my sister. Along the hedgerows the grass was growing straggly and turning yellow, and the last shrunken blackberries dangled at the ends of the briars. Through a gap in the hedgerow, on someone's allotment, the broad-bean pods were jet black.

At home, we called them *bobbelekh* and, on a winter's evening, Mum would boil them for ages and we would all sit around the table, peeling and noshing them, like sweets. The day before I'd rubbed a few beans out of a pod – and nearly broken my teeth trying to chew them. Perhaps one day after school I would collect a few and ask Mrs Clark to boil them for me.

I stripped a handful of grass seeds and threw them up into the air, watching them drift away into the mist, thinking about the bacon and Dad. If the Sabbath was for us to enjoy, as Granddad Ziyder said, why were there so many things we couldn't do?

'Don't dawdle, or we'll be late,' Rita called.

At the church hall, we parted as usual.

'Bye, David,' Rita called.

Still annoyed, I walked through the gateway, silent. After a few paces, I stopped and turned. 'Bye, Rita.' I waved. 'See ya.'

It was our daily ritual. Although I was furious with her, there was always the fear that she might suddenly not be there, that I would lose someone else close, like my friends Sid and Alfie, like Ziyder and Mum. And if she did go away, at least I'd have said goodbye.

Rita waved back and walked off into the mist. There was no spring in her footsteps: I knew she hated every day at the village school where the schoolmaster was nasty and vindictive. I heard Rita telling the headmistress one morning that she was sure he was *yidified* – the word we used for anti-Semites – because he had snapped that it was only the Jewish kids who talked in class. Barry said his billet lady had told him that the schoolmaster was bad-tempered because he'd been gassed and shell-shocked in Flanders. All the older class was scared of him, and Rita had told the headmistress that she feared, sooner or later, there was bound to be trouble. And there was.

The following week, when we were playing during morning break, Rita hurtled through the gateway, straight into the headmistress. Breaking away from the games, I edged into the porch and listened. My sister was half talking, half sobbing, stopping to catch her breath.

'It all started when Derek started coughing in the middle of morning prayers, Miss Pizer.' I already knew from Stephen that the headmaster held morning service each day with hymns and the Lord's Prayer. Miss Pizer had said that, while they shouldn't sing the hymns, they could recite the prayer because it could easily have been a Jewish prayer.

'Well, Derek couldn't stop it, honest he couldn't,' Rita went on. 'So Mr Stratton went mad, grabbed him by the collar and said he was making a mockery of the prayers. He held him over the desk and started hitting him with the cane and—' Rita broke down, sobbing. Eventually she went on, 'But Derek broke free and ran out the door. Then Stephen and Maurice joined him, the headmaster shouting that he would deal with them all later. I wanted to follow but waited till the break.' Then, after another burst of sobbing, she stamped her foot. 'I'm not going back there, Miss Pizer. I'm not. Ever. Nor will Derek, I know.'

For a moment there was absolute silence inside the hall.

'Well,' said the headmistress at last. 'It will be like truancy if you all stay away.'

'But it's the truth, Miss Pizer. You can ask Derek and the others.'

'Oh, I don't doubt you for one moment. But we have to resolve this in the best way. Rita . . .' She paused. 'Look, you can stay here today and help me with this new delivery of books and paper. Later I shall speak to the vicar. I'm sure he will help in this. And we can discuss it with your parents. They're coming this weekend, aren't they?'

'Yes, Miss Pizer. Thank you.'

Suddenly I heard footsteps coming and Miss Pizer saying, 'Oh! Good heavens. I must ring the bell!' I dodged out of the porch and ran into the playground.

That evening at supper Rita sat very still, her shoulders hunched. I felt really sorry for her and guilty that we'd had arguments. Perhaps the headmistress could arrange for her to go to a different school.

It was Thursday afternoon. Mum and Dad would be coming in two days. The previous weeks had passed so quickly but this one seemed to drag. With so many new experiences each day, I hadn't missed my parents as much as I'd thought I would but now, with their visit imminent, I was tense and impatient. I wanted to show them around the village – *my* village. I also hoped Mum would bring more comics – and some of her marvellous bread pudding, with raisins and cinnamon.

Rita was sitting on her bed writing a letter. I was sure she was telling Mum about the headmaster. Meanwhile, with the folds of the coverlet making a great battlefield, I had set up the few lead soldiers that Dad had bought me in Woolworths at Gardiner's Corner. At the time, I was annoyed with him for not buying me some knights in armour on horseback. They'd cost sixpence each, he'd said, and I could have three soldiers for that money. Now I was pleased. Who wanted knights in armour in a real war?

I'd never played with soldiers much at home but now it all seemed much more real and I wished I had more. Three of them had lost a leg in my hand-to-hand battles and I wondered why they made them hollow and of soft lead when they broke so easily. I wanted new ones because most of mine had the scarlet tunics and black busbies of the Grenadier Guards or brightly coloured kilts. Only five were in khaki. Did those soldiers outside Buckingham Palace fight in their bright red tunics and busbies?

I moved the three redcoats towards the enemy but they were surprised by two khaki-clad sentries held in my other hand. In the hand-to-hand battle that ensued, they retreated – and another lost a leg. Rita was still scribbling furiously.

'Can you ask Dad to get me some more soldiers, Rita? Ones in khaki, if he can.'

She nodded, then carried on writing.

After a while I grew bored, put the soldiers away in my tin box and went downstairs. Standing by the open front door, I stared at the bees humming around the Michaelmas daisies and wondered about that name. I couldn't tell Dad what they were called. Michaelmas was a Christian word, wasn't it?

At that moment a group of the older boys ran past with my friend Gerald struggling to keep up at the rear.

'Hi, Gerry,' I called, running to the front gate. 'Where you going?'

'Stephen's found a tree full of apples,' puffed Gerald. 'We're goin' scrumpin'.'

'Money doesn't grow on trees,' Mum would say, whenever we thought of buying something. But apples did!

Like most evacuees I'd thought that the fruit on the trees was just part of nature – free for all – and had no idea that farmers grew it for a living. All across England, city hordes let loose on the countryside had the same idea and, in those first two autumn months of the war, created havoc. It even prompted urgent questions in Parliament. But by the time the lesson was brought home by lectures – and, on several occasions, a cuff round the ears – it was too late. Many orchards had been stripped almost bare.

One day the headmistress had called us all into one class to be confronted by an angry, red-faced farmer. Orchards were now out of bounds. If a footpath ran through one, and the orchard could not be avoided, we were to take only windfalls – but the fruit on the trees seemed to taste much nicer.

It was now October and I was surprised that there were any apples left on the trees – and a bit anxious about what might happen if we were caught. But I was bored and it was something to do.

'Hang on. I'll tell Mrs Clark,' I shouted, and ran in to get my jacket.

'Just make sure you're back before dark,' she said, and I ran to catch them up.

At the end of a lane we came to a thick hedge around the orchard.

'Won't the farmer be watching?' I asked. If we were caught, we'd really be for it.

'It's okay,' Gerald reassured me. 'Stephen's scouted it out and it's all clear.'

Crouching low, we wound Indian-file between the twisted tree trunks, stopping every now and again to listen. There must have been about a dozen of us. When a blackbird flew across, clucking its warning cry, we froze and my heart thumped. So much for Stephen's confidence.

Eventually, we reached a huge tree and gathered under it in a circle.

'See? What did I tell you?' crowed Stephen. 'Tons of 'em.'

Barry looked up and wrinkled his nose. 'They're all green.'

'So what?' snapped Stephen. 'So are Newtons, ain't they?'

He jumped onto a low crotch, where the branches separated, then climbed up into the tree and began to pick off the largest he could see, stuffing them into his shirt. When he came down triumphantly, he handed some to the bigger boys. But after just one bite, they threw them onto the ground.

'Ugh,' winced Barry, wiping his sleeve across his mouth, 'sour as a bloody lemon.' Turning to Stephen, he shouted, 'Blinkin' idiot. You've led us on a rotten wild goose chase!'

'Yeh,' added Harvey. 'They're cooking apples, you clot. My mum bakes 'em with golden syrup. You can't eat 'em raw.'

'An' that's why they're still up there,' added Barry.

Stephen tried to justify himself and soon loud arguments broke out, boisterous voices echoing among the trees. No one was cautious any longer. I sat back on my haunches, smiling to myself at the older boys having a go at each other instead of at us.

Suddenly they stopped and froze.

'The farmer!' Gerald shouted. 'Scarper! It's the farmer!'

In a split second, everyone turned and fled, knocking me flying as a mass of bodies hurtled by, a tall man in pursuit. By the time I got to my feet they'd all disappeared through the hedge and beyond. I was alone and, to my horror, the man had turned round. He walked back to the tree and stopped.

Slowly I crouched into the tall grass again, looking at him through the grass stalks. If I stayed very still, perhaps he wouldn't see me. In the silence my whole body trembled as I waited for him to go. But he didn't. He just stood there, thick grey trousers, brown gaiters and a long stick in one huge hand. With his top half and head hidden by the foliage, I felt like the boy who'd strayed into the magic garden of the ogre. I imagined an ugly red face with warts and crooked teeth, ready to stuff me into a dark cupboard where no one would ever find me.

I don't remember how long we stayed like that. Around me, the twisted tree trunks grew more gnarled and contorted, fissures in the bark, black and ominous. The scar of a lopped-off branch grew into an ugly face leering at me. The man still didn't move, so thinking he hadn't seen me, I crawled gingerly to my left to get around the tree. To my dismay, the legs moved in the same direction. I cowered and silently began to pray, Please, God, don't let him hit me with that big stick. And don't let him take me to the headmistress. I wasn't sure which fate would be worse. My eyes began to water and before I knew it I was crying, tears streaming down my cheeks. I made no attempt to stop them, hoping he might take pity on me.

'Oooh . . .' I wailed. 'I'm lost. The big boys left me here . . . Oooh, I didn't take nothing, Mister. Honest. Oooh . . . I'm lost . . .'

Slowly the legs came towards me and the huge figure stood

over me. 'Stand up!' he snapped. 'An' stop that snivellin'.'

Slowly I stood up and raised my head, seeing first the striped shirt and brown jacket, then the weatherbeaten face with grey eyes.

'You pick those?' he growled, pointing to the apples on the ground.

'No, Mister. It was the big boys. Honest it was!' I was about to burst out crying again when he pointed the way with his stick.

'Go on then, scarper,' he said. 'An' if I catch you in here again, I'll tan your ruddy hide for you. D'you hear, lad? An' you can tell that to your mates as well!'

'Yes, Mister. Sorry, Mister,' I whimpered.

'Go on, then,' he growled. 'An' remember what I told you!'

I could hardly believe my luck but didn't wait a second longer. Haring through the trees until I reached the hedge, I found a gap, pushed through and ran as though pursued by a pack of wolves.

At the corner of the lane, the boys were huddled in a tight knot, anxious and silent.

'What happened?' asked Barry. 'We thought you were caught.'

I glared at them. 'Yes, I was. Cos you lot ran off and left me. An' now I'll get all the blame if he comes round to the school, won't I?'

'We thought you was runnin' with us,' said Gerald. 'Honest we did.'

The experience left its mark on me. As we began to walk back to our billets, what upset me most wasn't the farmer's rage but the sense of abandonment I'd felt when the others had left me. I would never trust those older boys again.

By now it was now growing dark and, realizing that Mrs Clark might be worried, I started to run along the lane. As I was passing the vicarage, my teacher happened to come out. I stopped short: grown-ups were always suspicious when you were running.

'Hello, David.' She smiled. 'Been out playing?'

'Yes, Miss,' I lied. 'With Gerald and some friends.' I hoped she wouldn't ask where.

Esther Pizer crouched beside me and straightened my collar. 'Best to tidy you up before you get home, don't you think?'

'Yes, Miss,' I murmured, as the comforting hands brushed down my pullover and smoothed back my hair. 'Thank you, Miss.' I wished yet again that I could have been billeted with her.

'Right. Well, run along now. See you in school tomorrow.'

I trotted off down the lane, still worried that the farmer might come to the school tomorrow. The sky darkened and a few drops of rain started to fall. I ran even faster when the rain came in earnest, my stomach still churning from the confrontation with the farmer. It took me till after supper to calm down.

Later, as I lay in bed with the light fading outside, my mood brightened as I looked forward to the weekend. Only two more days to go to Mum and Dad's visit.

Chapter 6

First Visit

Sunday morning dawned grey and damp. From my bedroom window I gazed at the low clouds filling the sky, eager yet apprehensive about the day ahead. It had rained on Friday and Saturday and I hoped it wouldn't that day as well. There were so many things in 'my village' that I wanted to show Mum and Dad: the stile, my 'secret' path across the meadow to the back gate, the acorns in their little cups, which I'd collected from the huge oaks around the churchyard – Miss Pizer had said some of the trees were hundreds of years old. I'd take Mum and Dad to the pond where the red-beaked moorhen stalked on its spindly legs, and show them the dense bracken in the woods where you could hollow out a cave and be invisible.

Mum would probably come in the smart black astrakhan coat and hat she had nagged Dad to make for her. I'd watched it take shape on the dining-room table, Dad cutting the cloth from brown-paper patterns he brought from the workshop, tape measure round his neck, lips pursed, then sewing it together on the Singer treadle machine he'd had since the First World War.

Mum made the buttonholes herself. She often took in finishing work on newly tailored jackets and coats and sometimes I watched her sticking a pointed bone bodkin through the round end of a rough-cut buttonhole and sewing tiny close stitches with black 'twist' thread around the thick black 'gimp' thread to create a neat finish. Occasionally I helped her carry jackets and coats up to the dingy top-floor workshop in East Tenter Street, with the old hunchbacked porter coming down the other way, muttering, 'Up an' dahn the bloody stairs, all day long . . .'

I couldn't wait to see Mum, but I had butterflies in my stomach about Dad: he would want to know if I'd said my prayers. Luckily the headmistress held a *Shobbos* service every Saturday morning so perhaps that would be enough. But would Rita tell him about the bacon? And what would he say if she did? I had to eat meat to grow properly, didn't I? Mum always made me eat my meat and Mrs Clark had said there wouldn't be much lamb or beef when rationing started – and the chief rabbi had said we could. I hoped Mum would tell Rita off for not letting me eat it. I was also worried what the Clarks would think of Dad's gruffness and his foreign accent.

Later that morning, after breakfast, I stood with Rita in the crowd of chattering children by the green outside the village pub, waiting for the coach. I'd wanted to go early and meet Ronnie but Rita, being bossy, kept me indoors and tidy until it was time to go.

'You're not going to get all muddied up just before Mum and Dad come,' she'd said. Mrs Clark had agreed with her. Now with my shoes polished and neatly pressed creases in my grey shorts, I stood among the crowd of children and the two teachers.

On the green opposite there was a tall granite cross with

names carved into the pyramid-shaped base. 'Lest We Forget,' said the large letters above them. They were the names of real men who'd once lived in the village. Did their widows still live there, or their children? They would be grown-up now – and without their dads.

I wondered how long you had to remember. For how many more years would Dad march to the Cenotaph each November along with thousands of Jewish ex-servicemen, his medals bouncing on his chest? Mum and we kids would stand in Horse Guards Parade, with the echoes of them singing the prayer *Adown Owlom*, which meant Master of the Universe, ringing around Whitehall. The men couldn't take part in the official Remembrance Sunday because it was a Christian church service, so Jewish ex-servicemen had their own march-past and a service the following week.

Dad had been with the Labour Corps at Ypres, in the hell of Flanders, conscripted with thousands of others from the East End. They were still foreign nationals and were promised naturalization when it was over. After a year in the mud, facing death, some never made it back to make use of it.

As more and more children arrived, the noise and commotion increased. Villagers appeared at nearby windows, perhaps annoyed by the disturbance of their normal quiet Sunday morning. Some had opened their front doors and stood watching.

Suddenly everyone turned to face up the road and the clamour strengthened as a coach came round the bend from the main road and approached at speed. I reached out and gripped Rita's hand.

As soon as it stopped and the door opened, the noise erupted again as tearful mothers hurtled down the steps, red-faced and panting, each eager to demonstrate how much more they loved their child than anyone else loved theirs. After a few seconds, Mum emerged from the crush in her black coat, with the matching hat planted firmly on her hennaed hair. Having got used to the villagers' ordinary clothes, I thought she looked very smart. Her brown eyes were damp but sparkling and a smudge of lipstick showed on her thin lips. More importantly for me, in each hand she carried a bulging oilcloth shopping bag. She dropped them, hugged me close and I buried my face in the furry cloth of her coat. Then she stood back and looked me up and down. 'But you're still so thin.' She squeezed my arms and thighs. 'Don't you get enough to eat? Do you finish all your potatoes, like I told you?' I just smiled and looked at the bags, wondering what was inside. I would have to wait to find out.

Rita came forward and she and Mum embraced for a long, long time. I looked around for Dad. Hadn't he come? Suddenly a heavy hand rested on my shoulder.

'*Nu*, Dovidle. How are you keeping?' I spun round. Dad! He always called me by my Hebrew name. He wore his new grey overcoat, bought from the Fifty Shilling Tailors – he made only ladies' clothes – and a grey homburg perched over his bushy, black eyebrows.

'Dad. Where were you?'

'Huh. I waited in the coach till they'd all rushed out. Like *meshiggeners* – madmen – they were,' he huffed. 'And so noisy. In front of strangers, *nokh*. A disgrace!' I found myself admiring his distaste for fuss – which I seem to have inherited.

Ronnie's father, who worked in the same workshop as Dad, came past and grinned at him. '*Nu*. What do you expect, Jack, with all those *yentas* gossiping?' He winced. 'I've still got a head-ache from the way they kept yakking the whole way down!'

The driver had climbed out of his cab and hurried into the sanctuary of the pub. More and more curious villagers were standing by their front gates, staring. I felt embarrassed and tugged at Mum's hand. 'Come on,' I whined. 'Let's go.'

We walked down the lane, passing groups of babbling, gesticulating parents and children. The whole village seemed to be on the move. Suddenly Dad stopped, pushed back his hat and took two deep breaths. 'Ah, the air. A *mechayeh* – what a blessing, Dovidle.' He drew another deep breath. 'Ah. So good, after the stink and heat of the workshop.'

I had been to his workshop in New Road several times, a long, dusty first-floor room dimly lit with bare bulbs. A row of women, some in headscarves, huddled over whirring sewing machines. Opposite them, standing by a long table, Dad and two other men would be marking out cloth from brown-paper patterns with thin cakes of waxy chalk, making sure that every inch of cloth could be used. He often brought the chalk ends home for us to draw hopscotch grids on the pavements. At the far end, a cloud of steam hung over the table where Yankel, the presser, finished off the garments, taking a fresh iron from the flaming gas rings as the last cooled.

'*Nu*,' Dad asked me, as we walked, 'how far is your billet?'

I felt so grown-up. Dad was asking me the way! In my village. 'Just to the end of this lane, then round a bend into our road,' I said proudly, taking his hand. He was holding one of the bags and I walked ahead with him. He didn't say much but I wondered when he would ask about my prayers and what I ate.

We passed the village school and Rita began telling Mum about the headmaster, her voice low – perhaps not wanting me to hear. Then, as we neared the Clarks' house, I began to wonder what they would think of Mum and Dad and how Dad would react if they offered him something to eat – he ate strictly *kosher*.

Mr Clark must have made sure he had leave that day because as soon as we knocked he and Mrs Clark were at the front door.

'Oh, do come in. We've wanted so much to meet you,' said Mrs Clark. 'And this is Mr Clark.' I thought again how strange it was to hear her call him by his surname instead of saying 'my husband' or giving his first name, like Mum would.

'Lovely to meet you, Mrs Clark,' said Mum, in her pronounced cockney accent. 'And thanks a lot for looking after them so well.'

'Oh. They've been very good, considerin',' said Mrs Clark.

We sat in the front room where I couldn't help noticing that the yellow wallpaper was a shade paler just above the table. They talked about the weather, the new ration books, the coach journey (which had taken nearly three hours), Mum doing most of the talking. Dad sat silent, looking around the room and through the front window. Then Mum went out to the hall, brought back a small package and handed it to Mrs Clark.

'Oh. You shouldn't have, Mrs Malina,' said Mrs Clark, blushing deep red as she unwrapped the blue tissue paper. It contained a yellow and green china set of salt, mustard and pepper pots. 'That's very kind of you.' She got up and went to set it in pride of place on the mantelpiece. 'Really, you shouldn't have. Thank you ever so much.' I was pleased. Good old Mum.

My delight was short-lived, though. Mrs Clark went into the kitchen and came back with a huge serving plate. I blanched, fearing what was going to happen.

'Please have some sandwiches.' She held out the plate. 'You must be famished from the long journey.' Everyone took one and started to eat. Except Dad.

I shrank into my chair as he muttered, 'Thank you, but you shouldn't have troubled.' He stood up. 'We brought some food with us.'

For a second or two no one moved. I felt so embarrassed. He hadn't removed his hat either. I dared not look at the Clarks. All that preparation and care, asking Rita what they didn't eat, then making cheese and cucumber sandwiches so as not to offend. What could be *treifa* – or unclean – about cheese and cucumber? Yet my strict father couldn't bring himself to relax his rules because Mrs Clark's kitchen wasn't strictly *kosher*. After just a few weeks in the country, I was beginning to feel I had more in common with Malcolm Clark than I did with my own dad.

Mum defused the situation by laying her hand on Dad's arm and he sat down again as she took two sandwiches for herself. 'We had something on the coach,' she lied, 'so my husband isn't hungry.'

I ate some sandwiches and so did Rita and, as we munched, the conversation flowed again between Mum, Rita and the Clarks. They were comparing life in wartime London with the village, Mum telling of digging shelters, making allotments in the parks, and sandbags everywhere. Then they moved on to the prospect of rationing.

Meanwhile I was growing impatient and fidgety. Mum noticed, went out to the bags in the hall and came back, handing me a small brown-paper parcel. Thinking it would be rude to open it in the room, I ran out to the hall. I opened it to find some lead soldiers – mainly in Grenadier red, but there were four prone figures in khaki. Just what I needed! Later, she told me that they were difficult to find now that all metal was being used for the war effort. They'd even started cutting down the iron railings around the parks, she said, to use in munitions.

I wanted to go upstairs and play with the soldiers there and then, but knew I had to go back to the front room so I left them on the stairs. When I did go back in, Dad was sitting in a corner, a human iceberg, saying hardly anything. At least he was drinking a cup of tea; he must have been really thirsty to concede that. I'd had enough of his rules and was glad that, once he had gone home again, I wouldn't have to suffer them.

Rita and Mum managed to keep the conversation going but, after about an hour, it lapsed. With handshakes, thank-yous and choruses of 'It's a pleasure', we left the house, the Clarks waving from the front door. I was relieved that, in spite of Dad, the meeting had gone well. Soon I was cajoling Mum and Dad into seeing the village – *my* village. Everyone was to meet the teachers in the school hall at three o'clock and, in the meantime, I wanted to show my parents the stile and the kissing gate, feeling sure they would never before have seen either.

Outside, the whole village seemed to have been taken over by the family groups from London. Through their net curtains, the villagers were observing the histrionic gestures, stylish clothes and loud voices, the dark homburgs, the coloured headscarves and bright red lipstick. Ronnie told me that his billet neighbour had assured him last week that grown-up Jews had horns and huge long beards, because she'd seen a picture of a statue of one. I suppose that, had we not come to the village, she would have remained with this impression gained from Michelangelo's *Moses* . . .

As we walked down the lane, I jumped up onto the stile. 'See, Mum, see, Dad,' I called, as they stood on the road. 'It's called a stile, so you can hop over the fence, but the cows can't get out.' As I jumped off, Mum hugged me and I could see she was pleased that I was happy. Then I pulled them along the lane to my favourite pond. Rita waited on the road talking to Dad, who must have been starving by now, as he munched sandwiches they'd brought from London.

I took Mum's hand to guide her past the muddy patches and we reached the water's edge but the pond was deserted, the water still and black. Just the occasional ripple of a dancing fly or falling leaf. The moorhens were in hiding and I was sure that all the visitors and noise had scared them into the bulrushes.

'Come on, David,' Rita called from the road. 'We all have to be at the school hall by three.'

Soon, we were in the midst of a noisy throng, all heading in the same direction. At the entrance gates, Dad paused. Glancing at the cross on the notice-board, his lips moved and I imagined he was saying a silent prayer, like he did when we passed the Mission in Spitalfields. But in he went.

In the hall, the dividing partition had been pulled aside and everyone was looking towards the stage at one end where the teachers stood. Ronnie and I disappeared into a corner and compared notes about the parents' visits. His father wasn't religious so, despite some awkward moments in which no one had had anything to say, he'd had it easier. Barry had said Ronnie's dad was a communist and opposed the war, but I had no idea what that meant. Much later, I learned of the Molotov–Ribbentrop Pact and that, until the German invasion of Russia, the British Communist Party had opposed the war.

The hall fell silent as the headmistress told everyone that the school had been split up and would not be reunited until we returned to London. Ronnie and I looked at each other: we wouldn't see our friends until after the war. The headmistress continued with other news, to which I didn't pay much attention. Then, at the mention of the chief rabbi, my ears pricked up.

'Obviously,' she was saying, 'we cannot expect the foster-parents to keep all our dietary rules. As some of you know, children have been excused from these for as long as rationing continues.' Then she read out part of the chief rabbi's letter. I winked at Ronnie and we smiled. Finally, she invited everyone to tea and biscuits, disappointingly adding, 'And please, children, wait until the end before helping yourselves.' I noticed that Dad and two or three other fathers didn't take any, fearing that they were not *kosher*.

Eventually, Ronnie and I managed to find a few broken biscuits while Mum and Rita were talking agitatedly with the headmistress, Rita stamping on the floor from time to time, as she did when she was annoyed. I couldn't hear what they were saying but I knew it must be about the village school again.

The meeting ended and we all filed out of the hall. In small groups, we strolled up the lane towards the green and the coach, but everyone was much less animated now, conscious of parting again. The coach would leave in less than half an hour, as it had to be back in London before the blackout.

A breeze had blown up. Overhead the huge oak branches creaked with the wind. Birds chirped as they sought shelter in the dark hedgerows and the last bees hummed home to their hives before the rain arrived that threatened from the ominous clouds.

With Rita still talking to Mum about her school and the headmaster, I found myself walking again with Dad. He hadn't yet asked any awkward questions and I was feeling relieved because it was nearly time to go. Suddenly, he stepped ahead, turned and bent down to me, his eyes sharp.

'Tell me, Dovidle. Do you say your prayers every day?' The abrupt question caught me completely off balance.

'Yes . . . Course, Dad. Course I do,' I blustered. 'We have prayers every morning in school and a service on *Shobbos.*' I began to sweat. I should have known Dad would find an opportunity and, sure enough, he had – right at the last ruddy moment, just when we'd reached the coach and I'd thought I'd got off scot-free.

'But you're not at school in the evening and at the weekend. Do you say your prayers then as well?' he pressed.

I stared at my shoes. 'Well. Yes. Usually,' I lied.

'And do you wear you *tzitzeh konfus*?' he asked, referring to the special fringed vest all Orthodox Jews wear.

'Course,' I said. Having been prepared for this one, I'd made sure to put it on that morning and raised my pullover to show him. After the first week, I'd deliberately stopped wearing it, fed up with the fringed tassels flying out of my shirt tails when I was playing tag. Very few of the boys ever wore it and I felt silly in mine. 'Look, Dad,' I chirped, pulling out one of the tassels.

He hadn't finished. 'And you say the *Shema*? That's the most important prayer, you know.' We used to say it in school prayers: '*Shema Yisroel, Adonoi Elohenu, Adonoi Ekhod*': Hear, O Israel. The Lord is God. The Lord is One. It was the only prayer I knew by heart.

I was becoming annoyed with Dad's interrogation and obviously my responses didn't satisfy him because he turned away and, striding forward, started to talk to Mum, angry and red-faced.

'Tell me,' he snapped at Mum, in a loud voice I couldn't help overhearing. 'What kind of a *mensch* will he be when he comes home? A complete *goy*!'

Mum looked around, embarrassed. People nearby must have heard. 'Look, Jack, the teachers are doing their best,' she said. 'What do you expect? There's a war on.'

'So what?' He snorted. 'Nothing else to eat? Only *chazzer*?' Pork. So he'd heard about the bacon. Dad started to walk forward again, fists clenched. 'Since Bible times, Jews have refused to eat *chazzer*. In Russia, the Cossacks used to force pork into Jews' mouths while they beat and tortured them. And now in Poland the Nazis are doing the same. You've heard the news. And I should let my son eat it? Eat *chazzer*? Because the *Englisher* rabbis can't take a stand?' He took a couple of paces. 'We'll have to bring him home,' he muttered.

Mum listened, then said firmly, 'You can say what you like, Jack, but he's still a kid, just a kid, and there's a war on. I'm not bringing him home, away from the school and away from his friends.' She shook a finger at him. 'He's staying here. Out of the war. And Rita can keep an eye on him.' She lowered her voice as if not wanting me to hear. 'At least here he's safe.'

Dad walked on with her, silent and brooding. I dragged my feet but Rita took my hand and we all walked in silence up to the green. When we got there, Rita and Mum talked about new shoes while Dad stood to one side of them. I was a few feet to the other, feeling guilty. Because of me, Mum and Dad had argued, which always upset me. If I'd done as Dad wanted, they wouldn't have argued – but I didn't want to do all those silly things. Ronnie didn't have to.

The coach driver appeared and climbed into his cab. I buried my head in Mum's coat, the cloth tickling my face.

'Bye, my angel. Be a good boy – and write.' She hugged and kissed me. 'Even if it's only on the bottom of Rita's letters.'

I was always drawing cartoons and adding them to her letters: Hitler getting heart attacks from Victory Vs on his wall; fat Goering tripping over his million medals into the sea.

'Yes, Mum.' I tried to hold back the tears. 'Thanks for the presents, Mum.' As she turned to say goodbye to Rita I looked at Dad. He was still morose and brooding.

'Bye, Dad,' I called. 'Thanks for the soldiers.' He started, as though roused from a dream.

'Oh. Cheerio, Dovidle.' He stepped towards me and patted my head. 'And remember what I told you. Promise?'

'Yes, Dad,' I mumbled. Yes, he was my father and I was sad that they were leaving so soon but I wanted him to be gone, to feel free again. 'Honour thy father, thy mother . . .' The teachers had taught us the Ten Commandments.

The driver, meanwhile, was fast losing patience and sounded his horn. With only a narrow slit of clear glass on his black-painted headlamps, he needed to be back in London before the blackout. No one moved, every mother wanting to be last on the coach. Eventually, he started the engine and revved it. There followed a mad scramble to occupy the front seats. The door closed and a forest of arms waved from the windows.

Slowly the coach drew away up the slope, gathered speed, turned the corner and disappeared. We hung around on the green as the haze of blue exhaust smoke dispersed into the trees. Then, as the first raindrops pattered down, one by one we walked away, towards our billets.

In front of us, little Marion was on her own, chin tucked into her chest and one hairgrip hanging loose. I was sad that Mum had gone but seeing Marion so miserable – only her father had come – I almost forgot my own woes and wished I could console her. But I was only a kid myself, struggling to make sense of complex, unfamiliar emotions.

It was dusk by the time we reached the house. Mrs Clark had the kettle on and made us toast while she and Rita talked over the day's visit. Malcolm had gone back to the RAF camp and the three of us had supper. Outside, the rain beat steadily on the windowpanes.

Rita was still downstairs as I undressed for bed. Whipping off the fringed vest, I stuffed it into the bottom of my drawer guiltily. I'd deceived Dad. But I wouldn't be a *goy*. I'd show him – and God would see, too. Putting on my school cap, I switched off the light and, in the darkness, prayed, '*Shema Yisroel* . . . Hear, O Israel, the Lord is God . . .' I said it right through to the end and felt better.

As I lay in bed, the rain grew heavier and drummed on the roof of the garden shed below. Trees hissed in the wind – they had real storms in the country. I hoped Mum and Dad didn't get soaked walking home from the coach. Did they have the same weather in London? Poor Mum. She'd looked tired and her face had been so pale when the coach left. Still, I had managed to show her a bit of the village – it had been quite a day out. I felt a rush of love for both of them. The bread pudding she'd brought was smashing and I was thrilled with my comics. I was looking forward to the coming week as Malcolm had promised to show me how to do headstands. He was a PT instructor, so I knew he must be really fit and strong. Mrs Clark was nice too. She laughed when Malcolm cuddled her, giggling sometimes when they whispered together.

Rita switched off the light and I lay in bed, listening to the rain beating against the window beyond the blackout curtains. Now, after a month or so, I was getting so used to being with the Clarks and they were so kind that I was missing home less – especially being reminded of Dad's religious restrictions after his visit. But the Clarks weren't my family – and they would have their own children one day. Mum and Dad were my family: I loved them and they loved me. When all this was over, I'd go back to them. I was feeling a bit guilty that I was so happy there. I wondered how the other children felt.

Thoughts continued to chase around in my head until, exhausted after the day's excitement, I fell asleep.

Chapter 7

Moving On

October drew to a close with fine rain and frequent mists. On the way to school in my short trousers, the morning chill chapped my knees and, with the days shortening, I became aware that the roads were so dark. At first I thought it must be the blackout but then I saw there weren't any lampposts. They had no street lighting even in peacetime!

In the East End, we still had gas lighting. Every evening, the lamplighter came round on his creaking bicycle. At certain corners he raised a hooked pole and pulled on a lever-tap high up on the lamppost and, as if by magic, in all the nearby streets the lamps lit up. Sometimes he had to lean a small ladder against the post and climb up to turn it on. Then he would mount his bike, shoulder the ladder and pedal away into the gloom. I often wondered what would happen if he fell ill or had an accident on his bike. Would the streets stay dark? And did he ride around again in the morning to put them out? What if he slept late? Would they burn all day? I never did find out. The heavy bombing of the Blitz destroyed so many lampposts and gas mains that soon after the war the system was renewed with electric lighting.

While we were having tea one day, I asked Mrs Clark how the villagers managed without street lights.

'Oh,' she laughed, 'you soon gets used to using your eyes in the dark. Any rate,' she added, 'there's often a moon or lots o' stars. They give light too, y'know.'

'But aren't people scared? Like of robbers or wild animals?' I pressed, giving vent to my own anxieties about the approach of winter.

'Well, I don't remember anyone bein' robbed.' She laughed again. 'And there ain't been any wolves an' suchlike in Buck'n'mshire for a long time, s'far as I know.'

Still, I felt I'd be scared to go out in the dark by myself.

After a few more weeks, we became used to the pitch darkness and I became aware of the myriad stars I'd never seen in London, as well as the phases of the moon. That kindled a keen interest in astronomy, which flourished in my teenage years and has remained with me.

I finished my tea and, leaving Mrs Clark in the kitchen, I went into the front room to leaf through Malcolm's PT book. I'd looked through it before and marvelled at the pictures of hand- and headstands. In one, the 'Leopard Stand', the head was slightly raised and the legs stuck straight back at an angle. To me, it seemed impossible for anyone to be able to balance on their forearms like that.

At that moment, the front door clicked.

'Hello, love.' It was Malcolm. 'Got away early tonight.'

I jumped up and ran into the hall. 'Mr Clark, can you really do all those headstands like in the book?' I chirped.

'Reading top-secret manuals, eh?' He ruffled my hair and laughed as he hung up his coat. 'Well, I ought to – else they're payin' me for nothin'.' He grinned. 'But p'r'aps you'll let me have my tea first.'

I went back into the front room and lay on the floor, waiting. Their voices came to me from the kitchen, Mrs Clark's excited, and I heard 'doctor' and 'pretty sure', then silence. I knew they were cuddling – I'd caught them one night when I came down for a drink of water. I'd never seen Mum and Dad do that.

I heard a slight scuffle then, and Mrs Clark gasping, 'Will you let me get on with the tea things, Malcolm? And go and get washed.' Then he laughed.

A short while later, Malcolm was still smiling as he came into the front room. He picked up the manual and I jumped up and pointed to the picture. 'Can you do that Leopard Stand?' I asked, eager. He perused the page and frowned.

'Hmm. Bit of a while since I did that one.' He rubbed his ginger moustache. 'Not as bad as it looks, though.' He hung his RAF jacket on a chair, glanced around, then moved an armchair and a small table to the linoleum at the side of the room. A small green glass vase stood on the table.

'Well,' he said, crouching. 'Let's see.'

He knelt in the centre of the floor, elbows under his chest, pressed his forehead to the beige carpet and gradually raised his legs into the vertical 'Tiger Stand'. I watched, silent, fascinated as he adjusted his balance, raised his face, lowered his legs to an angle and took the weight on his forearms for the final pose.

'There y'are.' He strained. 'Leopard Stand. Simple.'

He glanced across at me and grinned, but as he did so, one elbow slipped sideways and he lost his balance. His foot caught the edge of the small table. It tipped. The green glass vase slid across the polished top then dropped onto the lino, smashing.

I jumped up and backed away, my heart thumping. As Malcolm sat up rubbing his arm, Mrs Clark ran into the room. She looked at her husband, then at the shattered vase, and her hands flew to her face.

'Oh, my God. What have you done, Malcolm?' She started to cry. 'Grandmum's vase. The only thing of hers I've got left.' She ran over and started to pick up the pieces. 'Assin' about to show off to the young lad that don't know no better,' she shouted. 'Won't you ever grow up?'

Malcolm rose and went over to her. 'Please, love, don't be gettin' yourself upset. Especially now.' But she shook him off and continued crying, picking up the pieces and shouting at him.

I backed along the wall to the door, my stomach churning. I edged quietly out of the room, ran upstairs and fell onto my bed. I had made Malcolm do those headstands and now he was in real trouble and Mrs Clark was upset. I wanted to go down and tell her it was my fault but I was scared she might start shouting at me, too. So I lay there, leafing absently through my comics but not really seeing anything.

A short while later, Rita came home and I heard Malcolm talking to her. At suppertime, Mrs Clark wasn't at the table. She must have been upstairs in the bedroom. Rita helped Malcolm set out the plates and cutlery. It was all very quiet and I ate with my head down, too embarrassed to look at Malcolm and feeling really sorry for him.

At the time, I didn't connect the incident with what happened next, but about two weeks later as I came into school, my teacher called me aside. 'David, you and Rita will be moving to a new billet.'

'But I like it there,' I said, puzzled. 'And we get on well, don't we?'

'Of course,' she smiled, 'but Mrs Clark isn't well and she has to rest.'

I had noticed that Mrs Clark was paler than usual and often lay on the sofa in the front room. Then I made the connection between her illness and the vase. I'd made Malcolm do that headstand: because of me Mrs Clark had got ill and because of that Rita and I were being thrown out of our nice billet.

'You'll be moving to the Bakers',' Miss Pizer continued.

'When, Miss?' I asked, thinking it would be in a while. Her reply stunned me.

'Today, David. Simon already lives there and he'll show you around after school. Rita and another boy have already taken your things round.' So it was all decided. I had no idea where the Bakers lived and Simon wasn't a particular friend of mine. More than anything, I was really miserable at having to leave the Clarks.

By chance, a few days after we moved, Rita asked me to go round to collect a pair of socks from them. I was glad to be able to go and say goodbye. As I ran round after school, I toyed with the idea that perhaps when Mrs Clark saw me, and with Rita gone, she'd invite me to stay.

A neighbour answered my knock and opened the door. Mrs Clark was upstairs in bed and called down to me. She was leaning back on pillows and looked pale but she smiled as I came in.

'I'm here to collect some socks,' I said bashfully, 'and to say goodbye, Mrs Clark.'

'Oh. The socks are in your old room,' she said, pointing to the doorway – as if I didn't know where that was. She half smiled. 'Goodbye then, little 'un. An' be a good boy with Mrs Baker.' I ran in and looked around. My bed had already gone – only Rita's was there, with a new coverlet. Without our clobber the room was so tidy.

For one last time, I looked out of the window over the back garden to the hayfield beyond, feeling quite nostalgic – though I didn't know the word then. On the landing I called, 'Bye, Mrs Clark. Say bye to Mr Clark for me.' I wanted to say how sorry I was about the vase – that my dad would pay for a new one. Instead, I just hurried down the stairs, upset. I had really liked living with the Clarks and now I would never get Malcolm to show me the aerodrome or learn how to fire a gun.

It had taken a while to get used to the Clarks' household. Now, again, there was separation and uncertainty. I would have to get used to a new billet. Gripping the socks, in the gathering dusk I ran past the school hall and the rectory and up the lane to Rye Close.

With the move to the Bakers', the warmth I'd been surrounded by came to an end. From this point on, events – some pleasant, others less so – seemed to follow sharply.

If I was apprehensive about the new billet, I had no illusions about my billet mate. I hadn't liked the look of Simon (one of Sammy's cronies) from the start. Ronnie lived near him in London and called him Four Eyes because of his thick-rimmed glasses. He was podgy and cocksure and, beneath a sharp nose, his lips were set in a permanent sneer whenever he spoke.

'What's she like, Mrs Baker?' I asked, as I walked with him up the lane. We'd hardly exchanged a word since Miss Pizer had told him to take me round after school.

'She's all right,' he muttered, and that was that.

I hadn't noticed Rye Close before, even though it was almost opposite the village school, perhaps because the entrance sloped sharply away from the lane. It was a long cul-de-sac of yellow-stucco, slate-roofed, semi-detached council houses, probably built in the twenties as part of the 'Homes for Heroes' policy after the First World War. Similar estates may still exist throughout the south-east, the roughcast stucco perhaps hiding hasty brickwork. The houses were set back from the road and narrow tarmac paths led across a strip of grass and round to the front and back doors. It was a self-contained world that was to be my home for the rest of the school year.

'Is she strict?' I persisted, as we walked up the close.

'Not really,' he mumbled. 'You'll see.'

The Bakers' house stood at the side of a turning circle near the far end.

As we reached the circle, Simon abruptly turned aside through a small front gate. I followed him to the back door then into the kitchen, blinking in the dim light from a tiny window. At that moment a tall, buxom woman, wearing a blue flowered apron over a brown dress, came in from the next room.

'So. This is the new lad, eh, Simon?' I looked up to see a broad, ruddy face with small but kind brown eyes behind steel-rimmed glasses. 'Well, come in and let's be lookin' at yer.' She smiled, and I followed her into the dining room.

'What's yer name, then?'

'David,' I said. 'David Malina.'

The surname was often a problem to me. A Slavic name, my father placed the emphasis on the first syllable and pronounced the short *i* correctly. In England, the second syllable has the emphasis so most people pronounced the *i* as *ee*, making it Maleena. My present surname – Merron – is the result of a voluntary change to Hebrew, effected while a member of a kibbutz in my twenties.

'Well,' she laughed, 'at least it ain't no "ovsky" or "umpstein" for me to break me false teeth on.' She raised a hand to her cheek and looked down at me. 'But, my, we'll have to put a bit o' weight on yer, won't we, Simon?' My growing appetite and Mrs Clark's good meals all seemed to have translated into boundless energy. 'Any rate,' she concluded, 'Simon'll show you yer room.'

As I turned to follow him up the stairs, a small dog ran in from the rear garden and started yapping about my legs. It had long, honey-brown fur, floppy ears and a black snub nose. From one set of my cigarette cards I knew it was a Pekinese. I had nearly four sets of cards that Dad and Uncle Barney used to give me from their cigarette packets, and we would swap doubles in school. I also had a set of cricketers, including Don Bradman and Len Hutton, and a set of warships, like HMS *Hood*, *Warspite* and *Afridi*. Perhaps I could exchange some of my doubles with Simon.

The dog continued to bark, then ran outside and came in again, followed by an older girl or young woman. I was at an age when I couldn't distinguish. She had a round, pretty face – in fact, everything about her was round: shoulders, hips, legs. Not podgy, just rounded. Long fair hair hung down to her shoulders, like on the posters of the American actress Carole Lombard, which I'd seen outside the Rivoli. Her voice was rounded too – almost posh, but not as posh as my teacher's. And, as I found out from that very first encounter, heck, she was spoiled!

'Mummy,' she said, almost in a sob, as though the world was falling apart, 'the shop didn't have the right belt to match the dress you bought.'

'Never mind, my love. Father and me is goin' to town Sat'day. We'll find one there, I'm sure.' Like Mrs Clark, she didn't say 'your dad' but 'father'. It sounded so strange, so formal.

'Oh, would you? Thank you, Mum.' She simpered and kissed her mother's cheek. I was a bit put out because she didn't seem to notice me, as though I wasn't there. This was Doreen. I didn't hit it off with her – or her dog.

I followed Simon into the small front hall and he nodded to a door near the foot of the stairs. 'There's the lav,' he said, 'and we don't use the front door. Never.'

The house wasn't as new as the Clarks' and the stairs were narrow and quite steep. In the front bedroom, two beds were lined up side by side, parallel to the small window, which was painted white and divided into small panes. Simon had the bed nearest the door.

Immediately, I ran to look out but there were no far views as there were at the Clarks', only the road and a row of identical yellow-stucco houses opposite. When I turned back, Simon had picked up a large cardboard box from under his bed and began to spread out his soldiers on the bedcover in exactly the same way that I always did. But there the resemblance ceased. He had handfuls of soldiers in all sorts of uniforms, as well as tanks, lorries and four planes. I'd never seen so many – he seemed to have more than they had in Woolworths!

At that moment, Mrs Baker came in to sort out my clothes in the chest of drawers.

'Well, then,' she said, when she'd finished, 'you've got someone to play with now, Simon, haven't you?' He nodded and continued setting out his army.

'Bet you've got lots of toys, too – so you can both share, can't you?' Mrs Baker said to me. I smiled back but I knew that Simon would be the last person to share anything. His parents must be rich – stinking rich, as my brother Arnold would say – or they had a toy shop. Either way, I'd be too embarrassed to take out my few playthings.

To make matters worse, Mrs Baker was holding up one of my pullovers. 'Hmm. We'll have to darn them elbows,' she muttered. Simon turned to look and I felt sure he would have lots of new clothes. Later, Rita told me that his family was 'comfortable'.

After tea, we went up to the room again. Simon was reading some comics – new ones, I noticed – and continued ignoring me. Fed up, I went to the window and stared out.

Down below, a few doors away at the end of the close, Marion was skipping with her rope and, as the days passed, I often saw her doing that after school or at weekends. She never seemed to do anything else when she was outside – and she never smiled or sang jingles to the rhythm, as the other girls did when skipping. She'd skip for a few minutes, then stand stock still for a while, staring at the ground. I wanted to go and play with her, to comfort her but also – far less altruistic – to find myself a nearby playmate. We could play all sorts of games, like hopscotch or cat's-cradle, with string, but I didn't approach her for fear that Simon would poke fun at me for playing with a girl or, even worse, take the news to school for Sammy and his cronies to crow about. So I just watched, and wondered about her until she was called in.

That first evening, as it grew dark, there was still an hour until suppertime so I knelt by my bed and took out my few soldiers. Not wishing to lay them out alongside Simon's army, I clutched them in my hands and laid my head on the bedcover. Trying desperately to hold back my tears and wishing I could be back with the Clarks, I attempted to cheer myself with the thought that perhaps the war would be over soon and I could go home. There didn't seem to be much fighting reported on the wireless, and the newspaper headlines said Hitler was proposing peace talks.

At that moment, Mrs Baker's voice floated up the stairs and made me jump. 'Come on, boys. Supper's ready.' I stood up and pulled up my socks. 'And don't forget to wash your hands.' Just like Mrs Clark.

A few days later, as I stood with my nose against the window-pane, the evening came in early with heavy grey clouds that made it even darker than usual. As Marion was called inside, I noticed, on the far side of the road, a tall, stout woman with smooth black hair, dressed in a sweeping brown coat. She was talking to a neighbour at their front gate.

When they'd finished their conversation, she ambled along the footpath, hesitating at every front gate and looking in. Another woman came along the road and, as she turned into her gate, the stout woman started talking to her. I could see that the other woman, carrying a shopping bag, wanted to go inside and kept trying to extricate herself from the situation. Each time, though, the stout woman, Mrs Suffolk, started talking again until, eventually, the other managed to disengage and go inside.

Looking disappointed, Mrs Suffolk continued down the road, hesitating by almost every gate and peering through the lighted windows. Finally, at the far end of the close she turned into a gateway and went inside. With her beady eyes and mean face, I was glad I wasn't billeted with her. Later, I heard Mrs Baker mutter to her husband, 'A right gossip and nasty with it, is that Mrs Suffolk.'

November came. The evenings were drawing in and after school there was little chance to play outside before it got dark. I was thrown into Simon's company. We sometimes played Ludo or Snakes and Ladders together, either in our room or on the kitchen table when Mrs Baker didn't need it. But he was a bad loser: when he didn't win, he'd scoop up his toys and sink into a sulk.

As a result, I began to come downstairs alone, leaving Simon upstairs, and sit in the back dining room, watching Mrs Baker ironing or mending. Using a wooden mushroom she would darn the heels of our socks and I looked on, fascinated, as her fingers wove the wool first one way then the other. She worked with her glasses perched on the end of her nose, like Mum did when she made buttonholes.

Mrs Baker often listened to the wireless as she sewed, and as I read my comics, I listened too, remembering how our family used to sit together for *Monday Night at Seven*. Since the war, to accommodate people working longer hours, the programme had become *Monday Night at Eight* and I remember thinking how cleverly they'd fitted the revised words to the programme jingle; the content, of interviews, music and a play, remained much the same.

In the programme, I liked listening to Old Ebenezer, the fictional night watchman. Each time he began a story, I would croak along with his opening phrase: 'One night as I was sitting around my old fire-bucket, drinking a cup of cocoa . . .' So many interesting things seemed to go on in London after dark that I imagined myself being a night watchman one day.

In the short evenings after tea, I occasionally went outside to the back garden or the front of the house. Sometimes Marion would be skipping on the path. One day, when her rope became tangled, she pulled at it but didn't try to untangle it, just stood there looking down, defeated.

Feeling sorry for her, I went over. 'Here,' I said, 'I'll sort it out, if you like.'

She looked up and, without a word, held out the rope to me. I took it and managed to unravel the knot.

'Here,' I said. ''S okay now.'

'Thanks,' she said, then started skipping again. After a few minutes, she stopped and, again without a word, ran back inside the house.

The next evening, when she was on the path, I brought out a tennis ball. 'Wanna play catchers?' I asked.

She nodded and dropped the rope. We threw the ball from one to the other, again without her saying anything or smiling, strands of fair hair hanging over her face. After a few minutes, she threw the ball back, picked up her rope and ran inside on legs like matchsticks.

Most days, Marion was not outside and, despairing of ever becoming real friends with Simon, I began to spend more time alone in the Bakers' long back garden. Neat rows of vegetables, Mr Baker's handiwork, stretched away to the high, straggly hedge at the rear. A narrow cinder path led from the back door to one corner that was fenced off with high wire netting into a chicken run. Almost every day Mrs Baker threw the ashes from the kitchen range onto the path, but they seemed to sink into it without trace.

Like the countryside in general, that garden was a formative influence on my future life, giving me a love of gardens and plants and even igniting a desire in me to become a farmer. The only private gardens I'd seen in London had been full of flowers and lawns, like Uncle Sam's at Wembley, or the small triangular patch at the Rowsteins' corner house in our street – the only garden in our entire neighbourhood.

Whenever we played tag, Mrs Rownstein would yell at us to keep off her marigolds, so we looked on a garden as a luxury, something for show rather than a practical space. Here in the village, everyone seemed to have a garden. My interest deepened one day when Mr Baker, a lorry driver, finished work early. I was watching him digging over an old onion patch, admiring his smooth movements and steady progress as the weed-strewn, packed earth was turned into friable coal-black soil, glistening damply in the late sun. As he paused for a break he looked over to me. He was of medium height and slim, with thinning black hair and often with a Woodbine in his mouth, which he took from a square tin box he kept in his trouser pocket.

'Looks easy, I suppose?' He smiled, blowing out a puff of blue smoke.

I walked over to him. 'Can I have a go, Mr Baker?'

'Well, you won't manage with a spade, that's for sure.' He glanced behind him and pointed. 'Here, take hold of that fork there.'

I brought it over, stood it on the earth and thumped down hard on it with my tiny foot. Its tines hardly penetrated the solid earth.

'Here,' he said. 'No point in wastin' yer strength, lad. Do it like this, see.' He put his weight on his foot, rocked the handle back and, as if by magic, the tines disappeared into the soil. With a firm twist of his wrist, he turned the clod over. 'Right,' he smiled, 'just you do that, lad. Slowly. Nothin's as easy as it looks. Specially work.'

He watched as I tried again, then corrected me each time and, slowly but surely, with a sense of immense achievement, I began to turn the earth over on my own. It was a chilly evening and the light was fading but I didn't notice. By the time I had done half a row, he had turned over several. And I was puffed.

Resting my forehead on the handle, I breathed heavily. I felt a warm hand on the back of my neck. 'Reckon that's good enough for yer first time, lad.'

'I was just catching my breath, Mr Baker. I can go on, really.'

'Mebbe,' he said. 'But it won't run away.' He paused and took a drag. 'Work never does.' Taking up the fork and spade, he walked up the path to the house. 'And we'd better get washed for tea or Mother'll be havin' us.' He grinned. I scraped my shoes on the iron scraper by the back door, changed into slippers in the back kitchen and ran up to my room feeling six inches taller than when I'd come home from school. Mr Baker had treated me like a real grown-up.

Mrs Baker was folding some ironing into our chest of drawers. 'My,' she smiled, 'a bit o' diggin's put some colour into them cheeks, that's for sure.'

Simon was playing with some new tanks and planes that had arrived by post that morning. 'And you can both play with those new toys, eh, Simon?' she suggested. The boy mumbled something about wanting to save them for later and slipped them into his box under the bed. Mrs Baker went out and, after a minute or so, I took my comics and went down to the dining room.

She was talking with her husband and they didn't hear me coming down the stairs in my socks. 'See you had a willin' helper in the garden, Jack.'

'Yes. A real trier, that one. Needs a bit o' meat on him, though, don't he?' And they both laughed.

'Tried to get the two o' them to play together,' she said. 'But real tight with his things, that Simon.' She laughed. 'Real little Jew-boy, that's for sure.'

Standing in the passage, I tensed, wondering whether the Bakers were anti-Semitic. Feeling as I did about Simon, though, I didn't much care. Anyway, they'd never say anything like that about me. Looking back, I suppose their attitude stemmed not so much from anti-Semitism, but from the connection they made between Jewish people and cleverness with money – and, of course, we were different from them.

Chapter 8

Jack Frost

Mum always bought my clothes a size too large so that they would last longer. As November ended, with freezing nights and a white beard of hoar frost glittering on the grass verges on my way to school each morning, I was glad of my long brown coat. Usually I hated her money-saving habit but now, still in short trousers, I was thankful for it.

Simon and I rarely walked to or from school together but I often went with Marion, who came out at the same time as I did. We didn't talk much – I mean, what do boys talk about with girls at that age? The point is that it was company and she might eventually become a playmate, as Shirley in our street had been. But our budding friendship, like so many other things during evacuation, was not to last.

I was playing in my room one Saturday morning, when I heard Marion's voice coming from below – not her usual timid whisper but unusually loud and high-pitched.

'I'm not going,' she was shouting. 'You can't make me.' Then, a few seconds later, in a higher-pitched scream: 'I'm not going! I'm not going!' followed by a woman's coaxing voice. Running downstairs and out to the road, I saw Marion being held by her shoulders by one of those WVS women in green uniforms. She was being pulled towards a large white ambulance that stood by the verge. But it was not an ordinary ambulance. Its windows were blacked out.

As Marion struggled and screamed, her fair hair all over the place, one shoe fell off. A tall man in a brown suit picked it up, then grabbed her legs and lifted her. Somehow they managed to push the struggling figure into the back of the ambulance, where the woman held her down on the seat while Marion continued wriggling and kicking. I was amazed at the strength with which she resisted the two grown-ups; she always looked so thin and frail. Finally, the man managed to close the rear doors then hurried round to the cab and started the engine.

Shocked and trembling, I stood rooted to the pathway, wondering why and where they were taking her by force. Did her dad know – and the teachers? The van slowly backed up and turned. Then, with Marion still screaming and her feet drumming on the floor, it drove away.

As I turned to go back inside, Simon was standing a short distance away, a smirk on his face. 'Takin' her to the loony-bin,' he sneered, flicking his wrist.

I felt like punching his nose but I hated fighting so just walked past him. And I didn't believe him. Marion wasn't mad. She was just very sad about her mum. As I turned to go in, I noticed the bulky figure of Mrs Suffolk on the far side of the road, pointing after the ambulance and yapping to one of the neighbours. Yes, she would be there to watch.

As soon as I got to school on Monday, I asked my teacher why they'd taken Marion away. Miss Pizer assured me that she hadn't gone to a 'loony-bin' but to a convalescent home.

'Marion needs a rest in order to get better,' she said. Better from what? I never did find out. Knowing now the state of children's homes during the war, I still feel sorry for her, wonder what became of her and hope that, with help, she managed to get her life together afterwards.

All that week, as I walked to and from school on my own, I continued to brood on that shocking scene, hoping she'd soon be back. Even though we'd exchanged few words, I'd become quite used to her padding alongside me as I walked to school on the cold mornings.

One day, coming home from school at the end of the week, Simon was standing at the end of the close with two of Sammy's cronies. 'All on yer own today?' He smirked, trying to look big in front of the other boys.

'None of your business,' I snapped.

'Ain't there no crazy girlfriend, then?' grinned one of the others.

'She ain't mad and it's nuffin' to do with you, neither,' I replied, my head growing hot.

'But she's gone to the loony-bin, ain't she?' squawked Simon, pointing his finger at his head. 'She'll go to Colney Hatch, I bet.' In the East End, any lunatic asylum was known as Colney Hatch – the name of a large one at Friern Barnet, in the furthest reaches of North London.

I don't remember much else, except that a moment later I was at Simon's throat, punching and hitting. He hit back. His glasses dropped off and his nose started to bleed, but I didn't care as my arms flailed, mostly missing the target. It must have looked frenzied, though, because the other two boys took to their heels and scarpered.

At that moment Simon fell back onto the grass verge and I just stood over him, heaving and panting, my face stinging. A few of his punches had landed on me. Whimpering, he grabbed his glasses from where they'd fallen on the grass, jumped up and ran up the close towards the billet. Slowly, I followed, knowing that he would tell his side of the story first and anxious about what Mrs Baker would do.

There was a rainwater butt round the back of the house. Still breathing heavily, I stopped and plunged my face into the freezing water, then splashed it again and again, wiping it on my front shirt tails. My lip was still stinging but I felt more ready to face Mrs Baker.

She was waiting inside the back door, hand on hip. 'Well?' she said.

'He started it, Mrs Baker. Him and his mates, honest.'

'Simon says you jumped him from a hedge,' she said.

'How could I? There was three of 'em,' I protested. 'An' he needs to wash his lousy mouth out.'

'Now, now!' she snapped. 'That's enough of that.' She looked straight at me and I sensed a faint smile on her lips. 'Didn't know you were a fighter, David.'

'I'm not, Mrs Baker. He started it.'

'Well, never you mind, then. You'll make it up when Father gets home.'

She went inside but I didn't follow. I just didn't want to see that boy. Disconsolate, I wandered down the cinder path to where I'd been digging the day before but I was too scared to ask Mrs Baker for the fork.

The evening drew in and it was bitter, the congealed sweat clammy under my shirt. I crouched by the path and was pulling out groundsel to give to the hens when I heard a soft crunching on the cinders behind me. Mr Baker stood there and I thought I was for it. Instead, he just leaned down and spoke softly. 'Too late to start diggin' now, lad.'

I relaxed. His grey eyes twinkled and, tucking a cigarette between his lips, he added, 'Best be gettin' in for supper, hadn't we?'

As the weeks passed, Marion gradually faded from my mind. November moved into December through a dense white mist. I could only see halfway down the garden and on the way to school I felt as though I was walking through a cloud. Everything was silent and muffled, like the winter fog in my East End streets. But there the resemblance ended.

Fog in London was thick and yellow and made you cough. Even in the daytime, the street lights hung like yellow puffballs high above, barely penetrating the murk. The buses drove with full headlights on, their beams like searchlights in the gloom. In the village, fog or mist was full of mystery – and eerie because it was so silent. If a bull had escaped through a hedge, I'd never have seen it. A robber – even a German parachutist – could have been hiding anywhere.

I had little to do with Rita during most of the time that I was with the Bakers. Whether she was with Simon's older sister in an adjacent house or had already moved to a Mrs Roebuck, I can't remember. Perhaps it was because Mrs Baker was almost like a mother, kind, caring and reliable, that I had no need of anyone else.

On Saturday mornings I always arranged to meet Ronnie by the junction of the close: we had to go to the Sabbath service that the headmistress took for the whole school. It was held in the attic at the church hall because, Rita said, the parish council wouldn't allow us to use the main hall for religious purposes. I couldn't understand that. It wasn't as if the hall was a church, was it?

One particular Saturday, Ronnie wasn't his usual chirpy self. After a desultory 'Wotcher', he was almost silent as we walked through the freezing mist, water droplets dripping from the bare branches. In the light breeze the last shrivelled blackberries, cradled between purple, frostbitten leaves, swung at the end of thin briars.

'Whassup, Ronnie?' I asked. 'Trouble?'

'Nah. Just fed up.'

'Your billet that bad?'

'Nah. But tellin' me to take my shoes off, puttin' 'em here not there. Nah. Jus' wish I was back in London. Nothing to do here in this dump. No shops. No buses. No picture palace. No nuffin'.' I was surprised but said nothing. Though our friendship continued, this difference grew as the months passed. It was typical of what was happening to all of us. Most yearned to get back to their old streets and the excitement of London but a few, like myself, were already hooked on the countryside.

There was one thing, though, that Ronnie and I were absolutely in agreement about: we hated having to go to the religious service every Saturday. I was still resigned to it as part of school life and through fear of what Dad would say if I missed it. Ronnie, however, never went to synagogue in London and wouldn't have gone here either but daren't disobey the headmistress. He'd said his father didn't believe in God and I was puzzled. Surely everyone believed in God – even the Christians.

'Blinking cold up there in the attic,' I said, as we neared the hall. 'Lucky it ain't long.'

'Yeh. Blinkin' boring as well, ain't it?' he mumbled, then immediately brightened up. 'Anyway, we're goin' to climb those big elm trees in the paddock afterwards.' He grinned. 'In this mist the farmer won't be able to see us.' A bit of devilment always brought Ronnie out of a bad mood.

On the way to the hall, we had to pass a small clapboard-walled chapel. Inside the high black railings was a notice-board on which, every week, were printed Biblical quotations warning of 'God's Wrath to Come' and the like. That morning we stopped and stared. There were two rows of Hebrew print with verses in English printed below.

'What's Jewish writing doing on a Christian notice-board?' I asked.

Ronnie shrugged. 'P'r'aps it's for us. Trying to convert us?'

'Like that place in Fournier Street,' I added.

'Maybe.' He pointed to the chapel door. 'I saw the preacher standin' outside there the other day, mumblin' prayers and pointin'. Barry says he's a "religious maniac".'

I didn't ask what that was. I don't think Ronnie knew either.

At that moment, a thin, white-haired man dressed in a black suit came out of a side door, saw us and smiled. With one look at each other, fearing he would come over and try to convert us, we belted off down the lane as fast as we could run, my heart thumping all the way.

A small Valor oil stove was meant to provide heat in the attic, but its only effect was to give off an acrid smell of paraffin. As we came in, the headmistress stopped reading from her prayer book and gave us a fierce glance, as did Rita, who was already there. That Saturday, the attic was still full but, as the months passed, fewer and fewer children came. Many, like Ronnie, did so only because the foster-parents reminded them. Try as they might, the Misses Pizer were fighting a losing battle as apathy and separation from our parents nibbled away at our traditional beliefs.

Ronnie and I made for the back. Immediately the head-mistress called Ronnie forward to separate us, but I managed to sit on the wooden floor under the eaves, tucked away from prying eyes. As the service droned on, I discovered a pile of old magazines with yellow covers nestling between some dusty boxes: the *National Geographic Magazine*. Hidden by the boxes, I slid one out and was immediately entranced by the photographs and the reports, becoming completely immersed and only brought back to reality at the end of the service as everyone began to sing '*Adown Owlom*', the prayer with which the Sabbath morning service always ended.

From then on, I always tried to sit in that spot, Saturday after Saturday. While the headmistress droned on with the prayers – '*Adonoi melekh, Adonoi molokh, Adonoi yimlokh le'oylom ve ad. The Lord is king, the Lord rules, the Lord will rule for ever and ever*' – I would leaf through the magazines, deep in the jungles of New Guinea or soaring over the Potala Palace in Tibet.

My ever-present thirst for knowledge and my desire to travel the world must have been born from that magazine during those tedious Saturday services. My geographical knowledge came in very handy later when my brother was in the navy. While overseas, he was allowed to send aerogrammes, which were, of course, censored but he always hinted at where they had docked. From 'double coconuts' I knew that they'd been in the Seychelles and from 'Temple of the Tooth' I worked out that they had called at Ceylon. The 'Lady in White singing to the ships' was Durban. The censor didn't seem to notice these references and I enjoyed decoding them.

One Sunday morning I came down to breakfast to find the Bakers listening attentively to the wireless. Russia had attacked Finland and the announcer was telling us that the plucky Finns were fighting back. I knew that Germany and Russia had divided Poland and were 'at peace'. Why, then, were the Russians at war with the Finns? I'd always thought the war was between us and Germany. It was all a bit too much for me to grasp.

The following Saturday I looked at the pictures of Lapland in the *National Geographic Magazine* and couldn't imagine how anyone could fight in such heavy ice and snow.

That morning, after the service, Rita smoothed my hair and straightened my collar as usual in the courtyard. As she straightened up, she overheard Ronnie talking about a tree-climbing expedition.

'You're not going climbing in your *Shobbos* clothes,' she snapped, wagging a finger at me. 'And it's too dangerous in this mist. You'll break your neck.'

'Everyone else is,' I moaned.

'Well, you're not to. And if you do, I'll tell Mum.'

Ronnie and the other boys were already running up the lane and were lost in the mist. I was furious but said nothing as she walked me towards the close. But as soon as she'd gone into her billet, I ran up the road and into the paddock, my shoes getting soaked in the long grass.

'Blinkin' sisters,' I moaned to Ronnie, as the boys clustered at the foot of the huge elm tree, waiting their turn. Three of the older boys were already up there, lost to sight.

Given the task by Mum of keeping an eye on me, Rita was in a no-win situation. What could a young boy detest more? It created constant tension between us and an unfortunate rift that continued until well into my teens. Older sisters were spoilsports, controlling and bossy, I decided, my view later reinforced by Richmal Crompton's *Just William* stories.

Now, as the legs of the next boy disappeared into the mist, Ronnie and I grabbed a branch each and began to climb. With Ronnie just a few feet ahead of me, my heart pounded as I remembered not to look down. Up and up I climbed until I heard the voices of the big boys at the top. Suddenly I began to feel nervous. I'd never been so high before.

A few feet more and, perched in a fork, Ronnie and I clung to nearby branches, congratulating ourselves on being almost as high as the older boys. Grinning at each other, we began to sing:

> *We're the kings of the castle*
> *And you're the dirty rascals . . .*

We must have been there for some ten minutes when a breeze came up, swirling the mist around us, then blowing it away. Glancing down I could now see the ground – and, worst of all, Rita, in her blue hat, standing with another girl.

'David, come down this minute!' she yelled. 'I'll tell Mum on you. In your *Shobbos* clothes an' all. You just wait!'

I was furious, and at that moment I really hated her,

especially when the older boys began to take the mickey.

'Hey. You're for it now, David.' They laughed. 'You wait till you get down!'

'Blinkin' sisters,' muttered Ronnie. His elder sister had been evacuated elsewhere but he empathized with me.

Looking up, I saw there was room on the branches beside the older boys. In defiance, I began to climb higher, right up to where they clung to the topmost forks. That made Rita scream louder. I ignored her, feeling the exhilaration of accomplishment, with only the thin topmost branches and the sapphire sky above me, the ground far, far below.

The other boys began to climb down, leaving just Ronnie and myself singing, 'We're the kings of the castle . . .' until we were hoarse.

It grew chillier and damper. I started to shiver and knew we had to go down, too. But Rita was at the foot of the tree. We climbed down very slowly: first, because the downward climb was always more difficult and dangerous, and second, because I had to think of a way of avoiding my sister and getting a real mouthful. She would never larrup me, but her tongue-lashing would be just as bad.

On the lowest branch, Ronnie jumped down and I thought that would distract her, but it didn't, so I remained perched on the bough, wondering what to do next. At that moment a flock of sheep materialized out of the thinning mist. Thinking that the farmer might be behind them, everyone began to run away. As Rita turned to see, I seized the moment, jumped down and hared away across the meadow to a stile in the far corner. Rita was in no mood to give chase over the sodden grass, so I escaped into a narrow pathway leading to the close, lungs bursting, knowing how lucky I'd been. It was the only time I was thankful for the farmer.

Slowly, my heart stopped thumping and my head cleared. I leaned against the stile and looked around. Red hawthorn berries glowed like tiny cherries on the dense hedges. A thrush flew down, its spotted breast bright as it plucked a snail from a rotting log then flew back into the safety of the hedge.

I was exhilarated. For the first time I had disobeyed Rita. Here, among the high hedgerows and the dry bracken, I felt free. From now on I would do what I wanted, away from her, away from the *Shobbos* service, away from my father's rules. I was still a long way from cutting myself off completely and losing my faith, but as I strolled along the muddy path back to my billet, I knew that there was no way I wanted to go back to all that.

Overhead, a watery sun was trying to break through the mist, casting strange shadows on the billowing whiteness. In front were the yellow rear walls of the close and my stomach told me it must be lunchtime. Brushing a drip from the end of my nose, I ran up the path and back to the Bakers'.

The nights grew colder and each day, on the way to school, the hoar frost on the grass verges grew thicker and whiter. I now slept with just my nose peeping out of the covers and found it more difficult to get out of bed each morning in the freezing-cold room; English country bedrooms never had heating. On weekend mornings, I would linger, curled up in bed, until the smell of frying bacon or sausages lured me downstairs.

Even heavier frosts came, such as I'd never experienced in London, and one morning, I opened my eyes to a muted white light that cast vague shadows on the wall past Simon's bed. Turning my head to the window, I saw something magical. Each one of the small glass panes framed a different, translucent ice picture. Some were like ferns, others like the lace patterns on Mum's front-room curtains, and still others were like underground grottoes, hung with icicles. But it was those that looked like faces that were most startling – faces with sharp noses and pointed chins, wide-open grinning mouths, elfin caps and beards. As I turned my head, the pictures glistened and seemed to move.

The villagers sometimes joked about being visited by Old Jack Frost. Not understanding that this was just a figure of speech and still half believing in fairies and goblins, I wondered whether he really existed. Did his goblins come at night and paint these pictures? Had they been in my room? Anxious, I hid under the bedclothes for a while, then came up again and stared from one pane to another, fascinated, each time noticing more detail.

Then, as the sun rose further, the corners of the pictures began to melt and clear as, gradually, the whole wonderful tracery dissolved and vanished. I'd never seen anything so weird yet beautiful, and now that I was reassured they could not be evil or dangerous, I was sad to see them go. Perhaps if I stayed awake all night, I'd see who came to paint them. But if no one did, how could they have got there?

For many mornings after that, throughout the winter, I remained fascinated by them. Much later, I realized that the moisture of our nightly breathing freezing on the glass made those pictures. Today, with central heating and better insulated bedrooms, few children ever see those wonders.

'Breakfast!' Mrs Baker called up the stairs. I leaped out of bed, ran to the bathroom and dashed water on my face, got dressed and hurried downstairs. Simon was already there, spruced up because his parents were coming that day.

'Cleaned your teeth?' she asked, as I bowled in. Without answering, I turned and ran upstairs again. How did she guess?

After breakfast, I helped Mr Baker pick Brussels sprouts from the tall stalks at the far end of the garden. Soon the frost made my fingers sting and I could only pick with one hand at a time while the other warmed up in my trouser pocket. After that I took the bucket of ash from Mrs Baker and sprinkled it on the path, looking for the muddy patches and putting a good pile down at the entrance to the chicken run.

The parents' coach was due from London that afternoon. Mum had written to Rita to say they weren't coming this time, but had sent a parcel with Sheila's mum. Sheila was Rita's age and lived two doors away down the close. Simon's parents lived up in Stoke Newington, she wrote, so she couldn't send it with them. I hadn't yet met his parents but, after the visit that afternoon, I felt Mum had good reason for not wanting to take a tram ride up to their house.

Ronnie's parents were not coming either that day, so we arranged to meet by the village school after dinner.

'Ruddy cold, ain't it?' were Ronnie's first words. He was stamping his feet on the road to keep them warm. 'What shall we do, David?'

'Dunno, but I didn't want to stay in. Old Four Eyes' parents are comin'.'

As we started walking down the lane, he asked about the Bakers.

'They're really nice,' I said. 'But their daughter's a bit stuck-up. Never speaks to me, even.'

'Cor. Yeh. Doreen!' He laughed. 'She's the village beauty queen, my lady says. Got tons of boyfriends at the RAF camp, I heard her say.' Ronnie was only six months older than me but at least two years more sophisticated – or perhaps I was excessively naïve.

At that moment, he ran in front and started to 'shpraunce' down the road, waggling his hips. I joined in and we shimmied along, imitating Doreen's suggestive walk to the Laurel and Hardy theme tune – *Tarum tarum, tarum tarum / Ta ta ta rum, ta ta ta rum* – until we reached the vicarage where, conscious that our teacher might appear, we stopped and considered where to go next.

'Here.' Ronnie perked up. 'Let's go to them half-finished houses. There's s'posed to be dirty pictures on the walls!' I had no idea what he meant but we slapped our backsides and galloped off down the lane, past the Clarks' house.

Three unfinished houses stood by the roadside, red-brick walls and exposed window openings. Two had no roofs. With the builders away in the army, they would remain like that for the next four years.

Clenching our fists but with two fingers pointed, like detectives holding revolvers, we crept our way through the tall grass and weeds, where the older boys had tramped a pathway, and in through the front door. Sawn timber joists spanned the first floor above our heads and the inside walls were spread with smooth pink plaster. A flight of bare wooden steps led to the first floor where names had been scratched into the plaster, most of which I didn't recognize – probably village kids.

'Look,' whispered Ronnie. 'That's them there!' Etched in the plastered walls alongside the names were crude naked figures. 'Cor.' He sniggered. 'Barry says the village boys made 'em.' There were also outlines of what I supposed were girls as they had long hair.

I tried to imagine it for real. If little Sandra hadn't taken fright that day with Sid and me, I was thinking, I might have known.

Then I noticed two figures close together on a side wall.

'Stephen says that's how they make babies,' said Ronnie.

'How does he know?' I asked, sceptical of anything Stephen said since the scrumping fiasco.

'Says he saw it in a book. But Barry said he was makin' it up and they had a fight over it.' He laughed. 'Cor. Should 'ave seen 'em. Mud all over 'em.'

Although the day was sunny, it was bitterly sharp and frosty. My feet were freezing and I was shivering. Much as I didn't want to go back to the Bakers' with Simon's parents there, Ronnie and I left the unfinished houses, said goodbye to each other and made for our respective homes.

Chapter 9

First Christmas

As I walked up the close, the bulky figure of Mrs Suffolk hovered by her gate, watching me with her beady black eyes. There was something evil in those eyes – something hard to fathom. Nonchalantly trying to whistle a tune, I ignored her and carried on up the close, still reluctant to go into the billet but it was too bitter to stay outside.

Simon, his parents and the Bakers were all sitting in the dining room at the back of the house. His mother, Mrs Homel, was large and round and, from the way she was gobbling up the sandwiches and fairy cakes Mrs Baker had prepared, I could see why. Her brown hair was tinged ginger with henna and tightly permed under a small black hat.

Sliding round the table to take advantage of a fairy cake, I was now trapped in the corner by the window behind Simon's mother, and couldn't get past to go up to my room. Mrs Homel had draped a fox-fur stole over the back of her chair and its glass-bead eyes stared at me.

'Oh. What a terrible journey,' she was moaning, her hands waving in time with her words. 'A terrible journey it was.' I soon noticed that she repeated everything. 'That driver,' she continued, 'that driver took us all round the houses. All round, I tell you.' She mopped her forehead with an embroidered handkerchief, then carried on about the problems of the blackout in London.

Mr Homel, short and balding with heavy horn-rimmed glasses, didn't say much. He nodded now and again, made the odd remark to back up his wife's comments, then added a few sentences about the effect of the war on his furniture shop. Mr Baker sat silently near the door. Alongside him Doreen was keenly observing the smart clothes and fox fur.

Mrs Homel pulled over a small suitcase and brought out a tissue-wrapped package. 'These are for you, my darling,' she said, handing it to Doreen, who immediately opened it.

'Oh. Look, Mother! Silk stockings!' She whimpered with delight. 'Oh, they're lovely. Thank you, thank you so much.'

Mr Homel leaned forward, smug. 'Well, artificial silk, really, but you can hardly tell.

Doreen jumped up. 'I must try them on. Can I, Mother?' Without waiting for a reply, she hurried out into the passage and closed the door. Now I definitely couldn't get out.

'No. Not easy to find, that's for sure,' repeated his wife. 'But we had to bring something special for your lovely daughter.' It was as if they knew how the Bakers doted on Doreen. Then, turning to her husband, she added, 'Am I right or am I wrong?'

It was a phrase I came to associate with her for all time. Mum used to joke about it afterwards, too: 'Am I right or am I wrong, Mrs Homel?' She would laugh. 'Am I right or am I wrong?'

Delving into the case again, the woman brought out a brown

silk headscarf for Mrs Baker. 'For you, my dear. You're so kind to my Simon and he looks so well, bless him.'

Then she brought out a checked pullover. 'Real lamb's wool, Mr Baker. Just right for the winter, we thought.' She turned to her husband. 'Didn't we, Max?'

He nodded as his wife carried on, saying how cold it must be in the country in winter.

I felt so embarrassed for the Bakers – as if, like paupers, they needed clothes – but they took it all in good part. As the mother nattered on, making sure that everyone knew just how generous they were, I grew more and more agitated, but dared not show it. Mum had been to visit two weeks ago and brought with her a blue glass vase, which stood now on the mantelpiece. I'd been so pleased that the Bakers were appreciative. Now I had to watch all these gifts being showered on them, making her present seem insignificant.

Simon was sitting smug and self-satisfied. Waiting for his presents, I supposed. I wondered if they had a separate suitcase just for him. At that moment, with the Peke scampering after her, Doreen clattered into the room again on her high heels and spun around. 'Look, Mummy! Look how smooth they are! How sheer!'

I had no idea what 'sheer' was and just noticed that the stockings were almost invisible, a thin brown seam up the back of each leg. 'And look how they shape the leg,' Doreen was cooing, arching backwards and slowly raising the hem of her skirt to show off the stockings. I watched, fascinated, wondering how far up it would go, the image of that tapered leg somehow echoing the crude graffiti on those plastered walls.

At that moment, Doreen noticed me staring and, with a

frown, immediately dropped her skirt. My face grew hot and I turned away to look out of the window.

Eventually, after more tea, Mrs Homel dug out a cardboard box for Simon. I was feeling even more miffed but, luckily, as everyone shifted their chairs for him to take it to his room, I saw a gap by the rear door. Quickly squeezing behind Mr Homel, I slipped out into the back garden.

In the freezing cold I gritted my teeth but was determined to stay outside – I couldn't sit through any more of that. I wandered down the back path, twisted off a Brussels sprout and nibbled it, discovering that I liked the taste of the raw, frosted vegetable. I continued on to the chicken run, my fingers clutching the wire netting while I watched the hens scratching and comparing their varied plumage. The Rhode Island Red cockerel resented my coming so near and strutted by the netting door, crowing loudly. Whenever I helped collect the eggs from the nesting boxes, he would fly at me and I had to kick out in self-defence – yet I loved his brilliant colours: he was like an exotic jungle bird in my picture books.

Before evacuation, the only chickens I'd seen were the scraggy white bundles on Mrs Grossman's stall in Wentworth Street market, their necks dangling over the side of the table, blood dripping onto the cobblestones. Every now and again, the *shokhet*, the ritual slaughterer – skull cap, dirty bloodstained apron and long black beard – would come out with a brace or two in one hand and his razor-knife in the other. Meanwhile Mum, clutching her old leather purse in her fist, would haggle over the price of the giblets. On principle, she never accepted the first price.

Mr Baker kept several breeds of hen – brown Rhode

Island Reds, black-speckled white Light Sussex and also a few bantams – which were once Doreen's pets, he'd explained, and their small eggs were really tasty.

I picked some groundsel, poked it through the netting and was watching the hens pecking at it when I felt a hand on my shoulder.

'A bit too crowded in there, was it, David?' I looked up. Mr Baker had a wry smile on his lips.

'Well. It was a bit stuffy,' I tried to excuse myself, twisting my fingers through the wire netting. Then I looked up. 'My mum and dad like you just as much as Simon's parents, Mr Baker,' I said softly, 'even though they can't bring all them presents.'

The hand patted my shoulder again. 'Don't you let that worry you, lad. We know that and we treat you the same as Simon, don't we?'

'Yes, Mr Baker. It's just because they got more money than my dad.' Then, to make sure he really understood, I continued, 'Not all Jews have lots of money like they say, Mr Baker. Honest.'

He crouched beside me and turned my face to look at him. 'Never you mind what folk says.' He smiled. 'We don't listen to idle gossip.' After a pause he added, 'They jus' want to show their appreciation for our looking after Simon, I'm sure.' He took out a cigarette and lit it. 'Takes all kinds to make a world, David. Remember that.'

'Yes, Mr Baker.' I nodded as he straightened up.

'Anyway. Bit cold out here without your coat. And Mother's cuttin' a sponge cake. You wouldn't want to miss tha', would you?'

'No, Mr Baker.'

We crunched back up the path, past the frost-coated cabbages and the sprouts – they looked as though they'd had a light coating of snow. I glanced up at the heavy grey sky. Perhaps it was going to snow properly. It always snowed in the country in winter, like those pictures in my storybooks, didn't it?

That December night, heavy snow fell while I slept. When I woke in the morning, a brilliant white light flooded the room. Outside, the close was strangely silent.

Despite the cold, I jumped out of bed and ran to the window. Two cycle tracks and one set of footprints were the only blemishes on the smooth white blanket that covered the road. Simon was still sleeping and, without washing or cleaning my teeth, I dressed quietly and tiptoed downstairs, wanting to be first out into the new snow. Slipping on my wellies, I ran into the back kitchen to go out. Mrs Baker was preparing breakfast.

'My goodness! What's all the rush, then, so early?'

'It's snow, Mrs Baker.' I grabbed the door handle. 'Lots of it.'

'Oh, that.' She laughed, wiping her hands on her apron. 'I reckon it'll be here a while yet so it'll wait for you.' She touched my shoulder. 'What about a face wash and getting your jacket?'

I shrugged and went back to do just that. When I came down again I ran out through the rear door and round to the road. I'd never seen such a brilliant soft white carpet. We did have snow in London from time to time, but it was quickly soiled with black soot and usually trodden down by the time I went out.

Now I made snowballs, hurling them against the yellow stucco of the house. Then, beginning to feel the cold, my fingers red and tingling, I went back inside to have breakfast.

At the table, I could hardly hold the spoon.

'Forgot to take your gloves?' smiled Mrs Baker. I nodded. 'Well, remember to take 'em off for making snowballs, so they'll be dry to put on when you've finished.'

But the good advice went by the way as we had snowball fights at school, woollen gloves soaked and hands raw. At first, the snow was dry and powdery and I had to clench it tightly to form a ball, but after a day or two, it grew moist and balling was easy. After further snowfalls, the back and front paths to the house were completely blocked. As I helped Mr Baker shovel it aside, I realized why country people didn't get excited about snow. It was just a hindrance – and it meant they had to use more coal to heat the house.

After tea on the third day of snowfall, a few of the boys met on the paddock and we started rolling large snowballs, several of us at a time, heaving and pushing to make huge 'Chelsea buns' until they were too unwieldy to push. They were often bigger than ourselves and left caterpillar tractor tracks on the grass. 'Great, wa'n'it, Ronnie?' I puffed, as it grew darker. Just the two of us were left sitting on the fence, staring at the ghostly white shapes glowing in the night. 'Nothin' like this in London, is there? An' I bet it'll be snow for Christmas as well, eh?'

Wisps of our freezing breath drifted into the night but Ronnie was unusually quiet.

'What's up, Ron?' I asked.

'Oh. I dunno,' he muttered in a monotone. 'Jus' wish I was

home. 'Specially now it's winter.' He slapped his hands together. 'My billet lady's okay, but it ain't like home. I mean, I could always run in and Mum would give me something hot to drink. Or I could go in an' switch on the wireless.' He stared into the dark. 'She's not bad, but I can't do that here. And sometimes I have to stay outside and wait to come in if she's cleanin' up or somefin'.'

I walked with him to the end of the close where we said goodbye. On my way back to the Bakers', I felt sorry for Ronnie – and not only for him. What he said was true: nice as Mrs Baker was, there was no hug like Mum's, no nosh like Mum's, no feeling that I was special. By the time I reached my billet, Ronnie's sadness had rubbed off on me and, as I kicked off my wellingtons at the back door, I wished so much that Mum was inside, waiting.

The following evening, I was lying in my room reading comics when the smell of frying wafted up the stairs. It reminded me that the teachers had said it was Hanukah the next day, the festival of the Maccabees. 'Our own Christmas,' my older brother had joked once, as we fried potato *latkes*. I used to grate the potatoes on Mum's tin grater, a *rebasen* she called it, and wait for her to fry the fritters crisp. She also made small pancakes and rolled them in caster sugar.

Frying in oil was a Hanukah tradition in remembrance of the miracle of the holy oil lamp that miraculously burned for eight days in the reconsecrated Temple of Jerusalem. The eight-branched Hanukah lamp, the *hanukiah*, would stand on the mantelpiece and, as the youngest, I would light tiny fresh candles from the *shamash* candle in its centre, adding one each day until all eight were burning. Then we would place it on the windowsill, so that it shone into the night; most of the other windows around us were similarly lit.

That evening, as I looked at the heavy blackout curtain drawn across my bedroom window, I thought that now, because of the blackout, Dad wouldn't be able to put the lighted candles in the window. Suddenly I felt homesick for the first time in months. I wondered whether it was because of my conversation with Ronnie the previous day or because of the long, cold winter nights, when being in the country wasn't so exciting. As I was ruminating, Frank Baker called us down for a supper of fried liver and potatoes and the sadness vanished.

The next day in school, we lit Hanukah candles in a large nine-branched *hanukiah* and sang the traditional '*Moaz tzur Yeshuatee*' – 'Rock of My Salvation'. Afterwards, out of the teachers' earshot, we chanted our rhyming ditty in the playground: 'And the cat's in the cupboard and he can't see me!'

The following morning, the wireless announced that the German pocket-battleship *Graf Spee* had scuttled itself.

'Bloody cowards,' muttered Mr Baker. 'Couldn't even come out and fight.' He added: 'That'll show 'em who rules the waves!'

British warships had damaged the German battleship and it had been allowed temporary sanctuary in neutral Montevideo harbour. But, instead of coming out to face the British cruisers that waited outside, it had been scuttled to prevent it being captured by the navy! I wondered how they scuttled a big ship like that: did they cut a hole in the bottom? I had cigarette cards of HMS *Ajax* and *Achilles* and took them to school. It was the first large naval battle of the war, significant to us for the parallel between our smaller ships beating the huge German battleship and our ancient Maccabees defeating the mighty Greek armies.

At school we cheered at the news. If we kept winning like that, we'd soon beat them. As Malcolm Clark had said when we'd first arrived: 'It might all be over by Christmas, lad.'

Yes. Perhaps it would. But not just yet, I hoped. First, regardless of Dad, I wanted to see a Christian Christmas in the countryside. I'd expected to see scenes like those on the Christmas cards on the Bakers' mantelpiece but, to my disappointment, it didn't snow again. Gradually the snow melted away, leaving just our huge snowballs like white boulders on the grass and the countryside bleak and bare. It also grew much colder. A hard night frost brought the pictures to my window in the mornings, always with different designs – but I was no longer afraid of the strange faces.

As I looked out from my window each morning, come rain, snow or frost, Mrs Suffolk would be making her shuffling rounds of the front gates, talking to whoever would listen, her beady eyes forever darting this way and that as though not wanting to miss anything. Why didn't the villagers just tell her to go and mind her own business?

When school broke up for the holidays, I helped Doreen make paper chains with coloured paper strips and flour paste. Mr Baker stood a small fir tree in a bucket of sand in the corner of the dining room with a tiny doll perched on the top. Doreen hung silver-paper balls and cut-out stars on the branches.

The next day, Simon and I were in the bedroom reading comics when Mrs Baker called us down into the dining room. The family was sitting around the table, in the middle of which stood a large bowl of a dough mix with a large wooden spoon sticking up from the middle.

'Right,' she said, smiling, 'everyone makes a wish in the Christmas pudding.'

Frank Baker stood up and handed everyone a coin. Some got a sixpence, others a silver threepenny bit.

Doreen threw hers in first. 'I've made my wish and I'm not telling anyone!' she squealed. All she'd wish for was more silk stockings, I thought. At that moment, the Peke jumped up onto her lap. She hugged it. 'And you must make a wish too, my darling.' How soppy could you get?

'Come on, Simon,' called Mr Baker. 'Make your wish, lad.'

Simon twitched his glasses, threw in his coin and gave two desultory stirs.

'Give it some elbow grease,' said Frank. 'You won't get your wish that way, lad!'

Simon gave it two more stirs, then went back up to our room. Frank Baker handed me a silver threepenny bit. They were already quite scarce, having been replaced by the brass eight-sided new ones just before the war. If I got one in my piece of pudding at Christmas, Frank said, it would give me an extra magic wish. I stirred with all my strength and made my wish: I wished that rotten Simon would go home and leave me on my own at the Bakers' and that I would go home to the East End in the New Year – but only after I'd seen Christmas in the country.

Mrs Baker took back the spoon. She and Frank made their silent wishes. As she added dried fruit and carried on stirring, I remembered the many times I had helped Mum stir her cake mix – she often made a light, spongy *plaver*, a dark brown honey cake with ginger and lots of spices. Afterwards, she would give me the empty bowl to lick out, but I didn't feel confident enough to ask Mrs Baker for the same privilege.

At home, we never celebrated Christmas: after Hanukah came New Year. Yet last Christmas Mum had hung a Woolworths red-netting Christmas stocking filled with chocolate medallions and sweets from the bedroom mantelpiece. Somehow, my father hadn't objected. It was a small concession, but a sign that even her generation was accepting the rituals of the festival – for the children.

On Christmas Eve, I sat alone in the Bakers' dark dining room; they were all at church. Simon was upstairs playing with some new green tanks on his bed. As usual, he hadn't asked me to join in. Firelight flickered on the walls and on the silver balls that danced in the draught from the back kitchen.

I switched on the wireless. A choir was singing Christmas carols and I recognized the tune of 'Good King Wenceslas' from the ditty the older boys used to sing:

> *Na na na na na na naa,*
> *And* Yoysel*'s lost his trousers . . .*

Yoysel being the Yiddish pejorative for Jesus.

Most of the carols I'd never heard before but, as the programme continued, I found myself liking some of the melodies. With that pleasure, though, came a feeling of guilt. The carols must be Christian so I shouldn't be listening to them. If Dad found out . . . Again, I heard his gruff voice to my mother: 'Do you want him to grow up a *goy*?' Leaning forward, I switched off the wireless.

The back door clicking open woke me. Frank Baker came in stamping his feet from the cold.

'Right, then.' He smiled as he switched on the light. 'Call Simon down and we can all have some supper.' Turning to his wife he grinned. 'An' I'm starving, Mother.'

It was the first time I'd tasted roast goose – or seen or tasted stuffing. And with the roast potatoes, parsnips and Brussels sprouts, I was soon absolutely bursting. Then, with the plates cleared away, Frank went into the back kitchen and Doreen switched off the light. I waited expectantly, thinking that he was about to do some conjuring tricks, like when Uncle Sammy played tricks at birthday parties.

In the silence, I saw a strange glow coming from the kitchen, then heard a clunk – and Frank cursing as his foot hit the step. A moment later, his face appeared in the doorway, illuminated by a ghostly blue light from a flame that flickered and danced around the rim of a large plate he was holding. It shot round it two or three times as it came nearer, then suddenly went out – and, with another clunk, Frank walked into the table.

'Who the heck put that there?' he grunted, and we all laughed as Doreen switched on the light again.

On the plate was an enormous Christmas pudding, steaming hot, with a sprig of green holly on the top. 'Told you we should ha' put more brandy on the pudden.' He nodded to his wife. 'Went out too soon.'

'Any more an' the boys'd be under the table,' Mrs Baker countered.

My mouth watered as I waited to taste the pudding and custard. And when I did, it was like magic. On my second bite, my teeth bit on a coin. Pulling it out, I saw it was a sixpence and I jumped up, clutching the sticky coin tightly in my fist as if scared it would vanish.

'Hey,' laughed Frank. 'There's our millionaire, then. Most of 'em are old threepenny bits.'

Simon had a second helping, but I couldn't fit any more in. And more brandy must have soaked into the pudding than was burned away because soon after my head went fuzzy and I felt sleepy. I didn't remember anything else about the evening. Frank must have carried me up and put me to bed.

The next morning, I woke to the sound of rustling paper. Simon was unwrapping a parcel. I raised my head and saw a large sock at the end of my bed, from the top of which peeped the corner of a purple carton. I was sure it was the one the pedlar had brought that time.

Just before the snow had fallen, I had been in the garden when a thin, dark-faced man in a flat cap came to the back door carrying two large suitcases. I'd seen him before, selling things like lace trimmings, safety pins and combs. It must have been the dying days of the pedlar who trudged round the villages with bits and bobs not sold in the village shop.

As he had opened his cases on the doorstep, Mrs Baker had delved inside, turning over packages and bags. As she picked out a few things, she saw me looking and quickly hid them in her apron. At the time I couldn't understand why she was being so secretive. Now I knew. I'd caught sight of that purple box just before she'd hidden it.

As though it might vanish like the frost pictures, I stretched across the bed and pulled the sock to me. Simon was watching out of the corner of his eye but I didn't care: for once I would have as much as he had, that was for sure.

The purple box was a jigsaw with a picture of the King and Queen on it. I'd have preferred a battleship or a Spitfire, but I liked jigsaws so I didn't mind. She was so kind, Mrs Baker. She'd put an oil stove in our room that morning so it would be warm for us to play there.

I lay back in bed and held the box above my head, looking at the picture and thinking how wonderful my first Christmas was. I felt under my pillow and clutched the sixpence again, repeating my wish that Simon would go away and that the war would soon be over.

Chapter 10

On the Ice

As the New Year broke, fierce snowstorms blew across the countryside. At night the wind howled so loudly around the eaves that I put my hands over my ears and slept under the covers. On the first clear day, I went out into the back garden. The blizzards had left a deep covering of fresh snow. Apart from the bare trunks of the trees, everything was a brilliant white that glistened in the early sunlight and silence of a Saturday morning.

I'd come out with Frank to open up the chicken houses. Across the snow there were a number of tracks from animals that had been foraging before dawn.

'A strange dog's been in our garden, Mr Baker,' I said. Already it was *our* garden.

'No. Them's the fox. See?' He pointed. 'They're thinner an' one behind th'other. A dog puts 'em more side to side like.' He snorted. 'Good thing we had our chickens well shut up for the night, eh?' Suddenly the fox wasn't the naughty, mischievous character of the fables but a hunter with sharp fangs and an inquisitive nose. I felt a bit anxious that he'd been so close to the house.

The tracks led to a hole in the back hedge.

'There. He's come through that gap. I'll plug it later.' Frank gave a short laugh. 'Not that it'll make a lot of difference. He's a sly bugger is old Reynard.' Then he glanced around him, furtive: Mrs Baker told him off whenever he swore in front of us.

After we'd let out the chickens, I looked at the other tracks. There were sets of four-holed prints leading across the garden.

'Them is rabbits,' said Frank and, smiling, added, 'Which way were they goin', would you reckon?'

'That way,' I said, pointing to the pattern of smaller holes in front of the two longer depressions of the back legs.

'Wrong, lad.' He crouched down and spread his fingers. 'Rabbit lands on his front paws then his back feet come through and land in front, ready for the next hop, see?' He illustrated with his hands. He straightened up and lit a Woodbine. 'An' the little blighters have been at my kale.'

'Aren't they scared to come so close to the house?'

'Not when they're starvin',' he said, rubbing his hands together. 'Winter's fun on a full belly, throwin' snowballs. Ain't no joke when you're cold an' hungry, I can tell you. No fun at all . . .'

After breakfast, I wrapped up warm and wandered over the brilliant-white fields, following animal and bird tracks and trying to identify them, everything so much cleaner and crisper than the slush-filled streets of the East End after snowfall. It was indeed Saturday but in the school holidays there was no Sabbath service, so I was free to go where I liked, when I liked, and do as I liked, imparting a wonderful sense of freedom.

One Sunday morning, looking out of my bedroom window, I heard Barry calling across to his friend. He was billeted with Mrs Atkins across the close.

'The reservoir's frozen solid,' Barry was shouting. 'You can walk on it, honest.' Five minutes later I was washed, dressed and down to breakfast.

Mrs Baker smiled at me as I ran in. 'Well, then. Bed fallen in, David?'

'Please, Mrs Baker, can I go up to the lake? It's frozen solid, they say.'

She pursed her lips, hesitant. One of the village boys had almost drowned when he fell through thin ice near the bulrushes some years back, she told me later. 'Well,' she said, 'Doreen's going up there later. You get some warm breakfast inside o' yer and you can go up with her.' She wagged a finger. 'But you listen to what she says. Right?'

I wasn't overjoyed to be going with Doreen but at least I'd get onto the ice.

Wrapping up in my overcoat and gloves, I wound a long scarf round and round my neck and pulled on a navy balaclava helmet. I'd never seen one until evacuation but it was great – kept my ears really warm. Doreen wore a long green coat, red hat, mittens and ear muffs, and had ice skates slung over her shoulder. As we went out of the back door, the Peke scampered after us, a dark green doggy coat on its back. Doreen knelt down and hugged it.

'Sorry, my poor little darling. Doreen can't take you to the lake. It's too dangerous, my little Tootsie Wootsie.' Then she took it back inside to her mother.

'And you listen to what Doreen tells you,' cautioned Mrs Baker again, as we went out of the front gate.

If it wasn't big sister Rita, it was Doreen – always some older girl telling me what to do and what not to do. All the way to the reservoir, in case the other boys saw me, I walked a few paces behind her.

I'd often walked to the reservoir, a large lake created by a high earth dam many years before. It was surrounded by trees and bushes and looked completely natural. That day, as we came up the grassy bank to the top of the dam, I was amazed at the change. A solid covering of grey ice stretched from one end to the other. The thick beds of rushes that had swayed in the wind now stood still and brown, frozen solid into the ice, like hundreds of brown spears. Instead of the ducks and moorhens bobbing about, people were sliding, slithering and skating across the surface. I also saw why Doreen had been so keen to come. Nearby, groups of RAF men from Halton Camp were laughing and jostling.

Ronnie and some of the boys had made a long ice-slide near the trees. I started towards them but Doreen called me back. 'Now, don't you go getting lost,' she said. 'You're to go no further than those bushes there. Okay?'

'Okay,' I muttered, and hurried down to the ice. When I looked back, she was sitting on a clump of reeds and an airman was helping her to lace up her skates.

Joining Ronnie and the others, I slithered down the ice-slide and into the bank, then turned and slid along the return one. Both slides were well polished and it was impossible to walk on them without falling over. With everyone slipping and laughing and shouting, the time whizzed past.

Suddenly one of my classmates Harold's little sister Doris fell with a loud thump and a scream. When she got up, her right arm was hanging loose by her side, a bright blue mitten poking from her sleeve. 'It's broken!' Doris shrieked. 'It's broken, Harold. I can't move it!' She started to walk towards him, sobbing, but Harold was too petrified to be of any use. He backed away, as though she had some contagious disease. I was horrified. If Rita had fallen, I'd never have left her alone like that.

'Here,' shouted Ronnie. 'Let's find someone older. Quick.'

'Over there.' I pointed. 'Doreen went with those RAF blokes!'

We ran across the ice but I couldn't see Doreen anywhere. We told two other airmen what had happened and they hurried back with us. Together, they lifted Doris and carried her to the bank. Sitting her on a tuft of grass, one man crouched in front of her and gripped her wrist. With the other hand, he pushed against her upper arm and gave a slight twist. Doris jerked and screamed. The airman let go, then stood up, smiling, as Doris, whimpering softly, found she could flex her arm again. It was like magic. As the airman made a sling with her scarf, Ronnie and I stared at him as though he was a hero.

'Thanks, Mister. Thanks, Mister,' was all we could say as the pair turned away.

We returned to the slides but it wasn't the same. One by one the boys were leaving and going home. Then Ronnie went, and soon there were only a few people left. By now, my gloves and shorts were wet, freezing water had sloshed into my wellies and I was cold.

I looked for Doreen but she was nowhere to be seen. For a moment I panicked. Had she left me there? But she wouldn't have, would she? I stared across the deserted ice to the bare black trees and bushes. It was a brutal landscape. This was what Finland must be like, I supposed. The news was still reporting fighting between the Russians and the Finns.

A twig snapping nearby broke my thoughts and I heard someone giggle. It was Doreen. A moment later, she and an RAF man came out of the thicket. He had two bands on his shoulder epaulettes so I knew he was an officer. When Doreen saw me standing alone, she blushed.

'I thought you were all still playing on the ice,' she stammered. She turned to the man. 'What time is it, Geoffrey?'

He glanced at his wristwatch. 'About one thirty.'

Doreen clutched her face. 'Oh, my God. It's so late. I must go.' She whispered something to the man, then came over to me and led me up the slope to the road.

'Goodbye, young man,' the officer called after me. I turned and waved, wondering if he knew Malcolm Clark.

Walking down the road, I began to shiver. What had Mr Baker said? Snow wasn't so great when you were hungry – and I was that too.

As we neared the house, I feared that Mrs Baker would tell me off for being late for dinner, but Doreen was even more anxious. Was she worried I'd say something about her and the officer? As soon as we got indoors, she flopped onto a chair. 'Oh, Mother. Sorry we're late. It was so lovely out there.'

'You've both had a good time if you were out that long.' Mrs Baker nodded to me. 'An' I hope young David behaved himself.'

'Oh, yes. He was no trouble at all,' Doreen said sweetly. Could have knocked me over with a feather, as Ronnie would say. But I knew her secret, I told myself, and I'd remind her if she ever got nasty with me.

Dinner was a welcome treat and, as the Yorkshire pudding and thick gravy warmed my stomach, I thawed out.

While we ate, a news flash broke into the music on the wireless. The destroyer *Cossack* had boarded a German oil tanker, the *Altmark*, in a Norwegian fjord and had rescued hundreds of shipwrecked British seamen who had been taken prisoner. Yes, I thought, as I flicked through my cigarette cards of ships in the bedroom afterwards. If we carried on like this, we'd soon win the war.

During the week, a thaw set in and on the following Sunday I went for a walk by the reservoir again, but now it was deserted. The ice was thin and breaking up and the frost-browned bulrushes stood in dark, still water. A set of tracks ran along the bank in the thin snow and, recognizing the prints of a fox, I started to follow them hoping to catch sight of it. They went through the bushes and alongside a deep ditch, half filled with dry bracken and snow.

Suddenly I stopped dead. A patch of scattered snow revealed bloodstained grass beneath. Around it were the brown feathers of a pheasant or partridge. I caught my breath. The tracks led off into a clump of dark trees and, as I stared at the tiny drops of red sparkling on the snow, I imagined those sharp teeth tearing at the struggling bird, blood and feathers flying everywhere.

The late-afternoon sun shone low through the trees, a red ball wrapped in a fiery basket of ice-covered branches. The shadows had lengthened and grey hollows appeared in the snow. I was alone and, looking around, I became quite scared. This wasn't a game: the fox would be almost as big as me! I panicked.

Turning round, I ran like mad along my tracks to the lake and familiar ground. I no longer felt afraid but I was disappointed that I hadn't even caught a glimpse of that furry red coat and those pointed ears – from a distance, of course.

Chapter 11

Only a Dog

Why did it always rain when our parents came? A long thaw and steady downpours had washed away the last traces of snow, turning the fields and grass verges into a squelching quagmire. On that February Sunday I lay in bed and stared through the misted-up windowpanes. Mum and Dad would think it never stopped raining in the country.

Mum had been to see us last month but this time both she and Dad were coming and, as I dressed and had breakfast, I was hoping that the weather would clear up so we wouldn't have to spend too much time in the Bakers' house. I wanted to see Dad, but he always embarrassed me when he wouldn't remove his hat and refused to eat.

Rita called for me and, in the fine drizzle, we set off up the lane together. As we neared the village green, I heard a bark and the Peke scampered past, long ears flapping. Turning, I saw Doreen following and was puzzled: she was never normally out so early on a Sunday. And why was she going up to the coach? Then I spotted the tall RAF officer I'd seen on the ice. He was standing under the porch of the inn and Doreen was walking across to him. She'd obviously used our parents' visit as an excuse for her mother.

'Come here!' Doreen snapped at the Peke but the dog ran around in circles, sniffing at my legs then running back to her, sneezing and panting. If it hadn't been *her* dog, I might have liked it.

In the damp and drizzle, in raincoats and under umbrellas, we all crowded by the old elm tree near the inn. Then, through the Sunday-morning stillness, came the throbbing of an engine. The coach turned the corner at the top of the hill and rolled down towards us. I forgot about Doreen and the rain.

'It's our coach!' I shrilled, excited. I hadn't seen Mum for over a month.

With gears grating and engine whining, the coach began to slow down. Then, at the very moment it drew in towards the grass verge, a small black and white terrier ran out of the pub gate and across to the green. In a flash, the Peke scampered across the road after it. Doreen, who had been talking with her boyfriend, didn't notice at first but, as it started barking, she swung round.

'Tootsie! Come here! Come back!' she screamed, running after the dog as it dashed in front of the coach. Too late. Brakes screeched and tyres skidded on the wet road and, as the coach juddered to a halt, the engine cut out. Inside, parents standing near the front door toppled forward and fell in a heap against the front window.

In the shocked silence that followed, we heard the squeals of the Peke as it emerged from under the chassis, whimpering and dragging its mangled hind legs. It managed to reach the grass verge, a quivering, tangled mass of bloodstained fur. It tried to raise its head, then flopped down and lay still.

Doreen crouched over the dog, sobbing. 'My poor darling. My precious . . . my baby. What have they done to you?' Her shoulders heaved and tears streamed down her face as the coach door slid back and shocked parents spilled out, straightening their clothes.

The driver, ashen-faced, jumped down from his cab and approached Doreen, his hands outstretched. 'I didn't have a chance, Miss! It just came at me . . . Didn't have a chance!'

The innkeeper came out of the pub, went over to the driver and took his elbow. 'Saw it all from my window, mate. Nothin' you could have done, that's for sure.' He turned to a boy beside him. 'Here, Martin. You run an' tell Frank Baker. He'll know what to do.' As the boy shot away, he called after him, 'An' tell him it was over in a flash. No sufferin', like.' The boy raised a hand in acknowledgement and ran on.

The innkeeper began to guide the driver away. 'Come on, m'old mate. I reckon you could do with a drink.'

By now, all the parents had climbed down from the coach and soon became aware of what had happened. They stood in silence, looking at the sobbing girl and the ball of fur on the muddy grass, then dispersed towards their children, the happy reunions dampened. In small groups they began to walk away, talking in hushed tones.

I stood speechless and shivering, staring at Doreen and the dog, clutching Rita's coat. By chance, my teacher had joined us. She hurried through the crowd and gently laid a hand on Doreen's shoulder. 'Come, Miss Baker. Come. Let me walk you home.' Doreen shrugged off the hand, then lifted one of the Peke's brown ears and laid it over a staring eye. She stood up, head bent, shoulders hunched, hands hanging limply at her sides. Suddenly she straightened, swung round and glared at Miss Pizer, her eyes red and swollen.

'If your coach hadn't come, he would still be alive,' she snapped, clenching her fists.

Miss Pizer tensed, then reached out a hand towards her. 'I'm so very sorry. And very sad, Miss Baker. We all are. It was a terrible accident. Terrible. But, please. Do let me see you home.' Doreen looked down at the bundle of fur and, with the drizzle forming a mist on her hair, raised one knuckle to her mouth and began to cry silently.

'Please, Miss Baker,' Miss Pizer said. 'It was a terrible accident. No one is to blame.'

Doreen stiffened and stared into her face, eyes wild and bloodshot. 'It was *your* coach,' she hissed, through clenched teeth. 'If it hadn't come . . .'

Miss Pizer stepped back, fingering her necklace, and stood for a moment, silent. Then she walked slowly back to the crowd of parents.

I'd been so shocked that I hadn't noticed my father had alighted from the coach – one of the last – until I heard Rita say, 'Hello, Dad.'

I swung around as she reached up and kissed his stubbly cheek.

He was alone.

'Where's Mum?' I asked. Dad patted my head.

'She couldn't make it, Dovidle. Booba isn't well and she had to go round to stay with her.' Booba was my grandma, Ziyder's wife. My head was already spinning and now my stomach churned. Of all days for Mum not to come. 'Anyway,' he continued, holding up a large oilcloth bag, 'she packed a lot of comics and nosh for you both.' He smiled. 'Enough for an army.'

He stood for a moment, looking across at the dog and Doreen.

'Hmm. A pity,' he said, matter-of-factly. 'Looked a nice dog.' He put his hands on Rita's and my shoulders and started to turn us away.

'It's not just that, Dad,' I said. 'It's terrible. It's Doreen's dog – from my billet. And it was our coach an' all.'

'It was an accident, Dovidle.' Dad shrugged. 'Could have been any car.' He adjusted his brown homburg. 'Thank God it wasn't one of the children. Only a dog.'

I winced. 'But it wasn't *any* dog. It was Doreen's dog, Dad!'

At that moment, Mr Baker came up the road, walking swiftly towards us. He was dressed in his best Sunday suit, black over-coat and a bowler hat. Over his arm he carried the worn pink blanket from the Peke's basket. I tried not to catch his eye but I needn't have bothered. Frank Baker hurried past without seeing anyone or anything.

'Don't stare, David,' Rita muttered. 'It's rude to stare.'

After he'd passed, I began to drag my feet, dreading Dad coming to the Bakers'. Rita must have sensed it.

'We'd better go to my billet first, Dad. We can see the Bakers later when . . . you know.'

'All right, all right,' Dad huffed. 'But so much fuss over a dog.'

Just before we reached the corner of the close, Frank Baker overtook us. Doreen, head bent, was hanging on to one of his arms and the dog, wrapped in its pink blanket, was crooked in the other. From the folds of the blanket a damp, black nose peeped out, as though it was just asleep.

As they turned away up the slope, Dad pushed back his hat. 'Huh. So much fuss over a dog,' he said again, nodding towards the departing figures. 'For a *khaya*, an animal, only a *goy* would dress up like that!'

I was too shaken to respond but Rita nudged Dad's elbow. 'Ssh, Dad. It was like one of the family. And Doreen treated it like a baby. They must be so upset.'

'So what?' Dad huffed again and, growing more indignant, kept breaking into Yiddish: 'You only mourn a person, a human being. A man has a *neshumma*, a soul, but a *khaya* is a *khaya* – an animal!' In Dad's childhood *shtetl*, it must have been difficult enough to feed a family, let alone keep pets. 'You don't mourn a *hunt* – a dog,' he said finally. 'Ridiculous!'

His words made me feel even more angry and miserable. Of all days for Mum not to come . . . I had a terrible premonition that something was about to go very wrong.

Stretching out the time in Rita's billet was painful. Away from family and friends, Dad was no great conversationalist. Neither was Mrs Roebuck and long, awkward silences were punctuated with occasional comments about the weather or the war. When we eventually left, the drizzle had ceased but it was still overcast and grey when we came to the close.

'We'll have to drop in and see the Bakers, Dad,' said Rita, apologetically. 'Even for only a few minutes.'

Dad stopped on the spot and looked down at her. 'Of course I'm going to see the Bakers. Think I'd come to see you both and not drop in to say hello? It would be a disgrace not to go in and thank them for looking after you, Dovidle.' He held up the bag. 'Anyway, your mother has sent a small present.'

* * *

Despite the cool afternoon, as we neared my billet, my head and neck grew hot.

'Look, Dad,' I pleaded, 'Doreen was crazy about her dog. So were the Bakers. Please, don't show me up.'

Dad stopped again. 'I'm not a fool. I know. Of course they will be sad. Sure.'

I felt relieved and reassured, until we walked through the gate. 'Still,' he muttered, 'a dark suit. Hat? All that fuss for a *khaya*?'

My neck burned. Stubborn old-fashioned Dad. Please, God, keep his mouth shut. Make him stay quiet.

Mrs Baker wore a grey pinafore over her brown dress as she met us at the back door.

'Well,' she said, eyes red but trying to smile, 'we was wonderin' . . . We've waited tea for you.'

Dad touched the brim of his hat. 'Sorry we're late, Mrs Baker. My wife couldn't come this time. Thank you.' And we all went in.

Doreen was curled up on a pile of cushions in the corner, the Peke's corner, cradling the pink-wrapped bundle in her lap. A brown ear slipped out as we came in. She scooped it up and tucked it inside, then mopped her eyes with a large white handkerchief. Around her shoulders hung her father's black coat.

'I've made the tea strong,' said Mrs Baker. 'It's a raw day, that's for sure.'

Frank stood with his back to the fire. 'None for me, Mother,' he murmured, glancing at Doreen.

We drank tea – Dad as well, thank God. Rita and I nibbled some cake as, again, the adults chatted about the weather, the impending rationing and about Mum going to see her sick mother, with Mrs Baker wishing her a speedy recovery. The conversation came in short, disjointed sentences. Doreen's bleary eyes glared accusingly at every slightly raised voice, while the whole time I sat tensed, like a coiled spring, fearing that at any moment Dad would say the wrong thing.

Through the window, low clouds hung over the dripping, leafless trees at the end of the garden and, in one of the long silences, Dad reached into the bag and pulled out a small paper parcel. Mrs Baker thanked him and put it, unopened, on the table. I couldn't help remembering the gifts showered on them by Simon's parents. He must be upstairs, I thought, and wished I could be too, desperate for the visit to end.

Eventually, Dad glanced at his watch and stood up to go. 'The coach will be leaving soon,' he said, adding: 'I hate all the rush at the last moment.'

'Well, nice of you to have come,' said Mrs Baker.

Mr Baker leaned forward, nodded and shook Dad's hand.

As he reached the door, Dad turned, glanced down at the girl in the corner and touched his hat. Almost imperceptibly, Doreen nodded. Dad didn't seem to notice.

'Well, goodbye,' he said, still looking at her. 'And very sorry about your dog.' Then, after a brief pause he added, 'Still, it's only a dog. You'll soon be able to get another one, won't you?'

Oblivious to the looks of horror from the Bakers and darts of hatred from Doreen, he nodded again to Mrs Baker and left the house. Rita, red-faced, quickly said her goodbyes and followed, but I was furthest from the door and stood transfixed, my mouth open, wishing the floor would swallow me.

Why, oh, why did Dad have to come on his own today? If

only Mum had been here. And why did he have to say that? It was just so hurtful. At that moment, again, I hated him. Staring at the floor to avoid meeting anyone's eyes, I shuffled across the room, mumbled goodbye and ran out of the back door.

All the way to the green, hurrying along behind Dad, Rita tried to excuse him. 'Dad doesn't understand village people, David. He didn't mean to be nasty.'

Dad would have none of it. He turned and looked down at me. 'Don't have to make excuses,' he muttered. 'In Flanders, I was. Buried hundreds of dead. Ypres and Passchendaele. They were real tragedies. But this? A dog and a silly spoiled girl? For this to sit in mourning?' He coughed. 'An animal isn't a human being! You don't mourn a dog and that's all there is to it. You have to say so – and that girl should be old enough to know the difference.'

I knew he would go on and on but, thankfully, we had reached the green.

At the coach, we said our goodbyes. Rita kissed Dad but I just stood there, looking down even when Dad patted my head. I couldn't wait for him to disappear, for the coach to take him away. Far away. And for him never to visit again.

Miss Pizer had come back with a letter, which she gave to Mrs Marks to post in London.

'That was so sad about Doreen's dog,' she said to me, after the coach had gone.

'Yes, Miss. An' they're so upset. Really upset, Miss. And Dad doesn't understand, Miss. He made it even worse, Miss. Said such rotten things.' I was close to tears.

The teacher turned to Rita. 'Would you like me to see David home?'

Rita nodded. 'Thank you, Miss Pizer.' Suddenly and uncharacteristically – as though responding to my distress – she leaned over and lightly kissed the top of my head. 'Bye, David. See you soon.'

As Miss Pizer and I walked back to the close, my eyes began to water. I tried to sniff back the tears. Miss Pizer stopped and crouched beside me. 'You don't have to hide your tears, David. You must be very sad for the Bakers.' I sniffed again and wiped my eyes with the back of my hand.

'It's not that, Miss. It was my dad. He was horrible to Doreen and to Frank Baker an' . . .' In a torrent of sobs, I poured out what had happened. 'An' I wish I never see him again. I hope he never comes again. I . . .'

I stopped. 'Honour thy father and thy mother,' said the Ten Commandments. And he was my father. What would Miss Pizer think of me?

The teacher wiped my eyes with her handkerchief. 'I know how you feel, David, and how upset and angry you are. But he is your father. And the Bakers are just the Bakers. They are very kind and good and I know you like them. And, yes, your father has his ways but he loves you and wants the best for you.'

'I don't love him, Miss. Not now. Never,' I mumbled.

She smoothed my hair. 'That's what you feel now, I know. But we must respect his beliefs and his ways. They are our beliefs, too, and we must keep together and hold on to them always. We *are* different, David. You will see.'

She stood up and took my hand. She was so kind, Miss Pizer, but I would never forget what Dad had done. Never. Frank Baker wouldn't have said something like that, whatever

162

his beliefs. I'd always accepted what my teacher said but now I wasn't at all certain that she was right.

That night as I lay in bed the house was silent – and sombre. The Bakers had gone to bed early. Once more I saw the Peke's ear dangling from the pink blanket and felt sorry for the Bakers, desperately hoping they wouldn't blame me for what Dad had said. If only Mum had come instead . . .

I had never felt more miserable.

Chapter 12

Spring

Tiny bright purple-haired buds appeared along the bare hazel stems. They were the colour of Cousin Pearl's dress, which Mum had gone on about at Auntie Cissie's wedding. I couldn't believe that something growing naturally could have such a brilliant hue. It was a sign that winter had passed, and now March came in with bright sunshine and icy mornings. White hoar frost lay on the verges, but in the hedgerows, vibrant yellow catkins danced in the breeze.

Breaking off a few hazel branches, I was sure that Mrs Baker would give me a jam-jar of water to keep them in my room. When I got to the house, though, she quickly ushered me out of the back door.

'You can't have them inside the house,' she tut-tutted. 'Pollen all over the place.' Disappointed, I put them on the windowsill in Frank's tool-shed, which, sure enough, was coated with a vivid yellow powder the next day.

A week later, the wireless announced that the Russians had occupied a place called Karelia and the Finns had stopped fighting. Everyone felt sorry for the brave Finns and booed the Russian bullies, but still I had no idea what that war was about.

As for the real war, it was so quiet that nothing seemed to be happening. Perhaps we really would all go home soon.

Towards the end of March fierce winds blew for days on end, tossing the tall elms as though they were saplings. The windows thumped and rattled at night, and on the way to school one day, I was almost blown into the hedgerow. With the winds, it turned cold again – leaden skies and days of rain. Cold, heavy rain.

'March,' muttered Frank Baker. 'In like a lamb and out like a lion.'

At weekends, I lay in bed late, hugging my teddy bear to keep us both warm until we were called down for breakfast. The bear had materialized some weeks after Christmas. Mrs Baker had been sorting out Doreen's old toys to give to a war-effort jumble sale. Laying them out on our beds, she had asked Simon and me if we'd each like one. I'd waited until he had gone down to breakfast, then picked out a rag doll with brown woollen hair and put it into my bed with an equally battered white bear that had cross-stitch eyes and a smiling mouth. I'd never had dolls or cuddly animals at home – they were for girls. Here, though, on my own, I needed something to cuddle in the dark nights.

At first, I hid them under the covers each morning, scared that Simon would tell the other boys and they'd laugh at me for being a cissy. Then I noticed that he, too, had one – a fluffy dog.

Mrs Baker had reassured us when she came to switch off the lights one night. 'Tucked your little friends in tight, have you both?' she'd smile. Simon and I just glanced at each other, then sheepishly smiled back at her.

At the end of the month, the strong winds dropped. The sun shone again and April began quite warm – so warm, in fact, that on the way home from school Ronnie and I took off our coats and ran around swatting the clouds of midges that hovered over the lane. As I walked in through the back door, flushed and with my coat over my shoulder, Mrs Baker stepped in front of me, hands on her hips.

'What's all this, then?' she asked sternly, nodding at my coat.

'Cor, I'm sweatin'. It's like summer already, Mrs Baker.'

'Aye. P'r'aps you are but the sweat'll cool off soon enough and then you'll catch yer death of cold.'

'But it's so hot outside.'

'I don't care how hot it is. You keep yer coat on till I tell you.' She wagged a finger. 'Never cast a clout till the may is out. Just remember. An' that means the may flowers on the hedgerows.' Her glasses bobbed as she twitched her nose. 'An' I'll tell you when that is. Right?'

'Yes, Mrs Baker,' I mumbled. They seemed to have a saying for everything in the countryside.

Mum was supposed to have come the following weekend but Rita posted a letter through the door, which she'd just received. Mum couldn't make it because she had to go and get Cousin Issy out of a camp somewhere. She wrote that the government wanted to send him to Australia because he was German, which puzzled me. Issy was a refugee and Dad's distant relative. He'd escaped from Europe the year before and was staying with Uncle Barney. He hated the Germans, and I couldn't understand why England would want to imprison him. I learned later that it was Churchill's 'Collar the lot!' policy. Refugees – Germans,

Austrians and Italians – who had made a new home in Britain away from the Nazis were rounded up and locked away. Didn't matter if they'd previously been considered British. The government was nervous. The threat of invasion was very real in the early months of 1940.

I remembered Issy clearly from our last family holiday in Shoeburyness, Essex, just a month before we were evacuated. We were all on the beach and I was watching Dad and Uncle Barney playing quoits with a man I'd never seen before. He was bronzed, like no one could ever be from an English summer. He had black curly hair, a broad, squashed nose, and when he laughed, two gold teeth glinted in the sunlight. And, crikey, was he fit! Thighs like tree trunks, rippling muscles, and he threw the rubber quoit with a spin that could cut your head off if you didn't catch it. But he spoke hardly any English so they conversed in Yiddish. People of Granddad Ziyder's age often spoke mainly Yiddish but for someone so young it was strange.

'A refugee,' Mum explained. 'From Austria.'

'Lucky to escape from the Nazis.' Dad spat on the sand. 'A *kholera* on them all.' Cholera had been a fatal disease in the *shtetl* of his boyhood.

'Hey. Such *koyach*. Such strength!' Uncle Barney shouted, wringing his hand as he caught the quoit. He smiled at us kids. 'And what a voice. You should hear it. In the opera, he should be.' Flinging the ring back to the man, he called, '*Nu*. Issy? A song. Give us a song, eh?'

Issy flashed a gold tooth and shook his head. Suddenly, the strong face seemed sheepish. But Dad joined in. Then Cousin Lou and half a dozen more. 'Come on, Issy,' they chorused. 'Just one song. Like yesterday. Come on.'

Issy blushed and I felt for him. It was like me being made to recite a poem in front of the family. He stared at the sand, twisting the ring through his fingers. Then he flicked it aside, planted his feet wide apart and threw back his head. The mouth opened. The teeth shone. And out flowed a voice so powerful and clear that I paid no attention to the strange accent.

Vun day, ven vee vass young, some funderful mornink in Mai . . .
You tolt me, you luft me, ven vee vass young, vun day.

With growing confidence, Issy reverted to his native German, the words merging more easily with the music. Everyone nearby on the beach turned to listen, the song echoing from the promenade wall and out across the Thames estuary. They must have heard it over in Margate! It made such an impression that, as I think of that day, I can hear it now. When he'd finished, it was so quiet along the beach, you could hear the waves lapping. Then everyone began to shout and cheer.

Dad slapped him on the back and Uncle Barney shouted, '*Sh'koach. Sh'koach!* May God give you strength!' Then he glanced around us all. 'Didn't I tell you? Should be in the opera, he should.' Issy walked slowly to the water's edge and sat on the sand, gazing out into the distance, his face troubled.

I never saw him again.

As I put the letter back into the envelope, I noticed Rita's writing on the back.

David. Mrs Roebuck's niece is getting married on Saturday
and we're invited. I'll call for you at two. Rita.

Mrs Roebuck was Rita's billet lady, so I'd have to go but it felt strange being invited to a wedding on a Saturday: our weddings were always on Sundays.

Meanwhile, spring really had arrived. Every day, walking to school, I noticed something new: the bright green of the new hazel leaves breaking out of their buds, the birds singing in the hedgerows, and wild flowers along the grass verges. Mrs Baker had loaned me one of Doreen's old books about wild flowers and I began to recognize many of them: yellow primroses and cowslips, pussy willow buds by the ditch, the silverleaf weed – dark green on top and brilliant silver underneath – and many more. One day, when I asked Mrs Baker to tell me the names of some new leaves I'd found, she laughed out loud. 'My! You won't want to go back to them smoky old grey streets again, David, when this is all over!'

She'd touched a sore spot. Just a few weeks before there had been so many daffodils in the front gardens. In London, our only spring flowers were the three hyacinths that emerged from bulbs that Miss Pizer had grown in blue glass vases in a dark cupboard.

By now, I could no longer deny that I was becoming more and more captivated by the greenness and tranquillity of the countryside – and by helping Frank to grow things in the garden – all of which was further estranging me from my family's life in London. I sometimes wondered whether any of the other boys felt like I did. Most seemed to be like Ronnie, just waiting to get back to the East End.

One Saturday afternoon, Rita called for me, already looking so much older than she had done when we'd arrived seven months ago. Despite Mrs Baker making me wear a clean white shirt and my new checked pullover, I still felt a real *shlokh*, a scruff beside her.

Rita wore a new red dress and, as we walked down the lane, it seemed to glow in the sunshine, reminding me of a song about the girl dancing in a red dress that Uncle Barney used to sing:

> *Oy. The maidle in roit,*
> *The fellows go messhiger for the maidle in roit.*
> *Zingen unt tanzen . . .*

We hardly talked all the way down the lane and only when we came into Church Road did I realize that we would be going into the church. I looked up at the tall, square tower with its crenellations, like the Tower of London. Did they used to shoot arrows from the top? The bells were up there too, Rita said, but I knew they mustn't ring them until peacetime came. The tall tower and the grey stone walls seemed oppressive. For the first time in my life, I would be inside a Christian church and, despite my growing estrangement from Judaism, I felt anxious, certain that Dad would disapprove if he found out. Sure, Rita was going in too but she was a girl. Girls didn't seem to matter much in our religion, which was why they sat upstairs in the synagogue. Boys, however, took *bar mitzvah* and had to keep all the *mitzvahs* – the religious rules.

As we passed through the arched doorway and I heard the organ, I began to drag my feet and prayed that Dad wouldn't find out, that God would forgive me and that they wouldn't try to convert me in there. Rita must have sensed my hesitation.

She took my arm and smiled. 'Don't worry, David. It's just a wedding, not a church service, so it doesn't count.' Only partially reassured, I stared down at the old flagstones and followed her through the arched doorway.

At that moment, my teacher appeared. Seeing her there set my mind more at rest. She bent down towards me and smiled. 'Hello, David. You do look smart.'

Mr and Mrs Baker were there, too, with lots of the other villagers. Frank was in his dark suit, the one he'd worn to collect their dog when it had been run over. A week or two ago they had bought Doreen a black Pekinese pup.

Mrs Baker wore a flowered dress and a straw hat. Other villagers, too, were in smart clothes, but they were not over-dressed – unlike at our family weddings, where my fat aunts would bulge out of their strapless evening gowns, like Cinderella's ugly sisters. I also noticed that the men were bare-headed; only the women wore hats and they sat with the men, not separated as in the synagogue.

As we sat in a pew at the back, I was pleased to see some of Rita's friends and also Gerald, who'd come with Stephen. But as the vicar came onto the dais at the front of the church in his white robe, a cross dangling from his neck, my unease returned. I was glad we were at the back, far away from the huge stained-glass windows picturing saints, and from the golden crucifix on the altar table.

I looked at the massive stone pillars. Samson must have been really strong to pull down thick, solid blocks like those on to the Philistines. My eyes followed them up into the arched, timber-framed roof. And above that roof was God – for I still believed that He was up there – and he would be looking down on me and might punish me for my doubts.

Now the organ grew louder and the bride, in a simple light-blue dress, came down the aisle with her father. I tried to see where the organist was and, eventually, in the far front corner of the church I spotted a pair of hands moving over a white keyboard. The organ music stopped, the church grew absolutely silent, and when the vicar began to speak I was anxious again: '. . . and as we are gathered here in the sight of our Lord Jesus Christ . . .'

'Thou shalt have no other God but me. No graven image . . .' said the Commandments. So why did they pray to a wooden Jesus up there on the cross like that, like an idol?

As the bride and groom repeated their vows I glanced around. Despite the sunlight outside, the long stone nave was grey and sombre and everything was quiet, just the soft sing-song voice of the vicar. It was so unlike our family weddings, with the noise, the singing and the loud shouts of *Mazel tov!* as the groom smashed the wine glass for luck with a mighty stamp of his foot, and everyone singing '*Chosson kallah mazel tov . . .*' when the groom gave the bride a real smacker on the lips.

When the ceremony was over, the vicar announced a prayer for peace. There was a wave of movement in front of me as people knelt and put their hands together. In our row, we sat tight and watched. We wouldn't kneel. 'Thou shalt not bow the knee . . .' Yes, as Miss Pizer had said to me: we were different. But I really only felt it now in the church – not when I was outside with the flowers and the trees, nor with the Bakers.

The congregation was standing now, the organ playing, and the bride and groom walked back down the aisle. Everything appeared so peaceful. If the man hadn't worn a uniform, I wouldn't have thought there was a war on. But, without the war, I wouldn't have been there, would I?

Outside the church, I said goodbye to Rita and went home the long way round through the sunlit fields, watching the bees humming over the dandelions – the village boys called them 'pissabed' because, they said, they made you wet the bed if you picked them. The sunshine didn't last. Halfway home, thick cloud gathered. I started to run, then had to push through a hawthorn hedge to get onto the lane and kept running, hurtling in through the back door just as the heavens opened – straight into Mrs Baker.

'My, my,' she said, 'you look as if you've been pulled backwards through a haystack!'

'Beat the rain, Mrs Baker, didn't I?' I gasped. Tucking in my shirt and pulling up my socks, I flopped onto a chair in the dining room, catching my breath. While she made tea, the rain beat against the window and torrents streamed down the panes.

Frank was listening to the wireless. Suddenly he put down his cup with a sharp click, and turned up the volume. 'That means business, Mother,' he said, his face taut. 'Real trouble.'

Germany had invaded Denmark.

Despite this development, the war intruded only marginally into an almost idyllic existence, like when Mrs Baker complained about the new ration books.

'Takes him more time to cut out them silly bits o' paper in the shop than to get served!' she huffed, flicking the buff booklets across the table to Frank. I watched as he leafed through one: little squares and triangles on pages marked 'meat', 'fats', 'sugar', and so on, then more pages marked 'spare'. I wondered what else they could ration. What if you finished your rations before the end of the week? Would you have to go hungry?

One Saturday in April, as I dawdled back to the house after the religious service, I stopped by the pond. Moorhens were building an island nest of twigs and grass and the first swallows had arrived, skimming over the water, gulping mouthfuls of flies and midges. On the sill in Frank's garden shed, the frog spawn I'd collected in a jam-jar had already turned into tiny tadpoles, hanging by their mouths on to fronds of water weed.

'I reckon you could easily stay here, David,' Mrs Baker joked, as I was telling her about the pond and showing her the tadpoles one day. A month ago I had laughed nervously when she'd said as much but now it didn't seem so fanciful.

On her last visit, Mum had brought more comics and some Dinky tanks so I could have more realistic wartime battles with my soldiers. Apart from that brush with reality, the East End receded ever further into the distant grey haze beyond the Chiltern Hills that we could see from the reservoir dam. The only outward signs of war, apart from the criss-cross tapes on the school windows, were the boardless signposts at the cross-roads and the branches fixed to the monument at the crest of the hills to camouflage it as a huge pine tree.

By May though, the war was intruding more and more into overheard conversations – and my fears. The newspapers were full of the fighting in a place called Narvik in Norway, with smudgy pictures of Arctic fjords and battleships to accompany the reports. Then it was announced on the news that our troops had 'destroyed strategic installations' before evacuating Norway.

That positive gloss hid what I later learned had been a military fiasco that had allowed the Germans to occupy the whole of Norway. A government reshuffle in London followed.

Then, as I sat in the dining room one evening watching the sun set behind the trees at the end of the garden, the wireless reported the invasion of Holland. The announcer described the horrific dive-bombing of Rotterdam, with fires and terrible destruction. That frightened me. Holland was just across the sea, as Mum had told me when we'd sat on the promenade at Shoeburyness that last summer holiday.

That night, I hugged my little bear tightly and thought of Mum and Dad, Ziyder and Booba. They must be listening to the news as well. Would the Germans bomb London next? Perhaps they could all move out of London to the country and Dad could travel back to work each day. But Miss Pizer had said there were no more billets anywhere. I was worried: what would happen to the rest of my family if the Germans did bomb London?

Chapter 13

Granddad

A few days later, I was helping Frank to pack straw around the rhubarb clump in an old wicker skip when Rita called round.

'Hello, stranger.' Frank stretched up and smiled at her as she came down the cinder path. 'Come to see your little brother at work?'

'Good afternoon, Mr Baker.' Rita smiled bashfully. 'Can David come with me?'

'Is Mum comin' today instead of next week?' I asked, standing up.

'No. But Granddad and Grandma want to see you,' she said, not wanting to use their Yiddish names in front of Mr Baker.

'What – here?' I asked, puzzled.

'Yes,' she said. 'They came on Friday. Auntie Ciss brought them in the car.'

Aunt Cissie had a dress workshop in Fournier Street, Spitalfields, and often hired a large Daimler when travelling on business.

I stepped onto the path, puzzled and a bit annoyed because no one had told me they were coming. Once again, the matter of the penny loomed large.

* * *

Booba always made cherry wine for Rosh Hashanah, the Jewish New Year. She would stew the cherries, then squeeze the bright red juice through a special cloth into a white bowl. One day, she'd left them half squeezed while she went to get another bowl.

'Can I do it, Mum?' I asked. Mum was in conversation with Ziyder and absent-mindedly nodded, so I picked up the bundle and started to twist the cloth. The red juice squirted in all directions – into the bowl, onto the tablecloth and over me. Just then Booba came back in and glared at me, then she slapped me round the ear.

'It's got to be *kosher*!' she snapped. 'I have to wash my hands specially. Who knows where yours have been?' She might have landed me another, but Mum jumped up.

'He's only a *yingeleh* – a young one,' she said firmly. 'He didn't know.'

'He should know. He should,' Booba muttered and, gingerly picking up the cloth bundle as though it had been profaned, looked at it for a few seconds, shook her head and continued to squeeze juice into the new bowl. My ear stung for the rest of the day.

I never forgave her for that and we hardly spoke for the few remaining years of her life. But I loved Ziyder, especially after I heard him whisper to her that she shouldn't have hit me – 'After all, he's only a *yingeleh*,' he'd argued. He always called me that. Just like he had done the time I'd found the rosary.

My grandparents lived opposite the rear of a large warehouse backing onto Mansell Street, which was being used as a Jewish refugee centre. One day, Sid and I were playing hopscotch on the pavement when a window high up opened and a hand threw something out onto the street. Curious as ever, I picked it up. It was a silver chain with black beads on it and an ornate cross at the end. It looked like a piece of jewellery.

When Sid had gone home, I went into the house, spinning the chain on my wrist. Mum and Dad were there – talking about family, as usual – when Mum reached out, grabbed the chain and pulled me towards her. 'Where did you get this?' she screamed. 'Who gave you this?'

'It came out of the window of that warehouse opposite,' I said.

'It's a *Yoysel*,' she hissed, not wanting to pronounce Christ's name. 'Couldn't you see that, you stupid boy?'

She ran out, threw it down a kerb drain, dragged me to the sink and scrubbed my hands raw. My father had instilled in me that it was a sin even to think of Jesus Christ. Now I had picked up a Christian holy object with my own hands. As I sat in the kitchen, shaking and contrite, my chapped hands clapped between my knees, Dad had carried on scolding me.

'Such a stupid boy I have for a son. Like a *shtik goy*.' If I'd been at home I'm sure he would have slapped me. He didn't do it often but, with his heavy hand, once or twice was more than enough.

'*Nu*. One of the refugees must have used it to escape from Nazi Germany.' Ziyder sighed. 'Dovidle wasn't to know.'

'You're too soft on the boy. He's got to learn,' my father snorted.

'You think by shouting at the child you'll make him a better Jew?' said Ziyder. 'He's a *yingeleh*. He'll learn.'

The penny business had happened a week or so before we

were evacuated. Mum and Dad had left me with my grand-parents one afternoon while they went to visit Cousin Alf in hospital. I'd been to the hospital with them once and didn't want to go again: I'd been told off by the porter for riding up and down in the lifts. Cousin Alf had been sitting up in bed in light-blue pyjamas, listening to the wireless.

I didn't know it at the time but he had multiple sclerosis. Perhaps Mum's family had a genetic predisposition to the disease: after my brother Arnold was demobbed from the navy, he went down with it, too.

Well, that day, sitting on the carpet in Ziyder's small room and rereading my comics, I was getting bored. It was growing dark and Mum and Dad still hadn't come back. Granddad was studying the Talmud at the table, peering through his steel-rimmed glasses at the tiny-print commentaries in the page margins. It was typical of Ziyder that when he noticed I was bored he turned to me and smiled. 'Here, my *yingeleh*, they won't be long.' Slowly he got up and went over to the mantelpiece. 'Here. Go and get yourself a cake meanwhile.' Taking up a small blue china jug, he spilled out a few small coins and handed me a ha'penny. 'Here, take it.'

I jumped up. 'Cor. Thanks, Ziyder.' I ran out.

Old Fatty Isaacs's shop in St Mark's Street was always open late, a pale yellow light spilling out of his dusty window onto the pavement. The doorbell clanged as I went in and a fly-paper hanging from the ceiling spun in the draught.

'Can I have one of those, please?' I asked, holding out my ha'penny and pointing to a row of small fruit pies.

'They're a penny each,' grunted old Isaacs.

I pointed to another kind. 'They're a penny as well,' he

muttered. 'I've sold out of ha'penny ones today. Perhaps your mum will give you a whole penny.' He turned away to read the newspaper he was holding, then looked up again. 'But you'd better hurry. I'm closing soon.'

Disconsolate, I ran back to the house.

'They only got penny ones, Ziyder,' I said, putting the coin on the table, then sat on the floor again.

The old man rested a bony finger on his place in the tome and, looking at me through his glasses, smiled. '*Nu*. You want another ha'penny, *yingeleh*?'

'Just to borrow it, Ziyder.' I blushed. 'Mum will give you it back.'

He flicked his hand. 'Lend you a ha'penny? Lend you a ha'penny? Such a miser you take me for.' Getting up again, he went to the vase, put back the ha'penny and spilled out a penny. 'Here,' he smiled, patting my head, 'enjoy yourself, *yingeleh*.'

I ran all the way to the shop and caught old Isaacs just as he was winding up the sun-awning. Even now, as I think of that penny, I can still taste the raspberry filling as I munched the pie, sitting on Ziyder's carpet and picking up the crumbs falling on Beryl the Peril in my comic.

About an hour later, Mum came to pick me up and on the way home I happened to mention that Ziyder had given me an extra ha'penny for the pie. Mum gripped my hand and scowled down at me. 'You mean you took money from Ziyder?'

'Well, yes. I didn't ask. He gave it to me, Mum.'

'But you shouldn't have taken it,' she muttered, adding, 'You know how poor they are.'

Worse was to come when she told Dad. 'Huh. Such a *shnorer*

of a son he must think I have,' Dad fumed. 'You should be ashamed!' He said he would give me the penny to take back. I was to apologize and never do it again.

Not knowing what I was thinking about, and with Rita waiting, Frank Baker misconstrued my hesitation. 'Go on then, little 'un.' He ruffled my hair and smiled. 'The rhubarb won't run away.'

I went inside, washed my hands and face, changed into my shoes and took my jacket. On the way down the close, I questioned Rita. Why had they come? When? For how long?

'Well, the war looks more serious, David, so Mum and the aunts felt they should get out of London. In case . . .' She didn't continue. She didn't need to.

'But where are they goin' to stay?' I pressed. 'Miss Pizer said there weren't any more billets.'

'Here. In the close,' she said, then turned right and went through a rickety gateway.

A black crow flew across the road to an oak tree in the back meadow. With my head still spinning about the penny, I was so busy staring at the bird that I didn't notice where we were going. I looked back, saw the faded green paint and the black letter-plate askew – and immediately recognized the house. Mrs Suffolk's! Oh, God, no. Not there! My stomach heaved.

The Suffolks had never been allowed to have evacuee children – I'd heard Mrs Baker telling Frank so one day when she'd thought I wasn't listening. I had all sorts of suspicions as to why not. But now they'd taken in my old granddad. How? Why? Before I could say a word, Rita had knocked. The door creaked open and there stood the huge bulk of Mrs Suffolk.

'Hello, Mrs Suffolk,' Rita said.

'Well, then,' purred the woman. 'Come to see your granddad and grandma, then?' Her yellow teeth parted slightly in what passed for a smile.

'Er. Can we come in, please?' Rita said cautiously.

'Of course, my dear,' said the woman. She sounded just like the witch in *Hansel and Gretel*. 'Your gran'parents is waitin' for you.'

She waddled away and stood at the end of the passage, as Rita led me into the room on the right. Ziyder met us at the doorway, pale-faced, his little white goatee beard making him almost ghost-like.

'*Oy*, Dovidle. Rita. Come in, come in,' he said, his voice heavily accented but soft and gentle. He glanced up at the woman in an attempt to dismiss her. 'Thank you, Mrs Suffolk. Thank you.'

'Hello, Ziyder,' I said, and squeezed his hand. The shock of finding my grandparents billeted in this place had driven the penny clean out of my mind. 'I didn't know you were coming till today.'

Rita kissed his cheek and I went over to Booba, who sat in the far corner by the window, kissed her, then sat down on a small stool. The room was drab, with discoloured yellow wallpaper and scuffed lino on the floor. By the window there was an old table and a tiny oil stove on which simmered a blue saucepan. A series of trays full of crockery and china – they'd obviously brought all their own dishes and cutlery with them to stay *kosher* – lay alongside it.

'How will you manage to cook a decent meal?' asked Rita. The old man sighed.

'*Oy*. When you're old like us, you don't need much to eat.' He smiled at me. 'Not like you, *yingeleh*. You have to eat a lot. Keep up your strength and grow big.' I smiled at him but I was already worried lest he asked me about bacon and pork.

Booba got up, put a kettle on the stove and made tea. I noticed she moved slowly and heavily, as if her joints were stiff. As I took my cup, Ziyder offered me the sugar bowl.

'Don't take much,' Rita said to me sharply. 'It's their ration.'

'*Oy*. Don't worry,' Ziyder said. 'I mustn't, anyway. My diabetes.'

I couldn't help thinking that old Ma Suffolk was listening to us, just outside the door.

While Booba sat on a creaking, threadbare chair, which was far too soft for comfort, Rita and Ziyder talked a while. I learned that my grandparents had a bedroom upstairs and that the aunts and Mum were paying the Suffolks. I didn't hear how much but now I was sure that Mrs Suffolk had only let the rooms for the money.

Eventually, we got up to go and kissed our grandparents goodbye. As we went out into the passage, Mrs Suffolk was standing there and, behind her, the weasel face of her skinny husband – they looked just like Jack Sprat and his wife. My stomach turned. Poor Granddad. He was so old and frail, and Booba looked ill. As we went out, I felt guilty for leaving them there.

On the road and out of earshot I grabbed Rita's sleeve. 'Why are they at the Suffolks', Rita? They're horrible people. She's a witch – everyone in the close says so!'

'Oh, David. We searched the village for a place. Mum

wanted to get them out of London and the best thing is for them to be near us, so at least they'll have some company.'

'But Mrs Suffolk only did it for the money, Rita. She's horrible. Everyone in the village says so.'

Rita sighed. 'No one else in the village wanted to know. It was the last chance, and Mum and Auntie Cissie said we had to take it to get them out of London.'

We parted, and I walked back slowly to the Bakers', my sadness at the thought of my grandparents being with the Suffolks mingling with anxiety about not saying my prayers. At the same time I began wondering whether Mum and Dad had sensed that I didn't say my prayers every night and arranged for Ziyder to come here to keep an eye on me. What would I say if the old man asked me? I loved him too much to tell a lie. And if I told him the truth, would he tell Dad?

Hurrying in through the gate, I waved to Frank and went to change back into my wellingtons; the rhubarb strawing still had to be finished off. As I padded the straw into place around the red shoots, I couldn't get the picture out of my mind – my gentle, kind grandfather stuck in that dingy cottage with the witch . . .

Despite my good intentions, the days were so full that I didn't see Ziyder again until a fortnight later. I was coming home from school when I saw him walking down the slope from the close. He was dressed in a light-grey suit, stiff-collared white shirt and tie and using a thin walking-stick.

'Ziyder! Where are you going?' I called and ran up to him.

The old man turned to me and patted my head. 'Just for a little walk, *yingeleh*. Want to come with me?'

As I hadn't seen him for a while, I felt I should. 'Where to?'

'Oh. Just to the farm near here.' He pointed with his stick and I knew it must be Old Stent's farmyard.

'Have you seen much of the village?' I asked, as we walked slowly along the lane.

'Oh. A little. And you know what? I've found a barber here. He will give me a shave every few days.' He rubbed his cheeks. 'You can't have your Ziyder looking like a vagabond, eh?' I smiled back. The old man wanted to look neat even here, where no one knew him. Only yesterday Mrs Baker had said, 'A right gentleman he is, your granddad.'

In the farmyard, Ziyder walked me straight past the old sow's sty. Ronnie and I would sometimes go in and poke plantain seed-heads into the pig's nostrils for a laugh before giving her the weed to chew. She'd just farrowed and I wondered how big the piglets would be. But I didn't dare look towards them now.

By the lambs' pen, Ziyder stopped and asked me about my billet, the Bakers and school. I rattled away, telling him every-thing – it was the first time anyone had really wanted to know. I was relieved that he hadn't asked me once about my prayers, or what I ate – or the penny.

As he put his hand through the slats and stroked one of the lambs' heads a squeal came from the sty as the piglets fought over the sow's teats. Ziyder leaned on the fence and looked down at me.

'You see, *yingeleh*, how clean and peaceful the lamb is.' He nodded across the yard. 'And how dirty and noisy the pigs are.' He stroked my hair. 'That's the difference. Why our laws let us eat mutton but not *chazzer*.'

'But the chief rabbi says we can eat anything cos it's wartime.' I waited anxiously for some reaction. Instead, he just laid his hand on my shoulder.

'Yes. I know. I'm not telling you off, *yingeleh*.' He sighed and took out a large white handkerchief to mop his face. The sun hung low behind his head and made a halo around it. 'In wartime children have to grow up and be strong, and you have to eat what there is.' He raised one hand. 'But when the war is over, and you come back to grow up, you will keep all our laws. You're a good boy. I know you will.' He stroked the lamb again. 'That's what make us different from the *goyim*, all other people, Dovidle.'

At that moment, three swallows flew low between the farm buildings and we both watched their amazing twists and turns before they sped out again.

'You know, Ziyder, Malcolm Clark, the Bakers and even the vicar are all so friendly and kind to us.'

The old man looked around the farmyard, then smiled. '*Nu*. Of course. They are good people. I didn't say we are *better*. Or that they are *worse*.' He huffed. 'Huh. Plenty of *yiddisher* crooks – plenty, believe me. But we are *different*. Chosen by God to keep His word, His Torah. And for that we have been persecuted.' He straightened up and glanced at the clouds gathering over the sunset. 'Now we have the biggest villain of them all, Hitler, a *misseh mashinneh* on him. May God strike him.'

With the sun low in the sky, a lone Blenheim bomber droned on its way towards the airfield. I took his hand and we started to walk back to the close. As we passed the pigsty, I couldn't help glancing in as the pink piglets pushed and shoved. They were so comical and not dirty at all like the old sow. Ziyder must have noticed me looking, but he didn't say anything. No. Even though he was just as religious as Dad, Ziyder wasn't strict. Perhaps if Dad were like Ziyder, I thought, I wouldn't hate all those rules so much and maybe I'd say my prayers more.

At that moment, Farmer Stent came out of a barn carrying a load of hay on his pitchfork.

'Hello, Mr Miller.' He nodded to me. 'Yours is 'e?' He dumped the load on a cart.

'My grandson,' said Ziyder, smiling. The man smiled back and went into the yard. It was only a short exchange but I was so pleased at the way the farmer treated my granddad with respect, despite his foreign accent and beard. Everyone seemed to like him. Except the Suffolks.

We walked back to the close but, as we were passing the schoolmaster's house, I happened to glance up. The pale face of a young girl was staring out of an upstairs window and a tremor ran through me. The eyes were wide and anxious just like Marion's had been, but her hair was long and black. I hadn't heard anything about Marion since she'd been taken away. When I looked up again, the face had gone and I wondered who she was. I'd never seen her before.

As we came to the slope, Ziyder stopped and leaned on his stick. 'Tell me, *yingeleh*. Do you say your prayers every night?'

The question was unexpected and, as I sought the right words, my neck grew hot. 'Well. Sometimes. Er, not as much as at home, Ziyder. And we have *shul* – synagogue – on *Shobbos* with the teachers.'

'Yes. I know.' He leaned down a little. 'But you must keep saying your prayers. God sees us everywhere – here as well, you know. Otherwise you will forget them.'

I stared down at the gravel and shifted my feet. I didn't want to tell lies to Ziyder, but it would make him so sad if I let him know that I didn't pray at all in the mornings and only sometimes at night. I stayed quiet, hoping he wouldn't go on.

'Well,' he said, after a short silence, 'at least say the *Shema* – the most important prayer. And when you come home, it will be easier, eh?' He carried on walking slowly. 'And let us hope the war will soon be over.'

He took my hand, but as we slowly climbed the gradient to the close, I felt as though I was leading him, not the other way around. At the Suffolks' gateway, we said goodbye and I promised to come more often. I waited as he knocked at the door. They didn't even let him have a key, I thought, as the door opened and the woman stood aside to let him squeeze past. In a moment, Ziyder seemed to change from a wise grandfather to a shuffling old man. He turned, raised his arm and smiled. Then the door closed with a dull thud.

That night, as I undressed for bed, I heard the rain beating against the windowpanes beyond the blackout curtains. Simon was in the bathroom and it was very quiet. Then I heard Ziyder's words: '. . . not better or worse . . . But we are different. You will see.' I pictured him again in the Suffolks' passageway, old and bent. Placing my hand on my head, I closed my eyes and recited the only prayer I now remembered: '*Shema Yisroel* . . . Hear, O Israel, the Lord is God. The Lord is One!' I prayed for Ziyder and for Mum and Dad, for God to protect them if London was bombed. And to save Booba and Ziyder from the Suffolks. From then on, I silently recited the *Shema* every night.

Chapter 14

First Love

In the last week of May, the Germans invaded Belgium. I listened to the news and wondered yet again if there would be air raids this time. Each time another country was invaded, I awaited the dreaded sirens.

'Bitten off too much now, has Adolf,' Frank Baker snapped, as he read the newspaper at breakfast. 'Not the little Danes and Dutch this time. It's us and the French and we'll give 'em a bloody nose, like last time.' On the front page there were pictures of the Maginot Line, huge concrete igloos with concrete tubes pointing into the distance. I wondered how the soldiers inside could see their target. But, after a few days, everything calmed down again and the war seemed as far away as ever.

The first cut of hay had been taken and huge stacks rose inside the farmyards on the edge of the village. Now the meadows were covered with buttercups and daisies – the girls made daisy chains but my stubby fingers couldn't manage it. Ronnie said that if you held a buttercup under your chin, the yellow shadow showed whether you liked butter. It always did, but there was only margarine now – and dripping that Mrs Baker made when she roasted meat.

At the beginning of June, the German panzers struck into France. The newspaper showed broad black arrows curving out of Belgium and dividing to encircle the Maginot Line, then moving on across the page towards the Channel, as though those defences never existed.

'Ruddy Frogs,' Frank muttered. 'Never could fight.' He glanced up at the framed engraving on the wall: *Machine Gun Corps 1915–1918*. 'Had to sort 'em out last time. Now we'll have to do it again.' The wireless told of fierce fighting and of 'our lines holding against massive attacks' but, again, in the village it was as if nothing had changed.

I spent a lot of time wandering over the fields after school and at the weekends, watching the noisy rooks feeding their young high in the elms. As I walked back up the lane one day, a blackbird flew out of a hedge just past my head, cackling its warning cry. I pushed aside some foliage and discovered my very first bird's nest. In it were four light-blue eggs speckled with brown dots and squiggles. I was careful not to touch them because Frank had told me the mother bird would smell my fingers and not sit on them again. I told no one else and it became 'my' nest. Each day I peeped in and saw them hatch into ugly, bald nestlings that gaped their yellow beaks each time I jogged the nearby branches, thinking I was their mother coming to feed them. Most days I ran to the spot after school and waited until no one else was about, peeped in and watched as they grew feathers, then fledged. One day the nest – *my* nest – was empty. Although I'd known they had to grow and fly away, I did feel sorry.

Ronnie and I still met at weekends to roam around and explore together. Sometimes we sat on a grassy bank near

Halton airfield, watching planes taking off and landing. By the perimeter, two Lysander high-wing planes were parked, looking like giant dragonflies. I couldn't imagine them being much use in a war. One day, as we stared over the barbed-wire fence, a twin-engined Avro Anson came in to land. It was painted white and had red crosses painted on the fuselage and wings.

'Hospital plane,' muttered Ronnie.

'Yes,' I said. Trying to sound knowledgeable, I added, 'Malcolm said there was a special hospital here for casualties.'

As we were chatting, a lone figure came out of a gateway and walked towards the junction with the main road, turned and went back. He was dressed in a bright blue uniform and red tie, his left sleeve empty and pinned across his chest. The sight of him brought the war so close and, saying no more, we hurried back to the village.

The next morning, Frank was glued to the wireless again and this time he was fuming. 'Capitulated, they have, the ruddy Frogs. Surrendered. Stabbed us in the back. Would you believe it?' he thundered, hands clenched on the table. Now someone with a distinctive voice and a funny name – I later found out it was Alvar Lidell – told us that British troops were being evacuated from a place called Dunkirk.

That night, I huddled under the covers, clutching my bear. I'd seen the maps in the papers showing the black arrows right up to the English Channel. Dad had said that at Dover you could see from one side of the Channel to the other. I imagined thousands of boats ferrying German troops and tanks across the water and landing on the beaches. Hordes of grey uniforms swarming over the countryside and into London. What would happen to Mum and Dad – or to Booba and Ziyder when the Germans reached the village? The Nazis killed Jews, didn't they? Children and all, said Uncle Barney. Perhaps the Bakers would hide me and say I was theirs. But the Suffolks would never hide Ziyder. They'd probably join the Nazis. My mind ran riot.

The next morning, in the brilliant sunlight, I felt a bit better. The newspaper had pictures of deserted beaches at Dunkirk and smoke rising from the town. Frank was listening to the wireless again: lots of small pleasure boats had brought men off the beaches, victorious. I wondered whether the yellow-funnelled Eagle steamers we used to watch on the Thames, going past the Tower, had been there too.

'Some ruddy victory!' huffed Frank. 'Just about got away with our trousers on.'

Apart from a few bombing raids on the south coast, there was no more talk of invasion. As June rolled into July, Frank joined the LDV (the Local Defence Volunteers, who later became the Home Guard). He was gone two evenings a week to drill, which made me aware that, despite appearances, life was no longer as it had been before.

The real war still seemed as far away as ever when, one morning, the headmistress announced that at the end of the month the school would be going home for the holidays. I was excited. The country was great but home was home. And, anyway, it was only for the holidays, wasn't it? But before that happened, I had another surprise.

'How would you like a party for your birthday, David?' Mrs Baker asked one evening. I knew it was my ninth birthday the following week, but hadn't expected anything special.

'Really? Yes! Course!'

'Nothing grand, mind you, but we can invite your sister an' that.' I had no idea who 'an' that' might be.

Strangely I don't remember anything special happening on my birthdays at home, a small present perhaps but certainly no party. I know there must have been some celebration but I have absolutely no memory of London birthdays. It's this one that sticks in my mind.

On the day of the party, I ran home from school and made no objection when Mrs Baker sent me upstairs to get scrubbed and put on a clean shirt. When I came down, the dining-room table was laid with coloured serviettes and paper hats, plates of home-made biscuits and a huge iced cake. I wondered how she had managed to find all the ingredients with the now strict rationing and I couldn't stop thanking her.

Rita came round with a friend and brought me a set of coloured pencils in a painted wooden box. Then, just before we all sat down, there was a knock at the back door and two girls entered. I caught my breath. One of them was the girl I'd seen peering from the schoolmaster's window. With her was a shorter girl with fair, curly hair. They blushed as Mrs Baker introduced them.

'This is Eve,' she said, nodding to the dark-haired one I'd seen before, 'and this is her sister, Marilyn.'

Marilyn was much the prettier and, me being the birthday boy, she sat beside me. Eve was near Simon and I could see he was jealous, especially when the food was over and the games started: Marilyn and I hunted the thimble together, swapped paper hats and giggled. But when Frank Baker organized a quiz,

Marilyn kept jumping up with silly answers, always wanting to be the centre of attention. Eve didn't say much and looked down most of the time, except occasionally when she glanced at me as if she wanted to say something.

Without warning, Frank put out the lights and Mrs Baker came in with the birthday cake and candles. As she put it down, the candlelight glinting in her glasses and her face glowing, she looked just like a fairy godmother. And to me she really was.

After cutting the cake, Mrs Baker switched off all the lights again, except one in the standard lamp, and she and Frank, Rita and her friend sat near the wireless listening to a comedy programme. Soon Simon and Marilyn were laughing together, and in the half-light, Eve moved close to me. As we started to munch the slices of cake that Frank had handed round, she leaned against me.

'Thank you for inviting me to your party,' she said softly. I looked sideways and saw that she was a bit older than me and had smooth white skin. At that moment, she seemed much prettier than Marilyn. At first I was embarrassed that Simon would see and tell everyone about 'David's girlfriend' but he was too busy joking with Marilyn to notice.

'Your billet lady must be very kind,' said Eve.

'Yes. She is. She can be strict too, sometimes,' I added, lest she think I was having too easy a time. 'What's it like at the schoolmaster's?' I asked. Suddenly she stiffened and her lower lip trembled, almost as though she was going to cry.

'The woman's all right. But she's scared of him. He's a bully.'

'Is it like being in school all the time?' I asked.

'Worse,' she said. 'And I hate it. I hate him.' She took

my hand. 'And I'm glad I came because I can talk to you.'

At that moment Marilyn jumped up again, giggling at one of Simon's remarks, and Eve turned to me. 'I'm fed up with all this noise,' she murmured.

'Me, too,' I said.

'Can't we go somewhere quiet, just you and me?'

Where? How? Why?

'We're not allowed to use the front room,' I said quickly.

'What about your room?'

The bedroom! What if Mrs Baker came up? Desperately I thought of how we could possibly go upstairs without someone making a fuss, but I couldn't think of an excuse. Suddenly I had an idea. 'We could sit out on the hall stairs,' I said. 'No one could mind that.'

Eve agreed. I went out first and sat halfway up the stairs. She came out a minute later and as she sat down she leaned over and kissed me – a short, dry kiss. It was the first time I'd ever kissed a girl and I didn't know what to do. She put her arm around me and I held her other hand tight, and we sat like that, close and huddled together. I felt a mixture of warmth and comfort, while at the same time I was scared of someone coming out, switching on the light and seeing us sitting close like that.

On the dark staircase, Eve told me that she and her sister came from Ealing in West London and that her mother hadn't let them go away with their school because she would have been left alone. Her dad had been in the army in France and they weren't sure yet whether he had been lost at Dunkirk or taken prisoner. But now that there might be air raids, her mum had sent them to the schoolmaster's wife, who was her cousin.

I pictured those arrows moving across France and felt really sorry for her, a bit like the way I had felt for little Marion in the playground that day. To this day I am puzzled at my childhood empathy for other people's suffering – especially for women, it seems. Was it a reflection of my feeling alone and being away from Mum?

As Eve continued her story, we huddled together. By now I was anxious, feeling sure that someone would notice how long we'd been out.

'What's up, David?' she whispered, as I tensed.

'I'm worried Frank Baker will come looking for me.'

'It'd be nice without the grown-ups, wouldn't it?' And we began to talk softly about the billets, the parents, schools. Strangely, neither of us mentioned my being Jewish. I felt we could go on talking for ages. I'd never talked so much with anyone apart from Ronnie. And she was a girl. It was a completely new experience, my mind miles away from the billet, so deeply involved in the conversation that I didn't hear the footsteps coming from the dining room.

The door flew open, light shot into the hallway and Frank Baker came into the hall. I sat up, snatching my hand away from Eve.

'So there you are, you two.' He laughed. 'You're the birthday boy, y'know. You'd better make an appearance. And the girls have got to go home soon.'

'We were just talking about school and things,' I blustered.

He went back in, we stood up and Eve gripped my hand tightly. 'I hate them. I hate them all. All of them,' she hissed. 'Why can't the grown-ups leave us alone?' She stamped down the stairs and strode into the dining room, her eyes wild and her lips tight.

As they got ready to leave, Mrs Baker gave everyone a slice of birthday cake wrapped in tissue paper. Rita kissed her cheek and thanked her again and again as we all walked round the side path in the cool, moonless night. By the gate, everyone said their goodbyes and, as Eve and I parted, we clenched fingers tightly in the dark so that no one would notice.

'See you again soon,' she whispered, as everyone was calling goodnight. Then she and her sister were gone, shadowy figures melting into the darkness.

Rita and her friend left, too, and the Bakers went back inside. It had been a wonderful birthday party but I was a bit downcast. Eve went to the village school and lived behind that grey flint wall with the headmaster. I couldn't just go and call on her so how would we meet again? I stood on the path looking up into the sky with mixed feelings: delight at Mrs Baker's wonderful birthday party and anguish over Eve. It was a cloudless night: so many stars. I would have gone on staring at the sky, morose and thoughtful, if Frank hadn't come back round the corner.

'Long past your bedtime, birthday boy.'

I skipped around him and in through the rear door.

'Smashing party, Mrs Baker. Thanks ever so much.'

Up in the bedroom, Simon was reading the *Dandy*. 'Really pretty girl, Marilyn.' He grinned. 'An' she liked me, you know. Nothing like her sister. What a sourpuss. Hardly played one game all evening.'

At first I didn't respond, just slipped on my pyjamas. 'She's sad cos she doesn't know what's happened to her dad in France,' I explained eventually. 'You'd be sad too.'

'Well, he's Marilyn's dad as well, ain't he? She don't mope.'

I shrugged. People were different, weren't they? I climbed into bed and lay there thinking about Eve. How she'd taken my hand and how if she did it again, I'd squeeze hers hard and we'd talk for hours. Yes. If only we could meet again.

As I lay back, the sharp cry of a vixen came from beyond the meadow. I hugged my bear, then looked at him and smiled to myself. It seemed so babyish to keep him now. I was about to throw him on the floor when I saw him staring at me with his one half-stitched eye. Remembering how he had comforted me all through the winter, I sat him on the chair by my bed and tucked my vest around him to keep him warm.

Tomorrow I would give him back to Mrs Baker. After tonight, I wouldn't need him any more. I was a year older.

July blazed hot and bright but, despite the warm, bright country summer, the atmosphere was tinged with regret. I longed to see Eve again, and every time I passed the schoolmaster's house, I looked up at that window but she was never there. Perhaps she had gone back to London. By chance I happened to overhear Mrs Baker and Doreen talking about her one day.

'Sits on her own and mopes all day, his wife told me,' Mrs Baker was saying. 'Doesn't want to do anything.' They didn't know I'd heard and they weren't to know that I cared. If only I could see her and talk to her she would smile again, like that night at the party.

I did see Eve again, just once. I was coming down the lane with Ronnie when we met Gerald. He had a piece of chalk and, on a flat patch of tarmac in the road near the schoolhouse, we chalked out hopscotch squares and were soon noisily hopping and jumping across them.

Suddenly, from a side door, Eve came out. She walked through a brick archway towards the school and, seeing me, stopped for a moment and flicked her hand in recognition. I knew she was waiting and wanted to go over to her but didn't dare. Ronnie's reaction wouldn't have mattered but Gerald was sure to blurt it out in school. Why did it have to be when I was with the boys? I shot Eve a brief smile and my stomach heaved with frustration. She shrugged and went on her way.

'Come on, dreamy,' called Gerald. 'Your turn.'

I picked up the stone and threw it. Then, just before I hopped, glanced back. Eve had gone.

That evening after supper, I lay on my bed as late sunlight threw pale shadows on the ceiling, feeling really morose. I longed to be with Eve – to hold her hand and try to make her smile – and was certain that she must be thinking of me, too. Those few quiet minutes at the party with Eve were the first time I found I could really talk about the evacuation with anyone, about how I felt at the Bakers', about all sorts of things that I didn't even share with Ronnie. Was it my first experience of romantic love? Can a boy of nine feel real love – and for a girl of eleven? And the memory of her mournful face peering out of the high window – like that of the princess locked up in the stone tower – lingered with me long, long afterwards.

With the end of the month and holidays approaching, I grew increasingly excited at the prospect of going home. Ronnie and I often went to sit by the airfield now, watching the planes coming in and taking off, comparing them to our cigarette cards. I could already distinguish practically every type of plane that flew: Ansons, Blenheims, Spitfires and more. Once, three Hurricane fighters came in and we spelled out the large white letters on the fuselage. Looking back, they were probably the remnants of the few squadrons that had managed to escape from France.

A few days before we were due to go to London, we talked about the holidays as we sat on the grassy bank by the airfield.

'Going home on Sunday, ain't we, David?' said Ronnie, throwing a stone into the ditch. 'Cor. Can't wait, can you?'

'No. My stomach gets all tingly when I think of it,' I said. 'Wonder how long they'll let us stay.'

'Dunno,' said Ronnie. 'My mum says I can stay home for good, if I like.' Immediately he glanced around. 'Here. Don't tell no one, though, will you?'

'Course not,' I said. 'But will we be allowed to, then?' The headmistress had sternly told us that at the end of the fortnight we were to come back or we would lose our billets.

'Couldn't care less what they say,' he huffed. 'Had enough of this dump.'

'Oh. It's not so bad,' I said, but I didn't want to contradict him. Perhaps if he had someone like the Bakers looking after him, he'd feel like me. 'But what if they start bombing?' I added, perhaps justifying my own feelings. 'That's why we're here, ain't it?'

Two fighters took off one after the other and roared into the distance. We watched them go, then Ronnie shrugged. 'My dad says Hitler will attack Russia instead. He says that's what he always wanted to do anyway.' And again I recalled Mum saying Ronnie's dad was a Communist. And they were Communists in Russia, weren't they, so perhaps his dad knew something? Ronnie threw another stone into the ditch. 'Anyway, I'll be blinkin' glad to get out of this place.'

On the last Saturday afternoon before the holiday, I wandered across the paddock behind the close and into the large meadow beyond. There was clover among the grass and I searched for a four-leafed one on my hands and knees. But I couldn't find one. It was warm and sunny, and I lay flat on my back in the long grass so that no one could see me. Around me, grasshoppers chirped and birds sang from the hedgerows, but then I heard that magical trilling song again, directly above me in the cloudless sky.

As usual, at first I couldn't see it but then I spotted the tiny bird fluttering its wings and singing, rising a few feet, then hanging almost stationary before rising again, up and up, almost in a straight line, growing smaller and smaller until it was just a tiny speck and finally disappeared. Yet still I could hear its song, the song of the skylark, growing fainter and fainter. I wished I could be as free as he was – free as a bird to go wherever and do whatever I liked.

My stomach told me it must be near teatime. I jumped up, brushed down my shorts and ran back to the close.

Chapter 15

Home for the Holidays

The day before we travelled, Rita came round and helped Mrs Baker pack some of my clothes into a rucksack. We were going just for a fortnight, Rita said. I also stuffed in a few comics and my soldiers so I would have something to play with at home. That night, before she turned off the light, Mrs Baker came over and kissed my forehead.

'We shall miss you, little 'un,' she said.

'Well, I'll be back in a couple of weeks,' I chirped. She smiled, then went over to the door and switched off the light.

The next morning, excited, I jumped out of bed and came down early. Mrs Baker was still frying breakfast, so I went outside to join Frank in the garden.

'You just stay there by the back door,' he called. 'Don't want you look'n' like a ragamuffin when you go home.' He was coming up the cinder path holding a Brown Leghorn by its legs. With a swift movement, he slid one hand down its neck, gripped it tight between two fingers, then tugged and twisted, breaking its neck. The chicken fluttered its wings and jerked for a few moments as he held it at arm's length, then was still.

'There,' he said, stuffing it into a brown carrier bag, 'that's for your mum and dad. They can't be gettin' much meat in London these days.'

'Cor. Thanks, Mr Baker.' I took the bag from him. 'They'll be ever so pleased.'

'And there's half a dozen eggs in your rucksack.' He grinned. 'We packed 'em well but don't go sittin' down on it, now!'

As I tucked in to bacon and eggs and toast for breakfast, I wondered when I would be eating bacon again. Although I knew I shouldn't, I'd miss it at home.

Rita called round and, after a handshake from Frank and a hug from Mrs Baker, we walked away. As they stood on the path and watched us go, Mrs Baker looked a bit miserable, so I smiled and waved back a few times as we went down the close. After all, I'd be back in a couple of weeks, wouldn't I? It was not until many years later that I even thought about what a culture shock and an effort it must have been for those villagers, many of whom had never even met a Londoner, to take a load of boisterous East End Jewish children into their homes.

By the time Rita and I reached the green, most of the children were already there, including some of the foster-parents – some had been together for the whole year, so a separation of this length was really meaningful.

Ronnie was hopping around the war memorial, ginger hair glowing in the bright sunlight. 'First one on grabs a seat for both,' he said.

'You bet.'

About ten minutes later the blunt grey nose of the coach came round the bend and down the hill. Rita leaned down and kissed me goodbye. She was staying in the village to keep an eye on our grandparents and would go home after I came back. As the coach stopped, there was the mad scramble for seats and it was soon packed full. With everyone so eager to get going, the coach driver would have no opportunity for a swift half this time.

The engine roared, the coach pulled away and we all cheered. I waved to Rita who was standing with the Bakers – and was surprised to see that they, too, had come up to see us go. I slapped my hand on the window, they saw me and we waved to each other. Mrs Baker smiled and I saw Frank put his arm around her shoulders. Mingled with my excitement at going home was my sadness at leaving them – especially my fairy godmother.

Out on the main road, the coach wound over the hills, then down into the flat countryside. Tired from my early rising, I must have dozed for a while. I woke to a shout from Ronnie.

'Look,' he exclaimed, 'a real London bus!'

As we passed a red double-decker everyone cheered. I glued my nose to the window as we drove past red-brick houses with tiled roofs, then grey-brick and slate-roofed terraces. Trolleybus wires stretched across the roads. We were in the London suburbs. After the green and open spaces of the countryside, the streets seemed so dark and narrow. Were they always like that?

All the shop windows we passed were covered with criss-crossing, anti-shatter tape, and there were sandbags at the entrance to banks and office buildings. Green netting was stuck on the bus windows with just a small square left clear to look out. Yes, in London there was a real war on – and, suddenly, I felt it. It also made me anxious: I knew that if the Germans did drop bombs, it would certainly be on London.

The coach pulled up outside my old school. It looked strange – all grey and silent.

As we grabbed our luggage and spilled out, Ronnie clutched my arm, grinning. 'Great to be back, ain't it? See ya, David. Bye.'

'Yeh. See ya, Ronnie. See ya.'

It was good to have a real friend like Ronnie, but as the parents clustered around, I quickly forgot everything except that I was home and Mum was hugging me, then holding me at arm's length to look me up and down. 'Hmm. You haven't put on any weight, David, but you look so well.' She turned to Dad. 'Just look at the colour in those cheeks, Jack.'

Dad took the rucksack and patted my head. 'Good to have you home, Dovidle. Come.'

'Careful with the rucksack, Dad,' I called. 'Mrs Baker put some eggs in there for you. And a surprise as well!'

Mum pinched my cheek and hugged me again. 'Such a kind woman. I must send her something. Come. You'll be starving.'

Just then Ronnie and his parents walked past, heading for Brick Lane. 'Bye, David. See ya,' he called again.

'Bye, Ronnie,' I called. 'See you soon.'

But it was the last time I would see him. My best friend and I would never meet again. We no longer lived near one another and had no telephone. At first I really missed him, but new – and sometimes traumatic – events took place and we lost contact. Ronnie became yet another separation that would add to the sense of my familiar world falling apart – and my having to get used to a new one.

* * *

Mum took my hand and we went out to Leman Street to catch the bus, the hard paving stones under my feet feeling strange. I knew from Rita that Mum and Dad had moved a short while before, but it had been hard to think about London and impossible to imagine a new home there.

'It's a flat, David,' said Mum. 'In a large house in Stoke Newington.'

Until then, my London world had been bounded by Cable Street and Whitechapel Road. Anything beyond Shoreditch might just as well have been in China. Along with much of the Jewish community, Mum and Dad had intended to move out of the East End just before the war. Whether it was the threat of air raids on the docks – Mum had experienced the Zeppelin bombs on the East End during the First World War – or that Dad now had regular work making uniforms and they could afford the rent somewhere more desirable, I never knew. But moved we had.

We crossed Leman Street and, as we waited at the corner of Alie Street for the 647 trolleybus, I remembered how Rita and I had risen early one Sunday morning the year before to hurry to this same spot to see the first trolleys up and running. The tramlines were still in the road but now the trolleys had replaced them. As Mum and I boarded, I was excited about my first trolleybus ride. I remembered the clatter of the trams and it was strange to hear the click, click, click of the silent-running electric motor as the trolley accelerated or slowed down.

At the tall Victorian house in Amherst Road, Dad kissed the tips of his fingers and touched the *mezuzah*. As prescribed, every observant Jewish household has a small box or metal cylinder containing a tiny scroll of written prayers fixed at eye level on the right-hand side of the main entrance doorpost.

Mum opened the front door into a high-ceilinged but gloomy hallway. The house was divided into flats but, as in many large shared houses at the time, they were not self-contained. The basement and ground floors were occupied by the householders.

'We've got the first and second floors,' said Mum. I never did find out who, if anyone, lived on the top floor. After our three-up-two-down terraced house in Tenter Street and the houses in the village, the rooms seemed so large and the ceilings so high, with moulded cornices around the edges. The windows were huge, too, almost floor to ceiling – much bigger than me.

Mum took me to the first floor, where the kitchen was. It looked out onto an overgrown rear garden. 'I can dig it up and plant vegetables there, like at the Bakers',' I said excitedly.

'Well, we'll have to ask,' said Mum. 'It belongs to the lady downstairs.' Then I thought, it doesn't really matter. I'm only home for the holidays.

The kitchen seemed so posh after our tiny one in Tenter Street. Apart from a white Belfast sink and wooden draining-board, there was a blue and white cupboard and a small table and wooden chairs. Three tea chests packed with crockery from our old house stood against one wall. The shared toilet and bathroom were on the half-landing below, Mum explained.

'Dad's only managed to move some of our furniture,' she added. 'He'll hire a van and a driver one weekend for the rest, but we can bring small things from the old house every time we go there.' Our old house was empty and not relet, probably because the whole street was going to be redeveloped by the Co-op, our landlords. She leaned down and kissed the top of my head. 'It's good to have you home, my love. You can help unpack now as well.' I raised one hand and stroked her face.

As Mum began to unpack my rucksack, I looked out of the back window again. To the south lay the East End, the river, the docks and the house where we'd once lived. Now we were in North London, with trees in the street and houses with gardens. Real posh, I thought.

Mum took out the eggs, then the brown carrier-bag package.

'That's a chicken, Mum. Mr Baker killed one of theirs, just for us,' I said proudly, as the scrawny neck flopped out of the newspaper Frank had wrapped it in.

'Oh, that's so kind of them,' said Mum.

At that moment Dad came into the kitchen. He stopped and pointed to the chicken. 'Wait,' he snapped. 'How did they kill it?' and, before I could answer, he glanced at the neck and saw it had not been cut. 'Huh. It hasn't been killed properly!' He let go of the head and it swung from the neck over the table edge. 'It's not *kosher*, David. You should know better than to bring that home. It's *treifa*, unclean,' he declared, then immediately went over to the sink and washed his hands. Turning to Mum, he muttered, 'See? The boy's forgotten everything. A real *goy* he'll be!'

'Never mind,' said Mum, slipping the head back inside the bag again and putting it on a chair. 'I'll write and tell them we ate it and it was lovely,' she said. Turning to Dad, she added, 'I can swap it for something else with one of the women attendants at the baths. It won't go to waste.'

My stomach tied itself into a knot. I was furious. It was wartime. In the middle of rationing, the Bakers had killed one of their precious chickens for us, and stupid old Dad, with his silly old-fashioned rules, wouldn't let us eat it. The chicken was the Bakers' special present. Why couldn't he make an exception, just for them – or even just for me?

I stood there, my head boiling, hating him so much.

Yes. I was home.

A few days later, Mum took me down to the old house to collect a few odd things they'd left behind. Little appeared to have changed. The goalposts we'd chalked just before we went away were still on Fatty Marcus's wall. Old Isaac's shop, where I'd bought that pie, was still there. Dad seemed to have forgotten about the penny; Ziyder certainly had. There were probably more important things to worry about.

While Mum was packing some odds and ends into bags in the house, I wanted to go for a stroll around the old neighbourhood.

'Don't go far, David!' she called.

'Only up St Mark's Street,' I said.

I wondered why she was so anxious. In and around the village, I walked for miles and no one worried.

Opposite the house, the huge gates of the Co-op yard gaped open. Horses and carts and lorries were going in and out as usual. It was a sunny day but, above, the sky was a grey-blue haze and the air smelt musty. As I walked up South Tenter Street I wondered why it was so quiet, no kids playing in the streets. Hadn't they come home for the holidays? They couldn't all have moved.

The Rowsteins' garden, the one and only garden in the neighbourhood, which we used to think was so large and pretty, now looked what it must always have been – a tiny triangle of black earth and ashes, a sooty privet hedge, a few snapdragons and marigolds. There were no curtains at the windows and Mum told me that they had moved to Stamford Hill.

In St Mark's Street, the red pillar box was still there but its top, like all the others, had been painted a pale green. If poison-gas bombs fell, which the government feared they would, it was supposed to turn pink as a warning to us to put on our gas masks. The wireless news added that poison gas would smell like geraniums – a typically middle-class warning; as if any East End or northern industrial-town kid knew what geraniums smelt like . . .

At the corner of Scarborough Street, Ackerman's grocery shop had strips of brown paper glued across the dark windows. The old shopkeeper still rested her ample breasts on the counter, but the shop was half empty. Gone were all the boxes and barrels that had always stood on the wooden floor, in which Mum fished deep for salted herrings. The best ones were always at the bottom, she insisted, wiping her dripping arm with an old newspaper as she handed the chosen fish to the woman. I'd given up telling her that since all the other mothers did the same the barrel must have been turned over at least a dozen times.

Fingering two pennies in my pocket, I looked for the sauerkraut barrel, my chops watering as I remembered the long strings of pickled white cabbage dangling into my mouth. Perhaps she kept the barrel behind the counter now.

'Ha'porth of sauerkraut, Mrs Ackerman,' I chirped, holding out a penny.

The woman smiled. 'Huh. Sauerkraut? A ha'porth? I can see

you haven't been here for a long time.' She wiped her nose with a large red handkerchief and waved her hand around the shop. 'No sauerkraut. No *shmaltz* herrings. They used to come from Poland.' She leaned over the counter. 'And you wouldn't get much for a ha'penny now, I can tell you.'

I shrugged, disappointed, and wandered out. In Isaac's shop it wasn't much better. Just a few half-empty jars of sweets where there used to be a whole row and some dry-looking biscuits. No pies or cakes.

The shopkeeper looked at my coins. 'Two pennies?' He laughed. 'Won't get much for that. Sweets are threepence a quarter now. What there is.'

I bought a couple of chews and held on to the other penny.

The fruit shop was just the same. No bananas or oranges. Only apples, pears and plums – home-grown fruit. I wasn't going to waste money on those when I could scrump them for nothing.

As I came out of the shop, I heard high-pitched raucous voices coming down Newnham Street.

We're gonna 'ang out the washin' on the Siegfried Line,
'Ave you any dir'y washin', Muvver dear. We're gonna . . .

Recognizing Ginger Bernie's hoarse cackle, I ran to the corner. Everything about Bernie was ginger. He wasn't just red-headed, like Ronnie, his face, hair, hands and freckles were all red – and he was always laughing. Bernie was walking arm in arm with George. For some reason, they hadn't been evacuated with the school. Mum said George was half Jewish and only came to our school because his mother was fully Jewish. His father was a docker from Cable Street and George hung out with another gang who, although not much older than us, were a burly, rough mob. When they ran through our streets, we used to huddle in the doorways, quite scared.

As they spotted me, the two began to sing even louder:

> *If the Siegfried Line's still there –*
> *Wiv'aht yer trouziz,*
> *If the Siegfried Line's still there . . .*

We ran to meet, giggling and reaching out to touch one another and verify that we were real.

'When did you get back?' asked Bernie.

'Yesterday,' I said. 'Where's everyone?'

'Still evacuated, like you,' said George, scratching his short-back-and-sides fair hair.

'Or moved,' added Bernie. 'Everyone's movin'. Betty went last week to Dalston. The 'Orovitzes 'ave gone to 'Ackney.'

'Even old Fatty Marcus has gone,' said George.

'Yeah,' laughed Bernie. 'We'll 'ave to find someone else's letter box to throw fireworks in next year!'

'What about you two?' I asked.

'We were,' said George. They must have been sent with the other half of the school to the other village.

'Anyway, when there was no bombs and that,' said Bernie, 'our mums brought us back about a month ago.'

We all laughed, then set off together up St Mark's Street singing at the tops of our voices. And again I was aware that we were the only children around. I looked up at the sky. Over Tower Bridge, two barrage balloons glinted silver in the hazy sunlight, their cables trailing down towards the docks.

'Seen them shelters, David?' asked Bernie. I shook my head. 'In West Tenter Street. Come on, we'll show you.'

Two long, single-storey brick buildings, windowless and with vaulted, concrete roofs, blocked half of the road.

'Two foot thick, them walls,' said George.

'Yeah. Stop any bombs, they will,' enthused Bernie. Remembering the stories of the H. G. Wells film, I didn't feel so convinced. But with those new structures, the barrage balloons high in the sky and the deserted streets, I realized that, while not much had changed in the village, in London lots had been happening.

'Is everyone moving because of the war?' I asked Mum, on our way back to Stoke Newington on the 647 trolleybus.

'Well, people have been moving out for years, David, like Uncle Sam to Wembley and Auntie Esther to Tottenham.'

'Yes,' I pressed, 'but there were still lots of people around before I went away.'

'I know. Too many. Only a few years ago, two or three families lived in one small house. Now, as soon as someone manages to save some money, they move. And because the docks will be the first target – like in the last war with the Zeppelins – people are moving a bit sooner. And now that your father has regular work, we can manage to move as well.'

Before the war, Dad was sometimes out of work when the seasons or ladies' fashions changed, as were most East End tailors – though, as a good worker, he was 'in' most of the time.

Earlier, as the trolley had passed Spitalfields Church, I'd noticed that the iron railing had been removed. Today many low perimeter walls around parks and churchyards still show the stubs of where railings once stood. Ironically, after a huge stockpile of metal had been amassed, it was found to be absolutely useless for war weapons and dumped.

The trolleybus click-clicked up Kingsland Road to Stoke Newington police station, where we got off and walked down the road to our new home, hauling the carrier bags of possessions we'd collected from the old one.

Chapter 16

Blitzed

In the flat that evening, I sat on the floor reading my new comics. On the front of the *Wizard*, Sam and Spadger were building makeshift Spitfires somewhere in the jungle. Inside, the Finns were still fighting the Russians, even though that war was over. Mum was listening to the news on the wireless. Winston Churchill had visited troops on the south coast and announced that a Home Guard army was to be formed from the Local Defence Volunteers.

At bedtime, I got up and opened the blackout curtains. In the pitch-black darkness, searchlight beams swept back and forth across the sky to the south where our old house and the docks were. The barrage balloons were being lowered at sunset when we left the East End and I wondered if the Germans knew that – and would dive-bomb at night.

Footsteps echoed from the street and there was the distant sound of traffic on Kingsland Road. In London it was never really quiet like it was in the village and, as I stared into the darkness, I pictured Frank sitting by the wireless and Mrs Baker sewing, her steel-rimmed glasses perched on the end of her nose.

Dad had become a part-time warden and after supper he went out in his dark blue battledress and black tin hat with the white 'W' on the front. Mum said it was more to meet all his old pals but Dad was indignant. Didn't she know they were all old soldiers?

The next day, Mum took me for a walk over Hackney Downs.

'It's like the country.' She smiled. But it wasn't. There were asphalt paths and most of the open space had been divided up into allotments, all looking like the Bakers' rear garden. Runner beans hung from taut strings and old men were weeding rows of cabbages and lettuce. It was strange to see vegetables growing in London. By the fence there was a notice-board, and on a poster, a huge foot was pushing a spade into the ground under the words 'Dig for Victory!'

Nearby, behind some coils of barbed wire, there were two Nissen huts. Alongside them, a cable ran from a winch-lorry, which pulled the barrage balloon floating overhead up and down. In a shallow pit stood a huge searchlight with a generator beside it. Two soldiers were sleeping on the grass and three WAAFs, sitting on upturned boxes, were chatting to each other. It all looked so peaceful. Maybe the war would be over soon – though that might mean I wouldn't be going back to the country.

The first week passed, then the second. Neither Mum nor Dad mentioned anything about going back and I wondered what our headmistress would say. Rita had come for a brief visit and was already back in the village to keep an eye on the grandparents. After that scene with the village headmaster, she had transferred to a secondary school in Aylesbury, catching the bus there and back each day.

* * *

The days flew past. One afternoon I was reading the new *Film Fun* comic in the front room: Jack Keen, detective, was on a spy-catching mission and Laurel and Hardy were still 'assin' about', as Mr Baker would have said. Suddenly a mournful wail came through the half-open window, the pitch going up and down, up and down, without stopping. It was the first time I'd heard the siren for real and I jumped up, scared, and ran down to the kitchen.

'Don't be nervous, my love. It's gone off before,' said Mum. 'It's always a false alarm.' I was trembling, though, so she rested her hands on my shoulders, then hugged me. 'The all-clear will go soon.' She kissed my head and turned back to the sink. 'You'll see.'

I went over to the window and looked out to the south, noticing what seemed to be bees buzzing around the distant barrage balloons. Suddenly there were flashes and puffs of smoke and one of the balloons collapsed and started to fall. A few seconds later, the first reports reached my ears. Then the windows rattled.

Mum heard the noise and came over to look. Just at that moment, a plume of smoke shot up from the direction of the docks.

'Oh, my God,' she whispered, holding me against her and staring out. 'Oh, my God,' she said again. 'Come, David. Quickly.' She slipped on her coat as I got my jacket. Grabbing her handbag from the table, she took my hand and together we ran down the stairs into the road. Groups of people were already hurrying towards Hackney Downs, older children laughing but some of the younger ones crying. I had a sick feeling in the pit of my stomach as the siren's wail followed us all the way along the road.

Tunnels, shored with timbers and corrugated-iron sheets, had been dug in the park with the earth heaped over them in long mounds. At the entrances to the shelter, wardens were trying to regulate the scramble, but people crowded in as fast as they could. It was lit only by the odd hurricane lamp and we tripped over legs and feet until we found an empty place on the benches. It was hot and I was sweating as I nestled close to Mum, still in the apron she hadn't had a chance to take off.

Gradually the flow of people ceased. Here and there a torch flickered on and off as a hubbub of anxious conversation ran along the benches.

A woman opposite laughed. 'Blimey. Left me old man's tea in the oven. It'll be burned to a cinder when I get back.'

Further along the tunnel, a baby started crying.

'Give 'im a suck, girl,' a woman called out. 'That'll shut 'im up.'

Mum put her arm round my shoulders and hugged me close but said nothing. Dad was in the East End, working, and I guessed she was worried.

About two hours later, the all-clear sounded. We came up and joined the crowds going home. Through our back window, I looked south. From the docks rose a cloud of dense black smoke.

Towards evening Dad came home. 'They shot one Jerry down,' he said. 'Saw him fall south of the river.'

'You're all mad,' my mother snapped. 'Why didn't you go to my sister's shelter? It's near you.'

'Huh. Old soldiers. We don't run at the first bang.'

Mum thumped his plate of barley soup on the table. 'Bloody fools. What d'you think – it's a pantomime show?' They finished supper in silence.

Later, I sat and listened to Henry Hall's guest night on the radio; the music and the jokes made the air raid seem like a bad dream. Then I heard my parents arguing in the back kitchen. They were trying to speak quietly, often breaking into Yiddish, so I knew it was about me. I'd been wondering when I would be going back to the country and whether any of the other children had stayed at home. Miss Pizer had told us we must come back after two weeks. Perhaps I would ask Mum tomorrow.

The air raids settled into a pattern. Around mid-morning, the siren would sound and, at first, we ran to the shelters, like we had the first time. Sometimes there were planes and bombs but mostly there were not. 'False alarms,' everyone said, and after a week or so people carried on with whatever they'd been doing. I went with Mum by trolleybus to bring small items and clothes from the old house. Dad would hire a van with a driver that weekend to bring the rest of our furniture to the flat.

One afternoon, when we were down at the old house, the siren sounded, followed by two explosions. We ran along East Tenter Street to the basement of one of the tall red-brick houses from which Mum used to take work home. Girls from the workshops above and a few men hurried down the concrete steps into the dim cellar. After a few minutes, there was a squeal of laughter. A moment later, the ground shook and, in the absolute silence that followed, we heard the throbbing of bombers overhead and, *brrp, brrp, brrp, brrp*, the sound of machine-gun fire. Then silence again. Suddenly the warden called down the stairs: 'Got one. Got the bastard.'

Everyone cheered.

Some time later, at the all-clear, two girls pushed past us quickly to go out, their lipstick smeared and faces flushed. 'Bloody sight more dangerous down there than up here,' one said, and they laughed.

Out in the street, though, it wasn't so light-hearted. A thick pall of oily smoke rose from the docks beyond the Co-op warehouses. Red and orange reflections glowed from the underside of the smoke cloud like a flaming sunset. From the Co-op yard three men pulled a tender loaded with canvas hoses and fire engines were clanging their way down Leman Street.

We walked back up our road. A few windows were cracked but our house seemed safe.

'Got the bloody docks again, didn't they?' said Shirley's mother, standing at her street door. Shirley must have gone back to the countryside.

'Didn't get us, though, Mum, did they?' I said.

'No,' she replied, her face serious. 'I suppose not, my love.'

On the trolleybus home, I was dying to ask when I was going back to the country but Mum's face was taut and I didn't want to nag. Was that really what she and Dad had argued about? Since then, Dad had kept saying there'd only be a few air raids and the RAF would soon knock out the German bombers. But I thought he wanted me to stay at home because, in the country, I was forgetting what he thought was most important.

When the siren sounded the next day, Mum was taking no chances and we hurried to the underground shelters in the park. Many more people had come this time and we had to penetrate right inside to find an empty bench. The tunnel twisted and turned to minimize the effect of blast. It was damp and muggy and the air smelt of bad breath, like the synagogue on Yom Kippur, the solemn fast day, when no one drank or cleaned their teeth. With only the occasional crump of a distant explosion, people were relaxed and chatting softly.

Mum was talking to a neighbour and I strained hard to hear. 'I tell you, Mrs Levy,' she was saying, 'I'm not so sure I should have brought him home now, with all this.'

'Oh. I know how you feel, Mrs Malina. Mine's home, too. Mind you, I couldn't leave him there. So skinny he was. They starved him.'

'My David was well treated, I'll say that.' Mum sighed.

'*Nu*. Maybe I'm wrong,' Mrs Levy muttered, 'but a child's place is with his parents.' Her voice dropped as she continued, 'I tell you, he forgot everything, my Harold, prayers, reading Hebrew – even when it was Yom Kippur!'

Mum was silent for a moment, then said slowly, 'Yes. That's what my husband says.' She waved her hand around in the dim light. 'But at least he'd be safe – out of all this.'

'True. True. I don't know. Everybody has to make his own choice,' said Mrs Levy.

The long steady note of the all-clear followed us back to the new flat. After lunch, we took the trolleybus down to the old house again. In Stoke Newington, only a few windows had been blown out but, as we neared Shoreditch, the effects of the air raid were clearly apparent: smoking gaps between the houses, shop windows blown across the road and shattered glass everywhere.

At the top of Commercial Street the trolleybus stopped

for a long time and we wondered what was happening.

'All change,' the conductor shouted eventually. 'All change, please. This is as far as we go.'

'Change to what?' asked Mum.

'Dunno, Missus,' said the man. 'The overhead cables are down further on.'

We stood on the pavement and watched the driver and conductor pull, from under the bus, a long bamboo pole with a hook on the end. With it, they swung the long connectors on the top of the bus across the road to the opposite set of wires. Then, slowly, the trolleybus manoeuvred round to go back.

'We'll have to walk from here, my love,' said Mum, and we set off down Commercial Street.

With every step towards Aldgate, I grew more apprehensive, fearing what I would see – perhaps even bodies. Halfway along, two trolleybus posts leaned drunkenly over the road, their wires trailing on the ground. Alongside, a house had collapsed into a pile of smouldering rubble and a half-flight of stairs led up to nowhere. A chain of Air Raid Precautions (ARP) men and women was passing out clothing, pieces of furniture and blue crockery through an open doorway, trying to lay it in neat piles on the glass-strewn pavement.

A woman wrapped in a tattered grey shawl was sitting on a bentwood chair. She was mumbling to herself and kept sweeping away imaginary hair from her eyes with one hand. Nearby, on a handcart, two children were wrapped in army blankets. The little girl's eyes were deep set and black-rimmed, with a look of hopelessness. The boy, a bit younger than me, had black smudges on his face.

A few neighbours had gathered by the old woman.

'Lucky you got to the shelters in time, Mrs Harris,' a dumpy woman with a hairnet was saying.

'Lucky? What's lucky?'

'Lucky you got away with your lives. It could have been worse.'

The old woman threw out one arm, her sleeve tattered. 'Lucky?' She waved her hand over the few belongings heaped on the pavement. 'Lucky? My home, my furniture, everything, gone. A lifetime's work.' She hunched up on her chair. 'Lucky?'

The other woman stammered, 'Of course it's terrible. But thank God you're still alive.'

'I should thank God for leaving me this?' The old woman picked up a broken shard of blue crockery. Her eyes filled with tears. 'What life? I have no life any more.'

Mum pulled at my hand. 'Don't stare, David. It's rude – especially at someone else's misfortune.'

We walked on, but the picture remained imprinted in my mind. I wondered whether my aunt's house had been hit – she lived just around the corner from this one. Perhaps our old house had been bombed too. I was glad we'd moved.

When we reached our old house it was still in one piece, but beyond Prescott Street I could see smoke rising from the docks. It being Friday and the eve of the Sabbath, my father met us there from work shortly after we arrived. He looked paler than usual and neither he nor Mum spoke much. As we walked up St Mark's Street to the synagogue, the sun was setting behind a thick bank of clouds and smoke.

Mum turned to him. 'Thank God my parents are out of all this.'

If only Mum knew about the Suffolks, I thought.

Our small synagogue in Alie Street was half empty. Three men in uniform sat near us and, up in the women's gallery, two WAAFs looked over the balustrade. I saw only two other kids. The service was short. Instead of the *khozen* trilling songs, the rabbi read the whole service with just a tune here and there. After the usual blessing, I waited for the wine. It didn't come. Instead the beadle took a tiny sip and the prayers continued.

It was almost dark when the service was over and, outside, people exchanged anxious glances, then hurried off after a brief handshake. I thought of the previous years, how long it had taken to get home after the service, groups of men standing outside the synagogue's closed doors, talking in the darkness. Then the innumerable farewells at every street corner, as the families separated. Tonight, no one could get home fast enough through the blacked-out streets. I was glad I'd got used to pitch darkness in the country.

The smell of burning hung in the air as we walked to the top of Commercial Street to catch the trolleybus home.

Back home that evening, as always before the Sabbath-eve meal, Mum covered her head with a white cloth and circled her hands over the candles to bless the Sabbath. We ate fried fish and barley soup; Mum had managed to get some meat bones from the butcher. She was used to 'managing', and I was full by the time the candles were burning low. Tomorrow I would finish off the bread pudding. No one could make bread pudding like Mum!

The next day heavy rain fell relentlessly from an overcast sky. As usual, the Sabbath hung heavy on my hands. I couldn't write, draw or switch on the wireless and, as usual, the religious strictures irked me. I lay on the sofa staring up at the ceiling, thinking of the skylark disappearing into the blue until I could hear only its twittering song. There was no *choulent*, either. Mum said the baker hadn't lit the oven on Thursday because of the air raid.

In the evening, we prayed *Havdalah* – signalling the end of the Sabbath. Book in hand I recited the words of the prayers after my father but I'd forgotten most of them and Dad tutted over my mistakes. Then he took out the silver spice holder and shook it as he concluded the prayers himself. He gave it to me to smell, opening tiny windows in the ornate cylinder, the pungent aroma of cloves and nutmeg filling my nostrils, spices to remember *Eretz Yisroel* – the Land of Israel, the Holy Land. Before the war, the whole family would gather at Ziyder's house, passing the spice holder from hand to hand, and I wondered what Granddad was doing now in the village.

Later that night, I lay in bed, unable to sleep. The wind rattled the windowpanes and I thought of the country and Miss Pizer. I'd seen a letter with her handwriting on the envelope and a Buckinghamshire postmark. Mum had stuffed it into her pocket after reading it and I guessed it was about me because later, from the kitchen, I heard Dad raise his voice. They were arguing again.

The daily vapour trails that laced the skies above were our only witness to the Battle of Britain, which was being fought over the southern counties. At the weekend, the papers and wireless reported hundreds of German planes shot down. For a few days after that, there was only an occasional short-lived siren warning. Dad said he'd been right all along: the RAF would win.

Everyone was surprised, though, when a few days later the sirens sounded, this time shortly after sunset. Dad had just left for his air-raid warden's post in Shackwell Lane so Mum took me to the tunnels in the park. It was cold and damp but, wrapped in two blankets, I must have slept because it was still dark when the all-clear went and we came up into the cold air.

As soon as we reached our flat, I ran up to the kitchen and looked out to the south, towards our old house and the docks. Nothing much had happened near us, but down by the docks gigantic yellow and orange flames were shooting up into the sky, lighting up huge black smoke clouds.

In the meantime, Mum had been speaking to Fred and Olive, our landlords, who had offered us a place in their make-shift shelter under the stairs. 'Better a three-storey house over your head than a few feet of earth in the park,' Fred reckoned.

From then on, the sirens sounded every night, but we didn't wait to be woken. Instead, every evening at dusk, we took blankets and a Thermos flask down to the basement and went to sleep there. Once or twice, I went to stand with Fred by the basement door even after the siren had sounded. We looked into the night sky, watching the searchlights. I learned to tell the buzz of a fighter plane from the throbbing beat of the twin-engined Heinkel bombers. Yellow and orange bursts of anti-aircraft shells split the dark sky, and in the morning I ran into the street to collect jagged pieces of bright steel shrapnel.

One night there seemed to be many more planes than usual, and searchlights swept to and fro across the sky. Suddenly I saw a silver speck caught at the tip of a cone of searchlights. It looked like a mosquito with yellow flashes bursting around it.

'They've got one!' shouted Fred.

From doorways along the street came excited shouts and I joined in the cheering, waiting for the plane to fall. Suddenly, from way above, we heard a shrill whistle.

'Quick!' Fred pulled me back into the hall and slammed the door. 'Quick! They're droppin' them on us now!' In two seconds we were under the stairs and Fred pulled the door closed. A moment later came the crump and thump, and a slight tremor shook the floor.

'Not that far away,' muttered Fred.

I huddled against Mum as the candle flame flickered in the corner and the alarm clock ticked away in the silence. Then it started again, the shrill whistle growing louder and deeper, the final crump, and the floorboards trembling. After that, it didn't stop. Shrieking and whistling filled the night and my ears rang with the noise and vibrations. I stuck my fingers in my ears, but it didn't help. Like wailing banshees, the bombs whistled into my head, filling me with terror as the ground shook and the explosions moved ever closer. Then it came. The one I would never forget.

The noise seemed to start directly over the house, a thin, high-pitched whine, growing louder, the pitch dropping as it came nearer. I was sure it was heading straight for us. My heart pounded against my ribs and I hid my face in Mum's coat while she wrapped her arms tightly around me. Then a split second of silence – and the ground seemed to heave up and push against me. The explosion was so close I was sure they'd hit the house.

'Mum!' I cried. 'Mum! It's got us, Mum. It's got us!' Tears sprang to my eyes and I felt her warm arms around me, but my body convulsed as I waited for the house to cave in on us. In my mind's eye, I saw those two houses at the corner of Hooper Street, half a staircase, a scrap of wall and a pile of smouldering rubble, and wondered whether the rescue men would be able to dig us out. When Dad came home from his ARP stint, he'd have to direct them – if we were still alive.

Slowly, the tremors died away. I turned my head sideways. The candle still flickered in the corner. The bomb had missed us. Slowly, I sat up. Mum gave me a handkerchief and I blew my nose.

'Blimey,' said Fred. 'That one nearly had our name on it, that's for sure.'

I almost managed to smile but then the ground shook again. It wasn't over yet. Bombs continued to fall, but that one had been the closest. Fred flicked his lighter and looked at the clock. It was half past two. It was the last thing I remembered as, exhausted, I dropped into a fitful sleep.

Chapter 17

Flight

I woke with daylight coming through cracks in the blackout curtains. Mum or Fred must have carried me up to my bed at the all-clear. Perhaps the front door slamming had woken me. As I went out to the toilet, Dad was coming up the stairs.

His black ARP helmet with the white 'W' clunked on the floor and the chair creaked as he sat down at the kitchen table. 'A terrible night, Missus,' he was saying hoarsely. 'We got called out every minute. Block of houses copped it in Cecelia Road. What a mess! I'll be late back tonight.' Soon he would leave for his workshop in the East End – 'If it's still there,' he added.

After a moment's silence I heard Mum's voice: '*Nu*, Jack. Do you still think the boy should be here, in all this?' Through the back window she must have seen the black smoke blotting out the sky.

'We'll see. It's Rosh Hashanah and Yom Kippur soon.' They were our two holiest festivals. 'He should be here for those, at least.' It was now the first week of September. I had already been home for the entire month of August.

'Two or three weeks, in all this, is a long time,' said Mum, firmly. There was an unusual hard edge to her voice.

'Okay,' Dad mumbled. 'Let's talk about it when I get home.'

'Here. I've cut some sandwiches for you,' Mum said, as he got up. 'Who knows if there are any shops left near the workshop?' As Dad clomped down the stairs, she called after him, 'If it stays quiet, I'm going to see if sister Becky is all right.'

As I was still so tired, I went back to bed. It was past midday when she woke me. 'David,' she said, as I dressed, her face serious, 'I'm taking you back to Mrs Baker.'

I quivered with excitement, then anxiety. 'What about Dad?' I asked. Mum shrugged. She didn't usually go against Dad: he had such a temper – I knew there would be a real argument when he came home. But she had made up her mind. Scared of experiencing another night like the last, I was relieved that she had. Mum began to pack a few of my things in an oilcloth shopping bag.

'London's no place for children now,' she said. 'We'll drop in at Auntie Becky's for a cup of tea, then go to Liverpool Street station.'

Again we had to walk from the top of Commercial Road, but Auntie Becky lived in Fournier Street so it wasn't that far. And as we walked along, my heart was light. Back to the village. Cor, what a lot of stories I had to tell them! I thought of how I would show them my bits of shrapnel and felt for the piece in my pocket from the day before.

We walked silently past shattered windows and boarded-up shops, our feet crunching on glass. Mum half turned to me. 'You'll be glad to get out of all this, won't you, my love?'

'Yes. Course.' Then I looked into her face. 'Can't you come as well, Mum? Like Ziyder?'

Mum laughed, then kissed the top of my head. 'No, I can't. Your dad has to work here and I have to look after him. Anyway, who'd give a grown woman like me a billet, eh?'

We carried on along the road. People passed us, looking weary and without a word. Firemen were rolling up hoses and, at the corner of Fournier Street, Spitalfields Church had been hit; workmen were trying to fasten back flapping lead roofing sheets.

Auntie Becky was overjoyed to see us. She'd been worried. 'Thank God you're all right,' she said. 'Don't worry about us. We go to a deep shelter right near here.'

I sat in a leather armchair nibbling the jam sandwiches she'd prepared, while Mum told her of her plans.

'Well, it's your decision, Martha. You'll have to face Jack afterwards. You know how angry he can get.'

'I know. And I've thought of that. But the boy's life is more important than whether he forgets a prayer or two.' She shrugged. 'You know what our father always said: "*Pikuakh nefesh dokheh Shobbos* – saving a life comes first even on *Shobbos . . .*"'

Auntie Becky glanced at the clock and sat up. 'Wait. But you can't go to the country now, Martha. How will you get back to London afterwards?'

Most buses and trains stopped at nightfall. Mum's face darkened. In her anxiety, she'd not taken that into account. Even if we got a train now, she wouldn't be able to get one back. It might even be dark by the time we reached the village.

She turned to me. 'Never mind. We'll go home soon and leave early tomorrow, my love. All right?' I smiled and nodded, concentrating on the strawberry jam as the sisters talked. There seemed no urgency now and by the time Mum stood up to go it was nearly sunset.

As we walked up Commercial Street to catch the trolleybus, the sirens sounded – much earlier than usual.

'Already!' Mum glanced at her watch. 'Come, David. Quickly. We must get back to Becky's and go to her shelter.'

I never knew Mum could run so fast for so long – I could barely keep up and was gasping by the time we reached the house. Aunt Becky had been waiting for Uncle Barney to get home from work. She didn't seem that surprised when we hurtled through the front door and I fell into the armchair, catching my breath.

'I had an idea you'd be back,' she said, as Mum and she hugged each other. 'They stop the buses when the warning goes.'

'*A brokh*,' puffed Mum. 'Lucky I told Jack we were coming to see you. He'll guess we were caught here.' Then she thought for a moment. 'But if we do go back to the village tomorrow, how will he know where we are?'

'Don't worry. Barney's workshop is in New Road, just around the corner from Jack's. He can pop in and tell Jack in the morning.'

'That's good. In case I can't get back, I'll write a note for Barney to give him.'

Just then Uncle Barney burst in through the front door. 'Come on, Becky. Oh, Martha! You too! Quick! We'd better get to the shelters. Everyone's going down already.'

It was almost dusk when we left the house. Auntie Becky switched off the electricity and turned off the gas and locked the front door. We joined a stream of people, all carrying blankets, food and clothing. Strangely, there was no sound of planes yet and Commercial Street was as quiet as a country lane, just hushed talking and the scraping of shoes on the pavement and over the broken glass.

The shelter was in the cellar of a huge office block and warehouse. I followed Mum through the polished stone archway and down three flights of stone steps. All I could see was a mass of legs and bags before we emerged into a huge underground hall. Tall steel columns, painted red, reached up to a high ceiling and between them there were rows of wooden bunk beds. I'd never slept on a bunk before and climbed up to grab a top one.

'Hey! Where do you think you're going, young lad?' A woman dressed in a dark blue uniform and hat held out one arm. 'Where's your parents?' I ran back to Mum.

'You've got to behave,' said my aunt. 'It's a public shelter.'

I held Mum's hand and we walked the length of the huge hall, but most of the bunks already had bags on them, taken by regulars who slept there every night. Eventually, we stopped by some canvas camp beds placed along the wall.

'Here.' Uncle Barney smiled down at me. 'You're lucky. You've got a bed.' It sagged as I climbed on and I rolled to the centre. Mum came over and took off my shoes, then spread two blankets over me. I lay back listening to the drone of conversation.

'Just lie down, David,' she said. 'When everyone has settled, it will be quieter and you can sleep.' She kissed me and went to sit with my aunt.

Having slept till noon that day, I wasn't tired. I lay on my back and looked up at the red steel girders that spanned the ceiling from column to column. They looked like a gigantic Meccano set. I wondered how they'd tightened the big bolts on the joints – they had rounded heads on both sides.

About half an hour later, two small boys ran past. They stopped and looked at me. 'You're new down 'ere, ain't you?' said the older one.

'Yeh. Just came tonight,' I said.

'Wanna join in our game, then?'

I sat up. Mum and my aunt were sitting on a bench, backs against the wall, eyes closed. Mum wouldn't mind my going to play with the children, I was sure.

'Okay,' I said. 'What you playing?'

'Hide 'n' seek with my sister and another girl. When we find 'em, it's their turn and they gotta look for us.' Swinging my legs off the bed, I slipped on my shoes and joined them to run about among the columns and between the rows of bunks, looking for the girls.

'Here,' said the younger one, 'I bet they're behind those cupboards.' Slowly, we crept round, then pounced. With shrieks and giggles, the girls bundled out.

'Not fair,' they chorused. 'There's three of you.'

'Well, I'm chuckin' it in anyway,' said the pimply one. He pointed at me. 'He can take my place.'

I ran off with the other boy and eventually we squeezed under the bottom bed in a line of bunks. 'They'll never see us here,' I hissed.

A minute later, the white socks and black shoes of the girls ran past. They came past three times and still didn't find us. In the stillness, we could hardly suppress our giggles.

Abruptly, just when we were congratulating ourselves,

everything changed. Bunks creaked as people jumped down and, in an increasing hubbub, lots of feet hurried past just a few inches from my nose.

The other boy squeezed out. 'Gotta find me mum,' he shouted, and hared away down the hall.

I looked for the steel column where I'd left Mum, but there were columns everywhere – and in a regular pattern. I began to panic as a crowd of people surged past me. Try as I might, I couldn't force a way through to where I thought Mum might be. My stomach knotted and I felt like crying. I was lost.

'Mum!' I shouted, pushing against the jumble of legs. 'Mum! I'm here, Mum!'

Suddenly I was lifted off my feet, high into the air, and found myself staring down into the flushed face of a policeman. He winked at me.

'Can't 'ave you gettin' lost in all this, can we?' he said, his breath smelling of stale tea and his helmet pushed back on his head.

'I've lost my mum.' I sniffed.

'More likely she's lost you, I reckon.'

From that height, I could see around the hall, and there was Mum, searching along a row of bunks.

'There she is!' I rapped on the policeman's helmet, scared I would lose sight of her.

The man pushed through the crowd towards her. 'Here, Missus,' he called. 'This one of yours?'

Mum's face was pale. 'Yes. You stupid boy.' She tugged at my hand. 'Why did you run away?' Then she hugged me close. 'Never mind, David. Let's go and find Auntie.' She turned to the policeman. 'Thanks a lot. Thank you.'

Gripping hands, we tried to force our way through the crowd, but we couldn't see Auntie Becky anywhere. Forced towards the exit, we joined the crush waiting to go up the stone steps but the throng was being held back by a warden at the top landing.

'Wait a minute. Don't push,' he called, sweat streaming down his face. 'Only in small groups. Wait for another warden. Please.'

The crowd surged back and forth and a stout woman in a rough brown coat pushed against me. I wondered what was happening. Everyone seemed to know except me.

'What's up, Mum?' I jerked my mother's hand. 'Has the all-clear gone?'

'No. We have to change shelters, David. I don't know why.'

A second warden loomed out of the darkness. The two men exchanged a few words, then he sectioned off about a dozen people from those in the entrance, including us.

'Now then,' he called. 'Just follow me and keep close together.'

The fat woman pushed past us and her rough coat rubbed the back of my neck. Just then, a lone bomb whistled down in the distance and we waited for the explosion. Then the man shouted, 'Okay. Now! Go!' Mum gripped my hand and suddenly we were out on the pavement.

Instinctively, I looked up and my heart started thumping. The whole sky was a dull orange with pinpoints of yellow and red bursting high above. White searchlight beams swept back and forth, clustering and separating. My throat was tight with terror. Everywhere I looked there were fires, flames leaping through shattered window frames and reflecting off surviving glass panes.

As we hurried along, I glanced back at the warehouse above our shelter. Huge tongues of flame were licking through the upper floors' barred windows and black smoke billowed from the roof. Now I understood why we'd had to get out.

Following the warden, our group hurried in single file along the pavement, clinging close to the walls. Again I heard that whistling, first one, then another and another, louder and louder in a shrieking chorus. I let go of Mum's hand and clapped my hands over my ears as we all halted, huddled against a wall and waited.

The bombs fell at the far end of the road, deafening explosions followed by crashing masonry. The blast swept past us. On the opposite corner, a window blew out of a burning building with a sharp crack. We waited until the shuddering ceased, then the warden raised his hand. 'Come on,' he called. 'Let's move.'

We hurried on, keeping close to the walls and crunching over a carpet of glass. Despite the heat from the fires, my teeth were chattering.

Ahead, I saw the broad expanse of Aldgate High Street – we'd crossed it on our way to evacuation. But now no policeman needed to hold up his hand so that we could cross in safety. There was no traffic at all and the space seemed so wide and exposed.

As we sheltered in a shop doorway, waiting for a signal from the warden, a fire engine clanged by, followed by an ambulance. Then Heavy Rescue men, who searched bombed houses for survivors, ran along the pavement in their dark boiler suits, faces soot-streaked. Behind us, over the docks, huge fires spewed showers of sparks and flames into oily black clouds shot with orange. Towards Stepney Green, a factory was alight, explosions throwing drums of paint into the air where they burst in showers of red, green and blue, like a gigantic fireworks display. Everywhere, the crackling of burning timber and the smell of smoke.

Above the noise, we heard the steady throb, throb, throb of the Heinkel bombers as they flew unseen overhead. I boiled with hatred for the Germans flying above us. If I ever caught a Jerry pilot, I'd—

At a signal from the warden, our group hurried across the open road. I didn't dare to look up again and hunched my head into my shoulders. In the bright firelight, the bombers could surely see us – they might even machine-gun us. And if a bomb fell now . . . Mum put her arm round my shoulders and hurried me along. Her face was as white as chalk, the lines like deep furrows.

Pieces of burning wood and cloth were falling around us, hissing on the wet roadway. My feet slithered on the glistening tramlines as I tripped over the tangled web of canvas hoses, stretching in all directions. Many were empty, lying flat and lifeless on the paving stones. At Gardiner's Corner, water spouted from two large craters and ran along the kerbs into the drains. The mains had been blown up.

We were halfway across the high street when a warehouse collapsed with a tremendous crash, sending sparks and flames into the sky, like a volcano. Reaching the far side of the road, we took shelter in another shop doorway. It was the only thing left of a shoe shop. The back had been blown out through the front windows and sodden shoes lay scattered across the pavement. A child's red sandal lay by my feet, the buckle glinting in the firelight. I shivered and closed my eyes.

'Where we going, Mum? We'll all be bombed before we get anywhere, Mum. Where we going?'

'Ssh, my love. We'll be safe soon. Another shelter. Just keep near me and hold my hand. Not far. Not far. Ssh.' Her voice was calm, but her hand was shaking.

A white ambulance hurtled by, its bell ringing all the way up Mile End Road, towards the London Hospital.

We moved off again. My ears were ringing from the constant noise, and my eyes smarted from the acrid smoke. I puffed and wheezed, dragging on my mother's hand as I struggled to keep up.

Without warning, we were led into a narrow alleyway. Suddenly, it was pitch dark – like the night should be – and, with high black walls on either side shutting out the flames and noise, I felt safer. Only the narrow strip of orange sky directly above betrayed what was happening all around. About fifty yards on, as if someone had said 'Open Sesame', a steel door opened in the wall beside us. We clattered down a flight of metal steps, then through another door into a long, narrow cellar lit by a few oil lamps. The door clanged shut behind us and I stood still, shivering and sweating at the same time in the abrupt silence.

Mum crouched down and hugged me close. Her coat smelt of smoke and sweat. In all, we had covered just a few hundred yards but it had seemed like a hundred miles.

'There you are, my love. We're safe. Thank God. We're safe.' She kissed my face and stroked my hair to one side. A few moments later, a woman showed us to a bench at the far end of the cellar and, as I walked along, the people already there stared at us.

After we'd sat down, another woman came with a jug of water and two cups. 'Just a few drops each,' she whispered. My throat was like sandpaper. I took the cup and gulped it all down.

'Now then. Just a few drops, I said.' She wagged a finger at me. 'You might be in a state of shock and too much water is dangerous.'

Just then I felt a nudge at my elbow. Mum was holding the cup and, while the woman was distracted by her colleague, she gave me another drink.

When they had moved on, Mum murmured, 'Get more of a shock from her than the water, I should think.' And for the first and only time that night, she smiled.

At the all-clear, we came up and out into the alleyway. Mum hurried me through the smoking, shattered streets to our old house to get a change of clothes. When we got there, only the first two houses remained intact. Like the rest, ours was just a shell.

'Come,' she said, 'I'm taking you back to the country. You'll have to go as you are, David.'

We walked back up the street. It was deserted. Overhead, a Spitfire buzzed towards Tower Bridge. I gazed into a cloudy sky. Was God really up there? Old Klinger's house on the corner was one of the relatively undamaged pair. While we prayed all the time, he never came to the synagogue – a real *shegetz*, Dad called him, a non-believer. Why had God allowed his house to survive while ours had gone? I should never question God's actions, Ziyder always said. He knows everything. Would He know I was questioning Him? I felt a shiver down my back.

Aldgate station had been damaged and was closed.

'We'll get the Metropolitan Line from Liverpool Street,' said Mum, and hurried me up Houndsditch, again on a carpet of broken glass. I'd become so used to the smell of smoke that I didn't notice it any more.

As we crossed Shoreditch High Street, we could see that Liverpool Street station had been bombed too. 'Maybe the Underground is still working,' said Mum.

We went in and down the steps to the concourse. The roof lights were shattered and staff were sweeping glass from the platforms. It didn't look as though any trains were moving. At the far end, Platform One had taken a direct hit. A huge hole had been torn in the roof and, beneath, beside a large crater, an engine lay askew, steam hissing from a gash in its side.

Mum turned to go down to the Underground but an inspector held out his arm to block our path. 'Sorry, love. Shut. No electricity.' He jerked his head in the direction of the chaos. 'All switched off till they get this lot sorted out.' Two women came past pushing huge brooms, sweeping up the glass that lay everywhere. 'You might try the Central Line further up at Bank.'

Mum hurried me out of the Broad Street exit and towards the City. Her face was set: even if we had to walk all the way to the village, she was determined that I was going back today. As we passed through the rear booking hall, a woman sat on a bench holding a baby. The small boy beside her had a huge white bandage all round his head. Only one eye showed and it followed me as we walked by.

Nausea gripped me and, as we came up the ramp, I spotted a large drain grating, leaned over it and spewed up my guts.

I hadn't eaten much during the past day and night but what I'd had went down that drain. Mum patted my back, and as I straightened, she wiped my mouth with her handkerchief.

'Sorry, Mum. Couldn't help it.'

'Never mind, David. If it had to come up, just as well it did.' She kissed my head. 'Let's try Moorgate station.' But that was closed, too.

We walked on and on, then went into a tube station and down a long flight of stairs – the escalator was out of action – got onto a train, changed, then changed again, pushed through crowds and climbed more stairs, legs and baggage everywhere. Mum didn't stop and hardly spoke, staring straight ahead, clutching my hand, pulling me along. I'd never seen her like that, but I held on and said nothing, my legs moving mechanically.

Somehow we got to Baker Street, where the Metropolitan Line was running a skeleton service.

'When it comes, it comes,' said the porter. 'That's all I know, Missus.'

A train left at around midday and we had to change three times. Mum had bought four bread rolls at a stall and I munched through two on the way. Eventually, we arrived at Aylesbury in the afternoon, with just the clothes we stood up in and a brown-paper bag containing two dry rolls.

We weren't alone. Three other families alighted with four or five children. They weren't from my school and looked dirty and scruffy. I glanced down at my soot-marked, creased shorts. Did I look like that, too? I'd feel ashamed to meet Mrs Baker.

All the way back, I never doubted that I would be going to the Bakers. They liked me, and would be glad to have me again, I was sure. I could already see myself feeding the bantams and collecting the eggs. Would there be any plums left on their tree?

The grey clouds had thinned throughout the morning and a pale sun tried to break through as we waited outside the station. The one bus that came ran only along the main road; Mum didn't wait for another. We got off at the fork and walked the mile-long lane down into the village, but as we neared the first houses, Mum's pace slowed. I recalled the headmistress's warning when we'd left for the holidays, then the letter that Mum had hastily stuffed into her apron pocket. I guessed she was thinking of what to say to the teachers.

The headmistress wasn't at the vicarage when we knocked. Neither was my teacher, the vicar's wife told us, as she opened the door. Standing on the porch, Mum was about to step back onto the drive, when the woman raised a hand. 'Oh dear,' she said, eyeing us – we must have looked a right sight. 'You're welcome to wait. Mrs . . . ?'

'Mrs Malina,' said Mum.

'Well. Yes. They can't be long, Mrs Malina. Do come in and sit down.'

We went into the stone-flagged hall where she motioned us to a long seat by the wall and left us. A moment later, she returned with two glasses of cold water, excused herself and disappeared. A small wooden crucifix hung on the wall opposite. Mum seemed too weary to notice, and I half dozed until the front door clicked open and my teacher, Esther Pizer, walked in.

For a moment there was absolute silence. Then, half smiling, she said, 'Hello, David. You look as though you've been through it.' To Mum, she added, 'The headmistress will be here shortly. She'll explain the situation, Mrs Malina. Meanwhile, come and sit in the garden.'

I wondered what she meant by 'the situation' as she led us out of the back door. After seating us on a bench, she asked, 'Will you be all right here for a while, David?'

'Yes, Miss.'

While Mum and I sat in silence in the dappled sunshine, the weeks in London began to fade. It was almost as though I had never left the countryside. I remembered how, when I had last sat there over a year earlier, I had also been waiting for a billet. Now, again, the sun was shining, the elms sighed in the breeze and a blackbird trailed his wings across the grass.

Nothing much seemed to have changed.

Chapter 18

The Blacksmith's Wife

About half an hour later the headmistress came into the garden. She wasn't smiling.

'Mrs Malina. Good afternoon.' She went straight to the point. 'I don't know why you're here. The term has begun and David should have returned more than three weeks ago, as we informed you. My sister wrote to you when he didn't come back. And you didn't reply.'

It wasn't Mum's fault that I hadn't returned: my father deserved the telling-off, not her.

'You must understand the present situation,' the head-mistress cut in as my mother faltered. 'At the outbreak of the war, the vicar and local parish committee arranged the billeting and everyone was in the right spirit to take it on. Meanwhile, the mood in the village has changed. With all the rationing and shortages, people are less forthcoming than they were – and don't take to being messed around.'

She paused.

'Now,' she continued, 'I have no idea if Mrs Baker has room, or whether she will agree to have David back. We'll go and see. If not, I have no idea what we can do. And I must tell you, Mrs

Malina, that we teachers have enough problems without this!'

The headmistress set off at a cracking pace, silent and tight-lipped. When we neared the close, she said, staccato and annoyed, 'We did warn you, Mrs Malina. I have no idea whether Mrs Baker will consider having him back – and I must say I can't blame her.'

'I know,' said Mum. 'But it was so quiet at first, and—'

'But now things have turned nasty, you all throw the children back onto us. You are the fourth family this week. As if Miss Pizer and I haven't enough to do.'

'Perhaps I should have gone straight to Mrs Baker myself.' Mum sighed.

'Then she wouldn't have considered it at all,' the headmistress huffed. 'The villagers are just ordinary human beings, Mrs Malina. No one likes to feel taken for granted – not when they've put themselves out once.'

As we walked round the side path at the Bakers' house, I saw a curtain twitch, and by the time we reached the open back door, Mrs Baker was already there, in her blue apron and brown leather slippers. She didn't wait for us to speak.

'Afternoon, Headmistress. Afternoon, Mrs Malina. Hello, David.' She smiled at me, but it was a thin smile and my heart sank. 'I know what you've come for but I'm afraid I have to say no. You see, two boys is really too much for us.'

Rotten Simon must have come back on time.

'Well, perhaps it could be just for a while until we sort out another billet, Mrs Baker,' the headmistress tried, but without much conviction.

The sun glinted off Mrs Baker's glasses as she shook her head, then turned to Mum. 'Well, he was a good lad, young

David. And I wish I could, Mrs Malina. But what with the shorter rations and my Frank a sergeant in the Home Guard now, we really have enough on our plate.'

Mum tried to smile. 'Yes. I do understand, Mrs Baker. I'm sorry to have troubled you. And thank you for all you did for David. He was very happy here, I know.'

They shook hands, Mum stepped back and we walked slowly round to the front gate. A shiny-coated black Pekinese ran after us and, as Frank Baker called to him from the rear garden, I almost burst out crying. I had lost my lovely billet and my fairy godmother – and I was certain it was all because of Dad and his prayers. It was one more nail in the coffin of my beliefs.

We walked back to the vicarage garden.

'I hope you see what trouble you've caused, Mrs Malina, and that you'll let your husband know,' the headmistress said sharply. 'All I can do now is throw myself on the mercy of the WVS – and try to avoid those billets who are doing it just to make money and have the extra ration book.' Then she stalked off.

The fraught night and the long journey were taking their toll on us as Mum and I sat silently, waiting. I was so tired but, more than that, I was scared that they wouldn't find anyone for me to stay with and I'd have to go back to London. Then I must have dozed off. I woke to hear the headmistress and my teacher talking by the French windows. Apparently a billet had been found – at the Hunters'.

'But they already have two boys,' my teacher was saying quietly.

'I know, but the WVS woman speaks well of them,' said the headmistress. 'Anyway, we have no alternative. Two more are expected back tomorrow.' She flung up her arms. 'Heaven knows where they will go!'

Miss Pizer took Mum and me along the winding lane to the north end of the village. I only knew that area because it was near the apple orchard where I'd once been caught. She mentioned that Mr Hunter was a blacksmith. At that I felt less despondent and even excited at the prospect of seeing him shoe horses and make tools. Perhaps he would let me help him.

We turned through a large wooden gateway. It was Sunday and the wide courtyard was deserted. On the right stood a low, clapboard building with a tiled roof and a tall, smoke-blackened brick chimney. Rusting iron bars lay outside the double doors. Opposite, on the left of the courtyard, there was a large, red-brick cottage. Further down there were stalls and stables. It must be a farm, I thought.

The sun had dropped behind the tall trees at the far end of the courtyard and a stiff breeze whipped up leaves and dust. As we walked to the house, a fair-haired boy peered at us from a side window. Miss Pizer knocked at the front door and a short, thin woman, with smooth black hair, opened the door. She looked a bit younger than Mum.

'Good afternoon,' she said, and looked down at me. 'So you're th' new lad, then.' I thought I saw her lip curl as she smiled and her small black eyes darted from me to Mum, as though she was sizing us up. She didn't look unkind, but I didn't feel the warmth of Mrs Baker. Her accent reminded me of the northern comics on the wireless.

As Mum and the teacher made the introductions, I wondered where the other two evacuees were. Then Miss Pizer bent down to me. 'Say goodbye to your mother, David. She has to get back to London tonight.'

Mum hugged me. 'You'll be a good boy, David, won't you?' She kissed my head and cheeks. 'Dad or me will bring your things as soon as we can.' She was anxious to get back to London before the blackout – and the next air raid.

I held back my tears as I held her tightly. 'Don't forget my comics – and the soldiers, the ones in the new flat.'

'Of course. Goodbye, my love, and be a good boy.' She kissed the top of my head again, then turned to the woman. 'Goodbye, Mrs Hunter. Nice to have met you. And thank you so much for taking David in.'

I stood at the gateway and waved until she and the teacher were out of sight, feeling tired, dejected and lonely. But I didn't have long to contemplate my fate.

'Right,' a sharp voice called. I spun round to face the woman. Her whole expression had changed. 'Now let's be gettin' some o' that mess off yer. Y'look in a right state.' I looked down at my soot-streaked jacket and trousers, the crumpled socks and scuffed shoes. She wouldn't have looked much better after an air raid, would she? I brightened up when she added, 'Then we can get some tea inside yer.'

The other two boys were still out and I wondered why. Later, I would know the reason only too well but, for now, I was happy enough to tuck into some corned-beef sandwiches and drink a cup of tea before being shown up to my new bedroom. It had three beds arranged around the walls. At the end of a sloping ceiling, a small dormer window looked out over the back garden, which seemed more overgrown than Frank Baker's. It was still daylight when I dropped my clothes on to the floor and, in just vest and pants, slipped into my new bed. Exhausted, I was soon fast asleep.

In the middle of the night, I woke and heard the other boys breathing in their beds. A faint glow showed through the window. I got up, tiptoed across and looked out. In the starlight, I saw again the row of tall trees at the end of the garden. It must have faced south because beyond them were the humped black silhouettes of the Chiltern Hills, outlined against an orange-tinged sky. The fires were burning in London again.

Silently I whispered the *Shema*, adding, 'Please, God, don't let them burn down our new home. And look after Mum and Dad.'

Granddad Ziyder said that God heard your prayers, even if you whispered them. Then I prayed for my grandparents, slipped back into bed and stared up at the dark ceiling. It was so silent here, so peaceful. Was all that horror last night just a dream?

Loud whispers woke me in the morning. Across the room, a chubby boy of about my age was scrutinizing me as he talked to an older boy sitting on the bed by the window. I raised myself on one elbow, then sat up and pulled the covers around me, conscious that I was wearing only vest and pants.

The smell of frying wafted up the stairs. My stomach rumbled. I was really hungry.

'What's your name?' asked the chubby one.

'David,' I replied. 'What's yours?'

'Aubrey,' he said. 'And that's my brother, Saul.'

I didn't like the look of Saul. His lips sneered naturally, and long black hair hung over a thin, pimply face.

'I was asleep when you came in,' I said. 'How long you been billeted here?'

'Too bloody long,' the older boy snarled, and swung his feet out onto the bare boards. 'Time we was back in London.'

'Lucky you weren't,' I said, and proceeded to tell them about the air raids, bombs, fires, changing shelters, everything, the words gushing out in a torrent. I felt better when I'd finished.

The younger boy listened, wide-eyed and anxious, but it was the older one who responded. 'Huh. You wouldn't catch me scuttling back here for all of Hitler's bombs. I'm not scared.'

I didn't react. He looked like a bully.

Any further conversation was cut short by a shout from downstairs: 'Come on then, you boys. Breakfast won't wait for ever, y'know!'

'Crikey,' squealed Aubrey. 'We'd better get a move on!' For all his bravado, Saul whipped on his clothes pretty smartly, too.

On a stool by my bed I found a clean shirt – it must have been one of theirs – and my shorts had been brushed clean, though they were still creased. The woman must have done that, so perhaps she was kinder than she looked.

At the bottom of the stairs, I stopped to look for the dining room.

'Come on, then,' Mrs Hunter called, through a half-open door. 'Haven't got all day, y'know.'

I went in and sat at a table with the two other boys. The sharp voice came again, this time from the back kitchen. 'Used to bein' waited on, then? Well, you'll have to learn different a bit smartish, m'lad.' Aubrey nudged me and pointed. I ran out and the woman handed me a plate with bacon and fried bread.

'You'll find porridge on t'table. Should still be hot.'

I went back and sat down, and we ate in silence until she went through to the other part of the house.

'Cor,' I whispered. 'Bit strict, ain't she?'

'Not 'alf,' said Aubrey. 'But the old man's nice.'

'Rubbish,' hissed Saul. 'They're just in it for the money. Ten bob a week extra they get – an' all our rations.'

I finished my bacon, then scooped up the remains of the porridge. The atmosphere wasn't anything like it had been at the Bakers' – or the Clarks'.

'Here. Come on,' said Aubrey, sliding off his chair. 'We've got to get out.'

'But it's not time for school yet, is it?' I said.

'Nah. Course it ain't,' snapped Saul. 'But she chucks us out of the house anyway. We're always first in school.'

We trooped upstairs to get our jackets. Despite the woman's obvious attempts, mine was still so crumpled and dirty that I was almost ashamed to put it on. Out in the yard, I looked back through the window on the other side of the front door. Two boys sat with a heavily built man at a large table. Once again I saw the fair-haired boy looking at me.

'That's her spoiled brat, James – ruddy sneak,' muttered Saul.

'The older boy ain't bad – Donald, he's called,' added Aubrey.

The three of us wandered around the yard. I looked at the long shed with its wide, stubby chimney. The two enormous doors were closed. I guessed that was the smithy and couldn't wait to see it working. Bars of rusty iron and useful-looking implements lay around outside, as well as a large cutter with a huge handle pointing up into the air. I drifted back up the yard, taking everything in. On the left were pigsties, from which I could hear piglets squealing, and at the far end, a wire-fenced chicken run. Perhaps it wouldn't be so bad here after all.

Suddenly Saul's raucous voice came from the gateway. 'Here, Dozy. If you want to go to school with us, you'd better get a move on.'

I ran down the yard and we strolled up the winding lane to the church hall, where Saul left us to go on to the village school. And, as he had said, we were the only ones there for quite a while. It was early yet.

In the hall, the first thing I noticed was that there were fewer children: some must have stayed in London, like me. Most were in one big class on my side of the partition, including Simon. Why couldn't he have stayed in London? A smaller, older group was with the headmistress on the other side.

As the day wore on, the weariness from the previous days and nights caught up with me and I felt exhausted and despondent. There was no Ronnie, no Marion, no Gerald. I didn't even feel like running out to play when the bell rang.

Esther Pizer noticed me hunched over my desk as she walked through the room. She approached me and laid a hand on my shoulder. It was like a trigger. Suddenly, my shoulders heaved. I buried my head in my arms on the desk and burst into tears.

'There, there, David. You'll soon get used to being back.'

'P'r'aps I would, if I was with Mrs Baker,' I sobbed. 'An' if I had my things, Miss. I don't like Mrs Hunter. An' Mrs Baker was so kind.' I burst out crying again.

The teacher took out her handkerchief. 'Come, David. Wipe your eyes.' I did so and sniffed. 'It doesn't hurt to have a good cry sometimes, you know. You've been through quite a lot over the last few days – your mother told us what happened.' She smiled at me. 'Just give yourself a little while to settle down, that's all.'

My teacher looked at her watch. It was time to ring the bell.

I went to the tap in the cloakroom and washed my face. My eyes must have remained red, though, and Saul noticed as he met us in the lane after school. 'Well, well. 'Ad a weepy, 'ave we, little boy?' If only I were bigger. 'Got a cry-baby, 'ave we?'

'None of your business,' I replied.

He took a swipe at me. I dodged away and he pointed his finger at me. 'You mind what you say, Titch!'

I dropped behind and let them reach the billet first. If it wasn't Sammy, it was someone else. There was never any shortage of bullies.

The smithy doors were open when I entered the yard. Curious, I walked slowly through them, wondering if it was allowed. In the dim interior stood the massive figure of Mr Hunter, dressed only in trousers and vest, wearing heavy boots and a thick leather apron. In the glow of the forge, sweat shone from his rippling arm muscles. As he stood by the anvil, hammering at a length of glowing metal, he caught sight of me and rested the hammer on the anvil with a sharp clink. 'You must be the new lad.'

'Yes, Mr Hunter.'

'Well, stand well back so you don't catch a spark.'

I stood by the door and watched as he worked a long wooden bellows handle up and down. Air spurted through the glowing coke, turning it bright yellow, and sparks flew up into the huge cowl above. It looked like burning houses. My mind switched back to the fires of the Blitz.

The smith thrust a pair of long tongs into the fire. Then, taking his hand off the bellows lever, he pulled out a glowing piece of iron and started hammering it around a long spike at one end on the anvil. I stood transfixed – it was like watching a magician. Suddenly he looked up and nodded to me. 'I reckon you'd best be gettin' in for tea,' he said, smiling.

I ran across the yard, through the front door – and full pelt into Mrs Hunter's flowered apron.

'An' where d'you think you've been all this time?' she snapped, hands on hips and looking down at me.

'With Mr Hunter,' I gasped. 'In the forge, Mrs Hunter. I didn't—'

She cut me short. 'Never mind standin' in there gawpin'. After school you comes straight in here, so I knows you've got home, right?'

'Yes, Mrs Hunter. Course, Mrs Hunter.'

I turned to go down the passage but she grabbed my shoulder. It was like an electric shock: my body jerked and banged against the wall.

'An' who said you can use t'front door then?'

'Well, I came in there yesterday. Er, no one, er—'

She leaned forward. 'Never you mind about yesterday.' Her eyes narrowed to slits. 'You use the back door like the others. Always. That clear?'

'Yes, Mrs Hunter.' Since I was already in the front passage, I thought I could go on through to the back kitchen and made to pass her.

She stretched out her arm, blocking my way. 'Now where

do you think you're going? Out and round to the back door, my lad, I said, didn't I? I shan't tell you again.' I shuffled out of the front door. 'And wash your hands and face at t'same time,' she called after me. 'You look as if you brought half the forge in with you!'

I walked slowly to the back of the house and washed at the back-kitchen sink – a sink I would come to know only too well – all the joy of the forge with Mr Hunter knocked clean out of me. The despair that had gripped me in the classroom that afternoon returned and I ran upstairs and fell onto my bed.

The next thing I knew, Aubrey was shaking my shoulder. 'Come on. Supper time. She don't like waiting, y'know.'

In the back room, the three of us ate alone. Aubrey said the Hunter family ate later. After supper, I started to go upstairs but he grabbed my arm. 'Here,' he said. 'You can't go up yet!'

'Why not?' I asked. At the Bakers' I could go in and out as I wished.

'We got to go outside cos she wants us out of the house till bedtime, that's why,' muttered Saul. 'The rotten cow.'

Slipping on my jacket, I wandered out into the yard with the other two, staring at the leaves blowing along the cobbles. The sky was grey but the weather was still quite mild. She wouldn't send us outside after supper in the winter, would she? I hadn't forgotten the snow and frost of last year's country winter. If she did, where could we go in the freezing cold?

I wandered with Aubrey up to the pigsties. One of the sows had just farrowed and a row of pink piglets were thrusting their tiny snouts into her swollen red teats. One kept slipping off and couldn't get back into the scrum, making me laugh. It was like watching clowns at the circus. I remembered the time Ziyder and I had been to a farm and he had deliberately ignored the pigs. Now his kind face came into my mind, and I wondered how he was getting on with the Suffolks. Mrs Hunter seemed almost as bad as that woman. I ought to go round and visit him soon, I thought, though the house was on the other side of the village and the evenings were drawing in. Perhaps I'd see Rita at the weekend and arrange it.

Along one side of the yard beyond the house there was a large, glazed building beside two more pigsties. Aubrey said it was the 'paint shop'. I couldn't understand why it was called that because inside there were old farm machines, not paint. Opposite, on the far side of the yard, there were four cow stalls with split stable doors. We wandered across and I looked into one where a brown and white cow was lying on the straw chewing the cud. Another lay in the second stall but the other two were empty.

As we leaned over the door, Saul strolled up the yard, kicking at loose stones. 'Better be gettin' inside now, you two,' he snapped, as though in charge.

A short time later, I was reading a comic in bed when Mrs Hunter poked her head around the door. She glanced briefly from one bed to another, said, 'Goodnight, then,' and switched off the light. I was in the middle of a story and swore under my breath. It was still twilight and I wasn't tired. I climbed out of bed and stood by the window, staring at the sky. It grew dark and the stars came out. 'You can see by starlight as well,' Mrs Clark had said. Yes, in the village you could.

As I stared out, the southern horizon began to glow and orange light once again spread behind the dark silhouette of the hills. Recalling the kindness of Mrs Clark and Mrs Baker, compared with snappy Mrs Hunter, I wondered whether, even with all the fires and bombs, I would have felt better in London than with this woman – and whether it had been such a good idea to come back. The orange glow reminded me that Mum and Dad were still in those air raids, and I was silently praying for their safety when Aubrey hissed, 'Hey. You'd better get in. She'll be real mad if she finds you there.'

Adding a prayer for myself – 'Please, God, protect me from that woman' – I climbed back into bed. A moment later she came upstairs, glanced in, then closed the door without a word.

The first month back in the village slipped past almost without my noticing. I grew used to Mrs Hunter's rules and suffered her scolding in silence. I also found ways to keep myself occupied when thrown out of the house.

A small stream flowed behind the chickens with a muddy path that clung to the bank. Dark green water weeds nodded in the current, swollen by the last rain. A clump of hazels grew out of the steep bank near the water. Feeling hungry and remembering the year before, I looked for cobnuts to eat. Pulling myself into the tangle of branches, I grabbed a cluster. It was October and they were still green but I stripped the bracts and crunched the soft nuts between my teeth, the milky fluid trickling out of my mouth and down my chin. They weren't as good as ripe ones but I was pleased to have found something to nosh.

On the roadway, the wind had blown down some horse chestnuts. Breaking open the spiky green covers, I collected five large shiny ones to play conkers. The year before, the village boys had told us they were good to eat, then laughed as we spat them out. Thinking of that, I longed for the roast chestnuts that Dad had bought me in Petticoat Lane before the war. They came from Italy, he'd said.

Back in the yard, I picked up two rusty horseshoe nails by the smithy doors. With their square shanks and large, diamond-shaped heads, they were just right for boring holes in the conkers for the string. The next morning, at school, I joined the other pairs of boys, each aiming a conker against his rival's. With my tongue between my teeth, I took aim at Sammy's. He said his conker was a twenty-sixer, which meant it had won contests over other conkers with a combined total of twenty-six victories between them. You took the score of the conker you broke so, if I could smash his, I would have a twenty-sevener – the top conker in the school.

Smack! My conker made no impression. His was a lighter colour than all the others – and a bit wrinkled. It should have been weaker. But it wasn't. Ruefully, I held mine up by the string while Sammy took aim. His first crack made a slit in my conker's brown skin. I tried again. Smack! A good hit but it made no impression on Sammy's, while my own started to crack open. Sammy's second hit split it in two and the halves shot onto the mud.

'Got Dave's. Mine's a twenty-sevener,' he crowed, as he danced round the yard. 'I'm the champion!'

'You didn't play him, did you?' said Gerald, who'd arrived back two weeks after me.

'Why not?' I asked, taking a second conker from my pocket and stringing it.

'Cos he bakes his in the oven, bloody cheat.'

Sammy heard and laughed. 'So what? No rule against it, is there?' He danced around the yard again. 'No one can beat mine – I'm the champion.'

With Ronnie having stayed in London, Gerald had become my best friend. Previously we'd never been that close, and he'd never got up to the same mischief, so I still missed Ronnie.

After school, I hung around with Aubrey in the Hunters' yard. By now I'd got used to the geese – although every time I came near them, they stretched out their necks, cackling and hissing as though they were going to peck me. There were three white ones and two Peking geese which, with their elongated, scrawny necks and a bump on the base of their beaks, were the biggest menace.

I liked the piglets, but the boar, his top lip curling up where the short tusks poked through, was another matter. He lived in the far sty and was a dirty grey with lots of white hairs. He looked really fierce.

'Best keep out of there,' Aubrey had said, and I did.

The large pink sow and her piglets lived next door to him, and another litter, born in the summer, was in the adjacent sty. They pushed at each other, scrambling around, and seemed to me just like us kids in the playground. In the last sty there was an even earlier litter, now almost fully grown. Donald said they were 'barrow pigs'. I assumed that meant they were a different breed – until one traumatic day a few weeks later.

To keep clear of Mrs Hunter, I eagerly helped Mr Hunter around the farmyard. I took hay to the cows, loaded straw and fed the pigs with buckets of cheese rinds that Mr Hunter bought from a local processed-cheese factory. These were kept in a large wooden bin between the first two sties. At weekends

I helped him walk the cows, Joanna and Daisy, up a grassy track to the meadow and occasionally Aubrey would come, too. Near the far hedge stood half a haystack, one side sheer like a brown cliff where hay had been cut away. We watched, fascinated, as the blacksmith positioned the cart beneath the stack, then thrust in an enormous blade and cut off a huge slice of hay as though slicing a huge cake.

One day Mr Hunter said: 'Here. C'mon, you boys. Give a hand. Turn this 'ere cart for me.' Aubrey and I took one shaft each and dragged it round for the blacksmith to put the horse in between them. Then we climbed on board atop the hay for the short ride back.

'You don't 'alf spend a lot of time out 'ere in the fields, David,' Aubrey said.

'Keeps me out of 'er way, don't it?' I muttered.

'Well, you gets used to it,' he said. 'Just learn to keep quiet.'

'I do, but she always finds something wrong, always.' As the cart started down the track, I added, 'But y'know what? I wouldn't mind bein' a farmer when I grow up.'

Aubrey looked horrified. 'What? Out here? In this dump? No shops. No buses. No picture palace!' He brushed some gnats away from his face. 'Wouldn't catch me stayin' here for a thousand pounds.'

I wasn't surprised. His reaction was similar to Ronnie's. Perhaps most of the boys felt like him. And, again, I wondered why I felt differently about the countryside. All the boys had had a similar childhood to mine: the narrow grey streets of East London, playing knocking-down ginger, going to synagogue at least on high holy days, and many of us had to attend Hebrew classes after school once or twice a week. Perhaps they accepted smoke and greyness as the norm and viewed the countryside as aberrant. There must have been other evacuees who felt as I did – I couldn't have been the only one – but I seemed unique among the boys in my class.

That day, as the hay-cart bumped down the track towards the yard, spots of rain fell on our faces. We laughed, then spontaneously burst into a raucous rendition of 'Pennies from Heaven'.

Mr Hunter smiled at us. 'Noisy beggars!'

We collapsed in laughter, sprawling on the hay. And, as I lay on my stomach, staring at the green hedgerows slipping past, I was thinking, if I were grown-up I could live out here in the country. I imagined myself cutting the hay with that gigantic blade. Marvellous.

Chapter 19

Barrow Pigs

On Sundays we boys and the family had dinner together. At that meal we ate really well – chicken or pork chops, lots of baked potatoes, parsnips, greens and a huge chunk of Yorkshire pudding. Afterwards I was always full to bursting. We probably ate much better in the country than in the towns, where they had to rely on strict rationing at the shops.

On one particular blustery Sunday, about two months after I'd arrived at the Hunters', we were having our lunch when, through the window, I saw a wiry, grey-haired man striding up the yard holding a knobbly walking-stick.

'Oh, my God!' exclaimed Mr Hunter. 'It's Jeremy. I have to go.'

'Damn fine time to call, though,' snapped his wife.

'Well, he's hard to get hold of, so I must go, Mother.' I was surprised how passively she acquiesced.

She muttered: 'I'll put t'dinner in oven, though it'll be burned to a cinder by time you're finished.'

The blacksmith stood up, pulled his broad leather belt tight and hurried out into the yard. The two men huddled together talking quietly, then walked slowly towards an empty cow's stall where the 'playground piglets', as Aubrey and I called them, had been transferred yesterday to make way for the new litter. As the two men went into the stall, something glinted in the old man's hand. A few minutes later, despite the distance, we heard the most horrendous screech, then another and another.

As soon as dinner was over, Aubrey and I hurried out into the yard and edged towards the far end. There came a piteous squeal from a piglet Mr Hunter was lifting by its front legs to swing over a low partition into the next stall. I cringed. Blood was running down the poor thing's back legs and a blood-stained cloth covered its behind.

Overcoming our apprehension, we moved slowly towards the stall. Jeremy was holding a bloodstained blade, while Mr Hunter grappled with the piglet to hold it steady. Then, as the man made a swift movement with the knife, again came that heart-rending squeal. I clapped my hands to my ears and shut my eyes. Why were they being so cruel? Mr Hunter was usually gentle and kind but at that moment I hated him. Aubrey and I turned and ran back down the yard, unable to say a word to each other.

At that moment, Donald came out of the back door.

'Why are they hurting the piglets?' I asked.

'Making 'em barrow pigs, that's all,' he replied matter-of-factly.

'What's barrow pigs?' I stammered.

'It's so they can be fattened up. Else they'll all be boars, won't they, and you can't have that, can you?' Once again that farmer's matter-of-factness.

'But what's Jeremy doing?' I asked, wondering whether I really wanted to know.

'He's castratin'' 'em. Old Jeremy knows how to do it and he's a busy man. Does all the villages round here. That's why Dad had to leave his dinner.'

Donald grinned condescendingly. 'It only hurts for a minute – then they forgets about it.' I didn't want to ask what 'castratin'' was, lest Donald thought me even more stupid, so the mystery was no nearer being solved.

Donald walked off with a bucket of meal for the chickens. Aubrey and I followed and stayed near the birds for the next hour until the scene with the piglets was over. When the last squeal had faded and the men had gone, we crept up to the stall doors and looked in. Rooting around in the straw, about a dozen young pigs grunted and snorted, their flanks stained with clotted blood, some licking it off one another.

Seeing us, they scrambled over for food, ears twitching. Feeling sorry for them, we ran over to the cheese rinds bin and took out a handful but when we threw them in, the piglets started to jostle and scramble around and it must have hurt for they squealed again. I wished I'd left them in peace.

I had one more encounter with Jeremy, this time more personal. The following Saturday, I was squatting on my haunches by the brook staring into the flowing water, when I heard heavy footsteps thudding along the path from the road. A moment later, Aubrey, Saul and two older boys ran across the narrow wooden bridge there. When Saul saw me, he stopped and glared at me.

'Oh, my Gawd. That titch,' he snarled, 'he'll tell everyone now.'

'Oh, never mind about him. He doesn't know anyway,' said another boy.

'David's not a sneak,' Aubrey called, 'are you, Dave?'

'Course not. Why should I tell?' I didn't even ask what it was all about as the boys hurried off up the far bank and disappeared beyond the hazel thickets.

Curiosity getting the better of me, though, I followed, keeping my distance until they walked out into a bright green meadow. The field was flanked on one side by a row of tall trees with shiny green leaves, some of which were starting to turn brown. Small, spherical fruits hung in emerald clusters high above. I stood in the shadows and watched as Saul and another boy threw up short branches and stones to knock them down. Soon they were gathering handfuls from the grass and stuffing them into their pockets. Curious, I walked forward to see what they were. Saul saw and pointed at me. 'Told you that sneak would tell,' he sneered.

'I won't tell,' I said, my face reddening and indignant. 'Why should I?'

Saul thought for a second and must have reckoned it was better for me to be an accomplice. 'Oh. All right, then.' He wagged a finger at me. 'But you ain't takin' many.'

I picked up three fruits and looked at the bright green leathery skins. 'How do you eat them?' I asked.

'They're walnuts,' said Aubrey, full of importance. 'Gotta peel off the skin first, though.'

I tried to use my fingernails but it hurt as pieces caught under them. I was about to stuff them into my pocket when suddenly we heard a shout. Over the brow of the meadow came a wiry figure with a shock of white hair, waving his knobbly walking-stick. I caught my breath. It was Jeremy!

'Bloody 'ell!' Saul had recognized him, too. ''Ere. Scarper. It's the farmer.'

A few seconds later, we were running hell for leather down the path towards the bridge, me coming last. As my feet hit the boards, I had a brainwave. Diving sharply to my right, I ran along the brook towards the rear of the chicken run to distance myself from them. In my excitement, though, halfway down the muddy path, I slipped and fell headlong into the water. The last thing I saw was a flash of sky through the water weeds, before it closed over my head.

Luckily the brook wasn't very deep and, scrambling out onto the bank, I crouched on all fours, soaked, my teeth chattering more at the thought of Mrs Hunter's scolding than the bitter cold. But there was no time to think. Old Jeremy would soon reach the bridge. I scrambled on and ran into the Hunters' yard.

Mrs Hunter happened to be just inside the back door. 'What the devil have yer done to yerself?' she snapped. Instead of scolding me, though, she pulled me inside and pushed me towards the stairs. 'Tha'll catch tha death of cold. Get upstairs and get out of them wet clothes. I'll bring yer some dry ones.'

I stood rooted to the threshold, unable to believe my ears.

'Go on, then!' she shouted. 'Don't stand there like a ruddy scarecrow!'

Up in my room, after I'd slipped on the dry clothes she threw on my bed, I heard loud voices in the front yard. Creeping along to the passage window, I realized that my soaking had been a blessing in disguise. In the front yard, Mr Hunter had grabbed Saul and Aubrey by the collar and Old Jeremy was standing in front of them.

'Let's see your hands, then,' he was saying. 'No. Not like that. Palms up.'

I peeped over the sill and saw Jeremy poke his finger into Saul's palm. It had been stained a bright orange by the walnuts. Aubrey's was lighter, but still stained.

'Right,' said Jeremy, 'there's two of 'em. The other big lads I'll catch in school tomorrow. That stain never washes off.'

Mr Hunter's face reddened. His hand grasped his belt. 'You boys been takin' this man's walnuts, then?' He looked Saul straight in the eyes, hand still on his belt. Saul hung his head. 'Well, if you ever goes up there again, I'll tan the hides off you meself. Understand?'

'Yes, Mr Hunter,' mumbled Saul, and Aubrey nodded vehemently.

'An' I shan't tell you again.'

I couldn't help smiling to myself, seeing Saul humbled like that. Served him right, the bully. I continued watching as Mr Hunter and Jeremy strode to the gateway. The boys couldn't see them but I could: they were smiling and chatting to each other as though enjoying a good joke.

At suppertime, Mrs Hunter told her husband about my soaking.

He leaned back in his chair. 'Well, I wonder what made you fall in, eh, David? In a hurry, were you?' His eyes narrowed. 'Here. Let me see those hands of yours.'

Reluctantly, I lifted one. Telltale streaks of pale orange blotched my palm.

'Right. You must have heard what I told those two. Same

goes for you as well.' He wagged a finger at the three of us. 'I'm not having my 'vacuees upsettin' Old Jeremy.' Then his eyes twinkled as he looked at me. 'Still. That soakin' were a lesson to you, weren't it?'

'Yes, Mr Hunter.' I tucked my hands between my thighs and felt I'd got off lightly.

'Them stains stays for weeks,' continued the blacksmith. 'Gypsies used to stain babies' faces with it, when they stole 'em to make people think they was their own.' He glanced at me. 'So don't let Old Jeremy catch sight of your hands, young lad.'

In bed that night, I thought of what Mr Hunter had said. Did gypsies really steal babies? Why? The only gypsies I'd ever seen had been at the fair on Hampstead Heath. They had looked quite gentle. Perhaps in the country the gypsies were nastier. I'd ask Donald some time.

It had been a traumatic day and I felt drained. Gazing up at the dark ceiling, I grew drowsy, my freezing soaking mingling visions of the piglets' bloodstained flanks before, dog-tired from that day's events, I drifted off to sleep.

November broke with thick mists that hung around for much of the day. Guy Fawkes Night came and went but was hardly noticed as no large bonfires or fireworks were allowed. I remembered the huge bonfire we lit in the middle of the road in West Tenter Street: when the police tried to clear it away, the bigger boys threw fireworks at them then ran away. Ronnie and I used to throw Jumping Jack firecrackers at the girls' legs, giggling as they screamed and ran around with the corrugated tubes jumping at their heels.

My older brother paid a ha'penny every week for a year into

a fireworks club. How I envied him every November when he walked in with his huge brown-paper parcel of fireworks. I resolved that, after the war, I would save all my pennies and make up for the years I couldn't have them.

Double summer time – two hours ahead of Greenwich Mean Time – had been instituted to lengthen the evening daylight hours. So when the winter clock switched back to GMT it was almost dark on the walk home from school and with the damp chill, things seemed even more dismal.

I remembered how happy I used to be walking home to the Bakers', scoffing a slice of bread and jam as I sat in the warm back room listening to the wireless or telling Mrs Baker about school. Now the bare hedgerows and straggly yellow grass on the verges reflected my mood. I knew that as soon as I opened the door, Mrs Hunter would tell me off, for some minor misdemeanour, or order me to go outside and fetch something. Hardly a day passed without a scolding for nothing. I felt really homesick.

One day, on the way home from school, I suddenly thought of Granddad Ziyder. I hadn't seen him since I'd come back. Just the odd word from Rita now and again kept me in touch. I wondered if I dared ask Mrs Hunter if I could visit him.

When I walked through the yard gate, the firelight glowing through the open doors of the forge seemed to offer encouragement so after tea I looked for Mrs Hunter, rather than staying out of her way as I usually did.

'Please, Mrs Hunter, can I go round to see my grandfather?'

'Hmm. Don't see why not, now an' again.' My heart leaped. 'But don't go runnin' off there whenever it takes yer fancy.' She had to spoil it, didn't she? 'An jus' you make sure you're back well before bedtime.'

'Yes, Mrs Hunter. Thanks, Mrs Hunter.' Grabbing my long brown overcoat, which Mum had sent with the last coach visit, I ran out through the back door. Just walking back to the close made me feel better, again remembering happy times at the Bakers'.

When I reached the Suffolks' house, my breath ghostly white in the cold, shadowy night, a faint glimmer showed from a corner of the right-hand window. Hesitant, I went to the front door, waited, then tapped the letter box flap. There was no answer. I tapped again twice, a little louder. I heard rustling and mumbling, then the door swung open and Mrs Suffolk stood on the threshold, looming over me.

'Yes?' She picked at her teeth with a little finger as she looked down at me. 'Oh. It's you, is it?' She pursed her thick lips and wiped one hand on her greasy apron.

'Evening, Mrs Suffolk,' I piped. 'Can I see my granddad, please?'

She thought for a moment. 'Hmm. Just for a bit, mind you. It's late, you know.' She waddled along the passage and tapped on a door. 'Mr Miller. It's for you.' Then shuffled on to the kitchen.

The door opened slowly and the familiar face peered around the door frame. It lit up when he saw it was me.

'*Oi*, David. My angel. Such a long time. Come. Come.' I nipped into the room, thankful when the door closed, shutting out Mrs Suffolk. 'My, how you've grown.' He pinched my cheek. 'A real little *mensch*.'

'Where's Booba?' I asked, looking around the room.

'Oh. She's not too well. She's upstairs in bed. I don't want to disturb her.'

Ziyder motioned me to sit on a wooden chair while he sat on another. Those chairs and a modest table were the only furniture in the room, apart from a small cupboard on which stood an oil stove with an aluminium saucepan on top. Everything was dark and dingy. The rooms in North Tenter Street were small, too, but not like this and so much more homely and I was sad that my granddad had to live like this.

'Rita told me you came back. Better here than in the Blitz, eh, *yingeleh*?'

I nodded and told him where I lived now, and about the blacksmith, and he was really interested, but I didn't tell him about Mrs Hunter. He had enough of his own troubles living with the Suffolks. He asked about school and thankfully didn't mention my prayers.

'I can't stay long, Ziyder,' I said, after about a quarter of an hour. 'Mrs Hunter wants me home before supper.'

'Sure. And it's so dark outside.' As we stood up, he kissed my cheek and patted my head. 'Be a good boy, David. And come when you can, but don't worry. We are fine.'

As I opened his door, Mrs Suffolk tottered towards me and opened the front door.

'Goodnight, Mrs Suffolk,' I said. She didn't reply and the door closed as soon as I was on the path. Buttoning my coat, I ran off down the slope and along the lane, my ears tingling in the wintry night, glad to get away from the witch.

After school and in the evenings, the freezing wind whistled around the three of us as we huddled in the back porch or under the eaves of the pigsties. Mrs Hunter didn't seem to care. It was always tea and straight out, then in again for a short while before going up to bed. One evening, I overheard her husband say that we looked like lost sheep out there. She soon put him right.

'I'm not 'avin' them traipsin' their mess all around t'house all day. How am I goin' to keep it clean, tell me, if they're under me damned feet all t'time?' His reaction was a short grunt, to which she snapped, 'Aye. An' you can bury your head in th' paper, but I have to manage t'house. Clean and cook and laundry an' all. Won't hurt them softy Londoners to toughen up a bit.' She snorted. The blacksmith seemed to know better than to argue.

One evening he came into the rear dining room, sat by the table and opened his newspaper. I looked across to see the headlines: General Wavell was still advancing, chasing the 'Eyeties' out of Cyrenaica.

'A bit of good news at last,' Mr Hunter said, winking at me. 'Do with a bit of that desert sunshine here, couldn't we?'

As the days passed, the evenings grew darker and the winds became colder. Last winter, in the sanctuary of the Bakers' warm, friendly house, the white snow and cold mists had been fun. But what about this winter? Mrs Hunter wouldn't leave us outside in the snow, would she?

The following Monday, the teachers announced that they had moved from the vicarage to their own cottage and that we could come and see them after school if it was urgent. They added that a new Cub Scouts pack had been formed in the village and they hoped the boys would join.

I didn't take much notice of either announcement because

we were all too busy talking about Saul, who had suddenly disappeared. Aubrey said he had bunked off home through Aylesbury station. I was glad he had gone but his mother brought him back on the coach that Sunday. As soon as she'd left, Saul swore he would bunk off home again and became even more obnoxious, which made the evenings out in the yard yet more miserable. Then I remembered the teachers' move to their cottage.

Despite the offer, my teacher seemed surprised to see me standing on the porch early one evening. She showed me into their front room and left me in an armchair with some books and magazines. The arms were threadbare and the carpet looked worn but at least the room was warm. I was almost dozing when Miss Pizer brought me a cup of tea. I sipped it, staring at the fire in the tiny grate. Suddenly tears welled in my eyes and dripped into the tea. She noticed and, kneeling beside me, took the cup from my trembling hands.

'What's the matter, David?'

'Nuffin', Miss.' I sniffed.

'There must be something.' She laid a hand on my knee. I sniffed back my tears and wiped my eyes on my sleeve. And, once I started to talk, I couldn't stop. I told her about being shut out in the cold yard, the constant scolding, the hunger in the evenings and my fear of the coming winter.

As it all spilled out, Miss Pizer listened, her forehead creased. I knew they had placed me with the Hunters because they had had no choice. And there were probably even fewer alternatives now. Gradually I stopped weeping, wiped my eyes and stood up. 'Gotta go, Miss. Got to get back, Miss,' I muttered.

My teacher stood up too. What could she say? The bombs

were still falling every night on London. Going home was not an option. 'Listen, David,' she said. 'I help with the Cubs every Tuesday. Why don't you come along? All the boys enjoy it. And,' she added, '*it lasts the whole evening.*'

'Yes, Miss. I'll come next week, Miss, but please could you let Mrs Hunter know? She won't let me otherwise.'

'Of course. I'll drop her a note, David. It'll be fine, you'll see.'

As I ran home through the gloom, the icy wind hissed through the black hawthorn hedges and whipped at my bare knees. At the corner of the lane, I stopped and a sick feeling rose in my stomach: I'd have to face her soon. Perhaps, like Ziyder always told me, I should pray and God would listen. I looked around. I was quite alone but I didn't have my cap. Instead, making do by placing one hand on my head, I began to recite the *Shema*, breaking off in the middle to beg, 'Please, God, don't let Mrs Hunter shout at me for nothing. Make her kind and quiet – and let us come inside in the cold evenings.'

I continued the *Shema* as I walked along the dimly outlined roadway between the dark hedges: '*Ubelekhtekha baderekh*,' ran the prayer. 'And you shall remember it as you go along your way . . . and when you shall return . . .' But I didn't want to return. I wanted to stay with my teacher in her warm house.

At the first Cubs meeting, I copied the other boys as they crouched with their knees wide apart, pushing their finger-tips onto the bare boards, self-consciously muttering, 'Dib, dib, dib,' then jumping up, fingers by their ears, like wolf cubs, staring at the corrugated-iron roof of the old Scout hut. That struck me as silly but I liked the games and tying knots

– and learning about the forest animals, flowers and trees.

Miss Ives, a young woman from the village dressed in jodhpurs and a white sweater, took two of the Sixes, and Miss Pizer the other two, including mine. By the end of the evening, I felt as though I had always been in the group. I looked at the Sixer, with his deep green jersey and two yellow bands on his sleeve. If I came regularly, I could buy a Cubs jersey too, Miss Pizer said.

After the meeting, I could walk home two ways, each about the same distance. One would pass the vicarage, the other the back lane where the teachers lived. I chose the second way and, as I dawdled reluctantly homewards, was soon caught up by my teacher.

'Hello, slowcoach,' she said. 'You'll be late home at this rate.'

'Hello, Miss. Don't matter, Miss. The later the better for me. She don't know what time we finish.'

'Did you like it, David?' It was a still night. Our footsteps echoed together from the thick hedgerows.

'Yes. It was smashing, Miss. Really was. Glad you asked me, Miss. Thanks.'

'Oh, don't thank me, David. It's there for the boys to come. So we'll see you next Tuesday, then?' We had reached the gate to her cottage.

'Course, Miss. Wouldn't miss it for nothing. Night, Miss.'

'Goodnight, then. Take care.'

After three meetings, I became completely immersed in the activities. All the knots were simple, except the bowline – I couldn't get that one. Miss Pizer noted my enthusiasm and allowed me to stay late to help her clear up. As we walked homewards together a few weeks later, she asked me, 'How would you like to be a Seconder, David?'

My face glowed despite the chilly night. A Seconder. Me! I already had the green jumper and loved it because it kept me so warm. I paid sixpence a week for it from the spending money Mum had left with Mrs Hunter. She gave me the one silver coin every Thursday.

'I'd love to be one, Miss Pizer. Smashing. When can I get the stripe?' I could attach the gold ribbon myself: Mrs Baker had taught me to sew – and to knit. Last winter I had knitted a navy-blue T-shaped piece that she had made into a balaclava helmet, and a scarf that just grew and grew. She'd also shown me how to darn a sock, using a wooden mushroom.

'Not so fast,' said the teacher. 'I have to tell the pack first. Then Miss Ives can get the ribbon for you.'

We walked on up to her gateway, stopping once to listen to rustling in the roadside ditch. Soon I would be a Seconder – and perhaps, after that, a Sixer! I was overjoyed. My teacher could see how good I was at the knots and games but I was sure it was because she liked me. I convinced myself that no other boy talked to her like I did.

Despite the heavy rain and mud of December, I ran up to the hut every Tuesday and Thursday now, not caring whether it was for the Cubs, Miss Pizer or both. Afterwards, she would let me walk back with her, sheltering me under her big umbrella, listening to my chatter.

Young as I was, I fantasized. Perhaps, when she understood just how rotten to me Mrs Hunter was, Miss Pizer might let me come and live in their cottage.

In the pouring rain, I ran into the yard and round to the

back door, knowing that Mrs Hunter would moan about my wet clothes, but I didn't care any more. Miss Pizer would always help me. Suddenly I remembered that I'd forgotten to say my prayers on the road. I always prayed for God to protect me from Mrs Hunter as I walked home. I'd prayed yesterday, though, and anyway, now I had my teacher to protect me so perhaps I wouldn't need the prayers so much.

That night, I curled up in bed – head and all under the heavy blankets. I'd started doing that when the cold nights came to feel warm and cosy. I also felt so safe there; nothing could touch me. Nothing. I began to doze off, thinking of being made a Sixer. And, as my eyes closed, I saw the two golden rings of the Sixer's ribbons and, through them, my teacher's large brown eyes, smiling.

Chapter 20

The Cheese Bin

The first snow came in December. It didn't settle for long but the bitter north winds howling around the paint-shop eaves, together with the wet and slush, made the yard a wretched place. Around eight in the evening we were allowed back inside the house but it wasn't much better there. The three of us huddled around the dead grate in the back room, trying to conjure up some traces of warmth from the grey ash; Mrs Hunter wouldn't let us make up the fire again.

'You'll be in bed soon enough,' she would growl. 'Can't waste good coals on an empty room!' And that was that.

We sat on the hard wooden chairs in a semicircle, Saul with his feet up on the range. Mrs Hunter wouldn't half shout if she saw him; I wished she would. At the end of the long passage was the Hunters' front room where the family sat each evening with a fire – but we were not allowed in. I didn't understand her. She was a mother: my mum would never do such a thing – even to a stranger. When she had taken in Myer, the refugee, she was so kind to him. And this woman was being paid to look after us . . .

One evening, as we shivered, Aubrey muttered, 'Cor. I ain't 'alf 'ungry.'

'Yeah, me too,' I whispered, afraid that the woman might somehow hear from the far room. We shivered in silence for a few minutes.

'Could do with a big chunk of my mum's roast chicken right now.' Aubrey grinned, licking his lips at the memory.

'Yeah,' I added, 'with lots of baked potatoes and green peas.'

'Mmm.' The two of us smacked our lips.

'My mum does 'em with Brussels sprouts and thick gravy,' Aubrey continued, waving his hands. 'Makes your mouth water, don't it?'

'My belly's achin' jus' thinkin' of it,' I said, leaning forward and gripping my knees while staring into the bleak, empty grate.

The wind was moaning outside and a sudden downdraught blew a puff of white ash into the room. Saul swung his legs down from the range and dusted them off. 'Pack it in, you two,' he snarled. 'Bad enough feelin' 'ungry without you two natterin' about food.'

But Aubrey couldn't stop. 'Yeah, and for afters, a 'uge baked apple with raisings – and golden syrup in the middle.' He made a big circle in the air with both hands.

'I like my mum's bread pudden best,' I said. 'Lots of currants and sugar on top, mmm . . .' We giggled and, for a moment, I even felt warm.

Saul snorted. 'Cut it out, you two, or I'll clip your ears. Both of you.'

I hunched towards the dead grate again. No harm in talking, was there? Slowly the cold crept up my back and into my empty stomach while we sat on in silence, desperate to be allowed to go up and get warm in our beds. On some nights, the three of us played cards or Ludo around the bare kitchen table but Saul always cheated if he was losing. On other nights, I read and re-read my comics but often it was back to sitting round the grate, staring at the black iron bars and the grey ash and conjuring up a red glow in the lifeless cinders, as if it would help to make us warm.

Every few evenings, Mrs Hunter would appear in the doorway holding a blackened coal scuttle. 'Here. One o' you, move yersel' and fetch some coals for t'front room.'

We took it in turns to scurry out of the back door to the coal shed, load the scuttle with a small shovel and shoot back into the relative warmth of the kitchen, then through to the Hunters' front room. I would knock at the door. The Hunters and their two boys would be sitting around a huge open fire, the flames roaring up the chimney. In there it really was warm. A red patterned carpet covered the centre of the floor. I thought of the cold red quarry tiles where we sat in the kitchen.

Putting on my most pained expression I would hump the loaded coal scuttle to their fireplace, plonk it down and look around. No one would say anything – no thank you, nothing. James would watch me with beady eyes and red cheeks. Without a word, I would turn and slouch out, hating Mrs Hunter even more.

The cold evenings made us much hungrier – we weren't given less to eat. Sometimes Mrs Hunter would leave half a loaf and a bowl of dripping on the table. But only sometimes. I'd never tasted dripping before the evacuation and didn't like it at first, the greasy taste clinging to the back of my teeth. As the winter progressed, though, I was glad of anything to eat and actually came to like it.

One afternoon, as I was aimlessly wandering around the yard, I saw Saul shaking his fist at Aubrey over by the pigsties. Aubrey was clutching something behind his back.

''Ere, you little squirt,' Saul snapped. 'What you noshin'?'

'Nuffin',' said Aubrey, swallowing hard as he threw something away to his right. By chance it landed at my feet. It was a tiny piece of cheese rind.

'You can't eat that, you dirty pig,' shouted Saul, leaning over him.

Aubrey backed away, holding his arms over his head for protection. 'Jus' leave me alone. I'm starvin',' he whimpered. 'Leave me alone. It's better'n nuffin'.'

Saul lowered his arm as he saw me watching, then looked back at his cowering brother. Aubrey straightened up and poked out his chin. 'They delivered a new load yesterday. It's not that bad. You try it.'

As if colluding in a plot, the three of us crept up to the wooden bin and lifted the heavy lid. A pungent smell shot up my nostrils and made me blink. Aubrey was right. It was a new load and by chance there was a thick layer of cheese on the rinds, lovely yellow Cheddar.

Shrugging, Saul picked out a piece and smelt it. 'Hmm. Fresh,' he conceded, and I saw he was looking for an excuse to eat it. Suddenly, Aubrey's face broke into a smile.

'See. Told you.' He picked out a rind, broke its back, then pared away the cheese with his two front teeth.

'Like a bloody bunny rabbit,' jeered Saul, but soon he, too, was gnawing and I joined in. In the fading light, the three of us stood by the bin, gnawing and chewing for nearly an hour, then throwing the rinds back into the bin. At the end of it, I felt sick but my stomach was full – and I was warmer.

Saul closed the lid and leaned back against the bin, as if he was now in charge. 'Not bad. It'll do till we get home.'

I shot a querying glance at Aubrey.

Saul sneered. 'Huh. Don't think we're stayin' much longer in this bloody prison 'ole, do you?'

'Thought we weren't allowed back to London,' I said, puzzled and pulling the chin of my blue balaclava up to my mouth.

'Well, our dad is sortin' it out, that's what. And that old bitch,' he nodded towards the house, his hair dangling down to his nose, 'won't stop us, that's for sure.'

I stamped my feet to warm them and wondered whether it would be better or worse without the two boys. Saul was good riddance but I liked Aubrey and he was someone to play with. Maybe Mrs Hunter might not be such a cow if I was on my own. 'Cow' wasn't quite the right way to describe her, though. With her sharp chin, curling lip and rasping voice, she was more like a monster. Yes – that's what she was. A blinking monster!

The next afternoon, the forge was working late and I wandered into the old smithy. A shaggy brown horse stood motionless, one front leg bent double on the blacksmith's knee. Mr Hunter was shoeing Old Jeremy's horse in exchange for his help with the piglets.

The smith picked up a glowing red horseshoe in a pair of long tongs, tapped it on the anvil until it turned black, then pressed it onto the sole of the hoof. My nose twitched as the acrid smell of burning hoof hit my nose. Mr Hunter took away the shoe and glanced at the scorch mark on the hoof. Then, as he let the leg fall, he saw me. 'Hello, little 'un.' I watched as he pushed the shoe into the glowing coke, then picked up the leg again. With a short, curved knife, he pared away part of the hoof, then dug out the hollow part underneath.

I winced. 'Don't that hurt him, Mr Hunter?' I asked softly.

'Nuh,' he said, without looking up. ''E'd soon let me know if it did, I reckon. Don't you?'

I was still full of questions. 'That leg looks real heavy,' I said, drawing close.

'Treat 'im nicely, and 'e'll put his weight on the other three.' He dropped the leg again, his wide, weather-beaten face dripping with sweat. 'Animals knows you're 'elping them. More'n 'umans does, I reckon.' He paused. 'Feelin' fit?' He nodded at the bellows. 'Like to give me a hand?' I sprang across and grabbed the handle. Taking a deep breath, I pulled it down with all my puny weight, then let it spring up again, then again and again. Spurts of flame shot out of the coke and, a few moments later, the smith pulled a glowing white shoe out of the fire.

'That'll do for now.' He smiled. 'Plenty o' time to work when you grows up.' He placed the shoe on the anvil. 'Won't be so much fun then, I reckon,' he muttered, as he picked up a hammer and rained a series of light blows on the brightly glowing shoe. He placed it over the huge spike at one end and hammered it into a slightly smaller circle. As the metal cooled to a dull crimson, he fitted it on the horse's hoof again.

Instinctively I winced at the sound of searing and the acrid fumes but, this time, Mr Hunter seemed satisfied with the fit. He dropped the leg and threw the shoe into a nearby water trough. There was a hissing sound and a cloud of steam rose up into the blackened rafters. Then, taking the leg on his knee again, he placed the shoe on the hoof and hammered one of those square nails through the shoe and the hoof until it came through at the front. With a sharp twist of his wrist, he broke off the projecting tip and filed the end smooth, then continued all round the hoof. A small triangular lip on the shoe fitted perfectly at the front, like a toe. Then the smith neatly filed all around the shoe and the hoof until they looked like one piece. I stood there, fascinated, until he dropped the leg and stood up.

I'd already noticed that, as he worked, Mr Hunter wore the same totally absorbed expression as Dad had when he was finishing a new coat on the table – as though nothing else existed, just the piece of work in his hands. I recognized, even then, real craftsmanship and began to develop a deep respect for it, which remains with me to this day. Sometimes as I gazed over to the red glow of the forge and felt the moist warmth of the huge beast beside me, I dreamed that perhaps one day I might be a blacksmith – as well as a farmer – when I grew up.

At the next Cubs meeting Miss Pizer made me a Seconder and the following week I decided to make my way home with her and show her how I'd sewn the gold ribbon onto the sleeve myself. But as I waited for her, a soldier with corporal's stripes on his greatcoat sleeve strode up to the back door of the hut and went in. A short while later, he came out again, this time with Miss Pizer. She looked surprised to see me.

'David. You still here? Oh dear. I should have told you. I

won't be going your way tonight. It's getting late so you'd better run along now.'

'Okay, Miss,' I said, stepping back. 'Night, Miss Pizer.'

I sounded cheerful enough but I was heartbroken. As I trudged away, I turned for an instant and saw the two of them go back inside the hut. I didn't know whether the corporal was a brother or a cousin, but either way, he had been more important than me.

That Friday it snowed heavily overnight, and on the Saturday afternoon, Aubrey and I built a snowman. It didn't give us much joy. It was freezing and no one came to admire it other than Saul, who laughed at the coke eyes and threw a snowball that knocked off an ear. Snow covered the roofs and hung from the eaves. With little traffic to tamp it down, the lane was snowbound and the yard, too, had a thick carpet everywhere except on the trodden paths to the chicken run or the stalls. We stamped our feet and wandered around, seeking somewhere to keep warm. The blacksmith only worked now and again when a horse came for shoeing or he had to make harrow spikes, or repair some other implement a farmer brought in, so the forge was often closed, the great fire banked and cold.

Again and again my mind wandered back to the previous year at the Bakers', rolling huge snowballs and sucking icicles, safe in the knowledge that I could always run inside the warm house and dry my frozen feet, or forget the chill by helping Frank in the garden. Now, in the early dark evenings the icicles – Jack Frost's fingers – hanging from the shed roofs only added to the harshness of the frozen scene. My red nose dripped, in my wellies my socks were wet on frozen feet, and my fingers raw in damp gloves. All with no relief until nearly bedtime.

Aubrey and I resorted to the cows' stalls, burying ourselves up to our chests in the deep straw, while Joanna and Daisy chewed hay and stared at us with dark bulging eyes. But we couldn't stay there long: the straw was damp and didn't help much. So we hung around at the back door, hoping Mrs Hunter's conscience would prick.

Then, one evening, the back door flew open and her hatchet face poked out. 'If tha wants to get warm, tha can come inside and help out.' Aubrey and I didn't think twice. Anything to get into the warmth. 'And don't bring that muck and snow into t'house.' We slipped off our wellies and put on slippers that stood by the doormat.

'Right. If tha wants to stay inside, get stuck into them dishes, then.' A large pile of dinner plates stood on a wooden draining-board beside the stone sink. 'There's hot water on t'range – and don't go sloppin' it all over yerselves!'

I rolled up my sleeves and put some dinner plates into a large white enamel bowl that stood in the stone sink. Aubrey brought a kettle of hot water from the kitchen range and splashed it in.

'Here. Go easy,' I yelled. 'It's got to last for all them dishes.' Then I took up a small mop, dipped it into a china dish of soap powder and started to wash the plates.

Aubrey stood alongside and rinsed them under the running cold tap. Every few minutes, we both plunged our hands into the warm, soapy water, smiling at each other with the pleasure. Soon, however, all the hot water was used up but there were still three large baking tins lined with congealed white fat. Just then the woman barged in.

'Tha can leave those pots. Just get them knives and cutlery finished. Then tha can stay in t'kitchen till teatime.' My heart lifted and Aubrey and I grinned at each other. 'Just for today, mind you,' she added.

It was better than wandering around the freezing yard.

We dried our hands and sat quietly at the table, looking through yesterday's paper. It showed a large map of Abyssinia and, alongside, a report that British troops were driving out the Italians. It looked so far removed from the desert war in North Africa – or the Blitz – that I couldn't understand what was going on out there.

Sunday dawned with brilliant sunlight. It was still bitterly cold, though. Donald and Saul thumped into the yard, intent on going for a walk.

'Can we come?' piped Aubrey.

'Oh. All right.' Saul scowled. 'But we're not hanging about. If you can't keep up, that's it.'

I pulled up my baggy socks from the toes of my wellingtons for the umpteenth time and we trotted after the older boys across a ploughed field, then alongside a snow-filled ditch. I had never been that way before. After about an hour, we came across a large thatched cottage standing in some rough ground by a small wood. Where the snow was slipping off, the thatch showed grey and patchy and was hanging down at one end. There was no garden and straggly brambles grew against the walls. The door was made of wooden planks, bare timber showing through flaking blue paint. It looked deserted, but a thin wisp of smoke from the brick chimney at one end showed it was occupied. There was something creepy about the place but it was the knocker that grabbed my attention.

'Here, Aubrey. Look at that.' An old frying pan tied with binder twine hung from a rusty nail.

'Cor,' said Aubrey. 'Right dump. Who'd live in a place like that?'

Edging closer, we tried to peer through the heavily leaded windows but they were dirty and it was pitch dark inside.

Suddenly Donald, who was standing back, yelled, 'Look out, you two. It's the witch's house! That's her broomstick by the back door!'

The hair on the back of my neck bristled.

'An' that's her fryin' pan,' Saul cackled from behind me. 'Must be what she fries little boys in for dinner, like in *Hansel and Gretel*.'

Caught by surprise, we didn't stop to think. With a last, wide-eyed glance at the smoking chimney, Aubrey and I hared off across the field, not daring to stop until we had clawed our way through a thick, blackthorn hedge and stood panting on the far side.

A minute later, the two older boys ran up, laughing their heads off. 'You nippers didn't 'alf scarper!' Saul sniggered.

'Oh, God. My side's aching,' puffed Donald. 'Haven't laughed so much for years. Did you really think we've got witches out here?'

I smiled sheepishly, then both Aubrey and I burst out laughing, too. No. I didn't really believe in witches.

As we came into the yard, Mrs Hunter hurried out of the back door holding a pail. 'Here, you two. Tek this to t'chickens and geese.'

Aubrey and I grabbed it with one hand each and walked up

the yard. I didn't mind feeding the animals – in fact, I quite liked it. It was the way Mrs Hunter took us for granted and ordered us about that I couldn't stand.

'And don't be long bringing t'bucket back to t'house,' she called after us.

I scowled as she disappeared through the back door. When we brought the empty pail back, she took it from us and slammed the door in our faces. We had to stay out till lunchtime.

I looked at the closed door. No, I mused. That one back there wasn't a witch's house and there weren't real witches, but this one was as good as.

To pass the time, Aubrey and I began to throw snowballs against the paint-shop wall, then tarted up our snowman but, despite having heated up during our mad dash, we were soon freezing again. I consoled myself that I would see my teacher at Cubs on Tuesday and would tell her that we'd been thrown out again – and about the washing-up.

On the following Cubs night, I was dejected as I walked home alone from the meeting. In the brilliant moonlight, the trees and hedges were sharply outlined in black, white and grey, just like in the films Aubrey was always talking about. He and Saul had left abruptly the previous Sunday on the parents' coach. I was glad to see the back of Saul, but would miss Aubrey.

Mum had come on the coach. She said that I had to stay in the country because the air raids were still terrible in London. I would come home as soon as they were over, she said. I wished she could come more often.

It was a miserable week and to top it all, Miss Pizer hadn't been at Cubs and Miss Ives had taken the meeting instead.

She'd said I chattered too much and that she would take my Seconder's tapes away if I couldn't set a better example.

As I trudged along I noticed a large dark car by the teachers' gate, its blacked-out headlamps showing just a tiny slit of light, barely visible in the pale moonlight. On the porch, the corporal and my teacher were talking. My head spun. That was why she hadn't been at Cubs.

In the distance, a dog barked and another answered. I walked away as quietly as I could. When I glanced back, the tiny red tail-lights peered after me, like two angry eyes.

In mid-December, it snowed heavily again. I followed the fox and rabbit tracks across the white-carpeted fields. Blood-red berries shone from vibrant holly bushes. Soon it would be Christmas but, meanwhile, it was Hanukah. Rita appeared early one evening and took me round to the grandparents'. It was my second Hanukah away from home.

In the Suffolks' tiny room, Booba sat in the corner wrapped in a pink blanket. She watched us all with half-closed eyes, nodding from time to time as I haltingly recited the blessing, then lit three candles in the nine-branched *hanukiah*, two for the days of Hanukah already passed and one in the centre – the *shamash*. Already the second day and I hadn't even known – but I didn't tell Ziyder.

We turned out the light and sat in the golden candle-glow, singing '*Moaz Tsur*' – 'Rock of Salvation' – softly so that the Suffolks wouldn't hear. At the end, the old man kissed my forehead, then gave me two pennies for *Hanukah gelt*. I shrugged and made to refuse them, the cake penny still at the back of my mind. Ziyder sensed my hesitation and smiled. 'Hanukah, my angel. You must have *Hanukah gelt*!'

It was traditional to give money to children but, still anxious, I glanced at Rita. She just smiled, too, and I was struck by how adult she seemed.

I gave Grandma a peck on her cheek and giggled as Ziyder's beard tickled my neck when I kissed him goodbye. Rita saw me to the corner by the vicarage, then ran back to her billet, her footsteps muffled on the powdery snow. Looking back, I realize that, hard as it had been for me, it couldn't have been easy for my sister as she went through puberty, far away from her mother.

I carried on down the lane, wellingtons crunching on the snowbound road, ears tingling in the frosty night. Above, a halo glistened around the full moon. I stopped and looked back up the lane. Soon I would be at the Hunters' house. Making sure I was alone, I pulled my cap down firmly and began to pray: '*Shema Yisroel*... Please, God... *Adonoi Ehod*... Don't let her shout at me when I get in. Don't let her leave all the washing-up for me. Please, God.'

As I turned from the lane, the snow-covered roof of the silent forge shone in the moonlight, but the courtyard and the house were in deep shadow. Perhaps with Saul and Aubrey gone, Mrs Hunter would treat me better now that I was the only one. I hoped I could go straight up to bed.

Chapter 21

Jennifer

'I've moved yer things into Donald's room. You'll be sleepin' there from now,' said Mrs Hunter, when I came home from school a few days later. I wondered why she wanted my old room empty but didn't care: I got on well with Donald, despite the big age gap – I was just nine and he was about fifteen. Now, with Saul gone, he seemed glad of the company. On her last visit, Mum had brought a large bundle of comics, which made him even friendlier because I shared them with him.

We tramped over the snowbound fields together and he laughed at my attempt to make a bow.

'Not enough spring in hazel wood,' he said. 'Need a length of ash – though yew is best, but you can't take it from the one in the churchyard.' I asked why it only grew there. 'Its leaves are poisonous – and cows would chew 'em and die, wouldn't they?'

He had a store of country lore, and I was always happy to listen and learn. Donald helped me cut a stave of grey-barked ash and stretch a bowstring, and we made arrows of brown bracken stalks, tipped with elderberry stubs. His usually flew furthest.

He took me along a sunken, overgrown track lined with tall, ivy-covered trees.

'Know what this is?' he asked, pointing ahead. I shook my head. 'Well, it's an old Roman road, that's what. Runs dead straight, right over that rise there.' I became quite excited as I gripped my bow and pulled my balaclava down to my eyebrows, thinking it rather like a Roman helmet. At the top of the rise, the track broadened to a small clearing. 'And this,' said Donald, 'is where the chariots turned around.'

I imagined the plumed-helmeted and leather-skirted Roman soldiers with their shining breastplates, like I'd seen in my school book, and my stomach tingled. I was standing on the very ground that black horses had stamped on as they strained at the two-wheeled war chariots, waiting to go into battle. It was just a muddy track now.

Many years later, I looked at an Ordnance Survey map of the village. It showed that track as part of an old long-distance way to St Albans – the Roman Verulamium – so perhaps there was truth in Donald's story.

Donald's company distracted me from the bitter cold at the weekends but in the evenings he still sat with his family and I was alone. Trying to conjure up warmth from the black iron range, I waited impatiently for each bedtime to snuggle under the warm blankets.

One day, further snow fell during school time. On the way home I noticed the fresh tracks of a car down the lane and was surprised to see them turn into the Hunters' yard. Outside the house stood a long grey car with a model of a crouching leopard on the bonnet. I had never seen such a posh one in the village.

I stood by the gateway and watched as a compact, balding man in a fawn driving coat came out of the front door. He was followed by a woman in an ankle-length fur coat. She had auburn hair beneath a green plaid headscarf. They looked posh, too, like my Wembley uncle and aunt. As they poked about in the car, Mrs Hunter appeared in the doorway with a young girl. She had wavy chestnut hair, a round face and wore a maroon coat with white fur trimmings. As I walked into the yard, the man straightened up and turned to the doorway.

'So that's all fixed up, Mrs Hunter?' He spoke loudly, with an East End accent.

'Yes. Yes. That'll do fine,' she said, in such a soft, low voice that I wondered whether I was hearing the same person.

The girl touched her mother's sleeve. 'When will you be back, Mummy?'

'Next weekend, darling.' The mother kissed her cheek.

'Sure?'

'Sure as sure,' laughed the man, as he stroked her hair. 'And you'll be a good girl, Jennifer – I know you will.'

'Oh, I'm sure she will,' purred Mrs Hunter, just the way she had put it on when Mum and my teacher had first taken me there. Made me sick.

The two adults got into the car and slammed the doors. The girl leaned back against Mrs Hunter and the expensive car glided noiselessly over the packed snow. As it turned out of the gateway, an arm stuck out each side and waved. Jennifer waved back, and it disappeared up the lane, leaving a bluish haze in the air. I waited until Mrs Hunter and she had gone inside, then walked slowly round to the back door, my mind

295

full of questions. Who was the girl? Why was she coming to live here?

She sat with us all at the kitchen table for tea, then Donald and Mrs Hunter went out, leaving the two of us alone. I was tongue-tied and just smiled at her. In the end, she spoke first.

'Have you been here long?' she asked. She had pale brown eyes and I guessed she was a bit younger than Rita, maybe about twelve.

''Bout four months, I s'pose.'

'What's it like?'

I paused, wondering how much to trust her. 'So-so.' I used my mother's favourite phrase. 'Where you from?'

'Well, we were from London but we moved to Coventry after the war started. My dad's a furrier and now his workshop is making flying jackets all the time – or was.' She pulled a pink handkerchief from her cuff and dabbed her eyes. I felt awkward. 'Sorry.' She sniffed. 'It's all gone now. Last week, in that big raid. The whole city went – all in one night. Everyone just ran away into the countryside and they've only just started coming back. It was horrible. Horrible!'

I remembered the flaming warehouse over our shelter in Aldgate and felt really sorry for her.

'Well, not everything's gone, I suppose. Dad's workshop can be repaired, but all his stuff was soaked by the fire hoses. That's what Mum said, anyway.' She smiled briefly. 'Dad said she exaggerated but I don't know.' She was twisting the handkerchief between her fingers.

'Weren't you evacuated?' I asked. 'At the beginning, I mean.'

'No. Dad said the Germans wouldn't bother, apart from

London.' She paused. 'Mum said Dad forgot that there were all those big weapons factories around Coventry. I could hear them arguing about it.'

'What made you come here?' I asked.

'Dad went to your school in London when he was a kid and wanted me to go to a Jewish school.' The girl lowered her voice. 'Dad has to pay this woman. It's more than the government pays, Mum says. But we couldn't find a billet anywhere.' I nodded. That was just like Mrs Hunter. But with the mention of the school, I felt big.

'Here,' I said, excited, 'I can take you with me to school tomorrow.' I leaned over the table. 'How old are you?'

'Nearly twelve,' she answered, puzzled.

I thought for a moment. 'Some of the older children go to the village school.'

'I hope I don't have to.' Her eyes opened wide. 'I didn't like the kids in Coventry. I want to be with London children. And Dad wants me to be in your school.' She dived into a red purse that hung on a thin strap around her shoulder. 'See? I have a letter for the headmistress.'

That night, I thought about the new girl as I lay in bed. Perhaps we would become real friends. I thought how wonderful it would be to walk to school and back with her. Mrs Hunter wouldn't snarl at me and maybe Jennifer would help with the washing-up. Then I caught my breath. I wouldn't be able to pray out loud on the way home if she was with me. But maybe I wouldn't need to pray for Him to protect me from that woman.

Fresh snow fell again that night and bulged from the eaves as we left together next morning. I looked back at our two sets of footprints: mine smaller with pointed toes and Jennifer's broader, with chevron-shaped ridges from her crêpe soles. Like the rabbit and the hare, I was thinking, remembering Frank Baker explaining tracks last year. My face glowed cherry red and I blew clouds of steamy breath into the frosty air. The red pompom on Jennifer's woolly hat bobbed about as she laughed when I told my corny jokes.

At the church hall, I took her straight up to the headmistress. 'It's a new girl for our school, Miss Pizer.' All the children were looking at us and I felt really important. 'She's staying at my billet, Miss.'

The headmistress smiled down at me, then turned to the girl. 'What's your name, my dear?'

The girl handed her the letter. 'Jennifer Black, Miss.'

The headmistress seemed puzzled as she ran her finger down the register. 'Black. Hmm. I have a note about a Jennifer Schwartz.' She looked up and took off her glasses.

Jennifer blushed. 'Yes. That's it, Miss. My father changed our name when we moved from London, Miss.'

'Well. No matter,' smiled the headmistress. 'We'll soon clear that up.' She glanced at me. 'Thank you, David. You may wait outside while I take down Jennifer's particulars.'

'Yes, Miss.' I smiled briefly at Jennifer and ran out to tell the boys.

I didn't see Jennifer all that day and supposed she was in an older class that met in the store room behind the stage, before going to the village school. After lessons finished, I waited long after all the children had gone but she still didn't appear. Then my teacher came out, pulling on her coat. She stopped and smiled at me.

'Hello, David, still here?' She came up to me. 'It's quite late, you know.'

I was still peeved with her because she hadn't walked home with me after Cubs and I hadn't been regularly since. I melted at her smile. It wasn't her fault she had grown-up friends. I was just a nipper, after all.

'I'm waiting for Jennifer. We live in the same billet, Miss.'

Her face clouded. 'Oh. Jennifer. Of course. You wouldn't know, David.'

'Know what, Miss?' My stomach turned.

'She has to go to the village school,' she said softly.

'Why, Miss? Is she too old for ours?'

'No, David. You see . . . Jennifer isn't really Jewish and we can only take in Jewish children.'

'But she is, Miss. They lived in Aldgate – an' I saw her dad. And she says she is, Miss.' I began to grow indignant.

'Well, you see, David,' Miss Pizer brushed back the hair from her forehead with an awkward movement, 'her father is but her mother isn't – so Jennifer isn't Jewish.'

'But George was only half Jewish, Miss, and he came to our school, didn't he?' I had pinned my hopes on Jennifer and I being friends and walking home together.

My teacher saw I was upset and crouched down beside me. 'I know that, David. But George's mother is Jewish. And that's what decides it, I'm afraid.'

I bit my lip. 'But why, Miss? What's the difference? I mean, her dad wants her to go to our school and . . .' Nothing I could say would change anything. 'I'm sorry I brought her along, Miss, that's all.' I stared down at the trampled snow.

'It's not your fault, David.' She reached out and straightened my coat collar. 'The school board insists that all children have to go to the village school and we can only stay separate because we are a school for Jewish children.' She smiled down at me. 'Oh, by the way, I haven't seen you at Cubs for a while.'

'No, Miss.' I glanced around the snowbound courtyard, then looked up into her face. 'I'll come again after Christmas, Miss.'

She smiled again and smoothed down my hair. I slipped on my balaclava. 'Good. I'll look forward to seeing you there.' Then she was serious again. 'And, David, I'm sorry about Jennifer. Really I am.'

I rubbed my nose. ''S all right, Miss. Bye, Miss.' I ran out of the gate, my eyes moist.

At teatime, Jennifer and I talked a little but neither of us mentioned school. I felt she was still friendly but the common bond had snapped. With her there, Mrs Hunter let me sit in the kitchen and listen to the wireless, instead of throwing me out as usual. It was a forces' programme variety show with the Crazy Gang. I mouthed the words along with Flanagan and Allen singing 'Underneath the Arches', but it no longer seemed so funny to sleep underneath the arches. Certainly not in the winter: I knew now what it was like to be stuck outside in the freezing cold.

I giggled with Jennifer as Arthur Askey quipped, 'I thank yew,' and we both cackled loudly as Archie asked Susie, 'What did Horace say?' Suddenly Donald's hoarse laugh joined in. I looked round, surprised, as he came in from the passage and sat down. Donald wasn't usually in the kitchen after tea. As the show went on, I noticed him glancing at Jennifer and his presence began to make sense.

Next morning, it was the last school day before the Christmas holidays. I walked up the lane, kicking at the snow between the tyre tracks, my balaclava pulled over my face, leaving just my nose and eyes free. Only yesterday, Jennifer and I had laughed our way to school. Now I was alone. The village school started earlier than mine and there were just her bootprints in the snow ahead of me.

She hadn't said much at breakfast and my neck grew hot as I thought of yesterday, all the fuss over whether it was a father or mother who determined where you could go to school – the rabbi's stupid regulations. Once more my mind churned over the many dos and don'ts of our religious laws. In the frozen tongues of snow that hung from the bare hawthorn hedges, I saw my granddad's white beard and mournful eyes. Ziyder would have let Jennifer come to my school, I knew he would.

By the vicarage, the road to the village school branched off to the right. A few paces on, I turned and looked back down the lane. There were my wellington-boot tracks and her chevron soles side by side until they parted at the turning, Jennifer to go one way, I the other.

The Hunters killed a pig for Christmas. It was one of the 'barrow pigs' and I was amazed by how quickly they'd grown. I was also glad that I didn't know which one it was and felt a little guilty as it hung there in the paint shop, gutted, one eye staring straight at me. I had spent so many hours watching their antics to pass the time in the freezing yard. Each time I lifted the bin lid to take a few cheese rinds to nibble, they would run across the pen and snort, ears twitching, waiting for their share.

Donald helped Mr Hunter prepare the pig. Everything was

used, from snout to trotters, except, as Upton Sinclair wrote in *The Jungle*, the squeal. With so little meat on the rations, it was a real treat.

Donald carved the meat off the head from which Mrs Hunter made brawn, boiling it for a long time with some of the bones. It cooled into jellied meat and I loved the crunch of the stringy bits between my teeth. Even the long gut was washed out and cooked and, much to my surprise, I really enjoyed the rubbery chitterlings with thick gravy. Nothing *kosher* about any of that.

On Christmas Day there was no party like we'd had at the Bakers' – just a few decorations around the walls and a lot of food. I didn't mind. At least I could stay indoors, listen to the wireless and eat with the others for a change. For a few hours, I felt warm and full. It was as much as I wanted at the time.

But on Boxing Day I was sent out again in the afternoon, crunching over the frozen snow in the lane and watching the sun setting through the hazel thicket, a deep crimson ball that made the branches glow like a basket of fire. By the vicarage gates, I stopped and looked up the driveway. The lights were on, but the blackout curtains were not yet drawn. Through the large bay window, a group of people was standing by a towering Christmas tree draped with tinsel. It looked so cosy and warm in the rich yellow light, just like at the Bakers' the year before. I felt painfully alone as I stood there, my damp toes slowly numbing in my chilled wellingtons.

The sun disappeared and my face began to smart with the cold. I felt like the Little Match Girl, thrown out in the snow at Christmas. She had frozen to death. If I died of the freezing cold, I thought, Mrs Hunter might go to prison – or be hanged.

Serve her right. But as I stared at the Christmas scene, a woman in a long dress came to the window and drew the blackout curtains. The picture vanished and, like the Little Match Girl, I was alone in the cold winter evening. It seemed that no one cared.

On the way back down the lane, I began to pray. There was no one on the road and I called out, desperate, '*Shema Yisroel* . . .' I prayed that there would be no dishes to wash and that I could stay inside in the warmth. But, as always, God didn't listen to me.

When I came in through the back door, the wooden draining-board was piled high with plates and another heap stood on the small table alongside. In the stone sink there were blackened pots, pans and baking tins. I'd never seen so many dishes in my life. With no Aubrey, I would have to do it all on my own. Mrs Hunter didn't let Jennifer lend a hand and I guessed it was because her father paid so much for her to stay there. The previous weekend he had brought Mrs Hunter a pair of fur gloves and she had crowed all evening about how lovely they were.

As I wondered where to start, Mrs Hunter's grating voice came through the doorway: 'You can stop gawpin' and get stuck into it,' she fired off, as she brought in a saucepan of boiling water. 'An' there's another kettle on t'hob. If it's too heavy, you call me.'

I glared at her departing back and stuck my tongue out.

Dipping a rag into the soap powder I started on the plates. Over the weeks, I had become more skilled and the china soon disappeared from the sink, but the water in the bowl looked like milky coffee. I ran to the passage and called several times.

Eventually, she bustled in, took up the blackened kettle and poured fresh water into the bowl. Then she picked up two or three plates and looked at them.

'Hmm. Could do with bein' a bit cleaner, but it'll do for now.' She flounced out. As I stuck out my tongue again, she seemed to sense it. Without turning, she called over her shoulder, 'An' you can stop makin' them faces and get on wi' it. Won't hurt you to earn yer keep a bit.' Her voice trailed away down the hall. 'Ruddy mollycoddled Londoners!'

I was furious. She got ten shillings a week for me! And at nine, I was being made a skivvy! Leaving a load of cutlery to soak, I started wiping the plates with a dishcloth. I'd learned to put two plates together and switch one behind the other, drying the top of one and bottom of the other then switching them around. Now I tried three at once and it went fine until the middle plate fell out and clunked into the stone sink. It cracked, one half falling into the sink, the other onto the floor.

I'd broken a plate! Petrified, I waited to see if Mrs Hunter had heard. No one came. I picked up the two halves, crept out of the back door and buried them under some potato peelings in the dustbin. Tomorrow, I would retrieve them and throw them into the woods. Trembling, I carried on, scouring the pots with a brass pan scrubber, then finishing off the cutlery.

I had no idea how long I had been there but by now my shirt front and trousers were soaking and I was rigid with cold – the kitchen range had long gone out. As soon as I'd finished, I went straight up to bed.

I lay there looking through the dark window into the black sky. Why didn't God answer my prayers? Why didn't He soften the woman's heart and stop her scolding like he'd softened Pharaoh's heart for Moses? Why didn't He stop her making me wash up? No answer came.

The following afternoon, Rita dropped off a parcel of comics and a bar of chocolate that had come by post from Mum. I took them upstairs when I went to bed and tried to read as much as I could before Mrs Hunter switched out my light. Jennifer's parents had come to visit so she might be up late – and when she was up late, Donald stayed up late, too.

All the stories in the *Wizard* were about the war. Cricket captains had become officers. Jack Keen, detective, was hunting spies instead of dockland villains, and even the comic characters were being dropped by parachute behind Nazi lines or driving irate sergeant majors crazy instead of dodging cane-wielding headmasters. In the *Dandy*, only Desperate Dan carried on as usual, as did Laurel and Hardy in the *Film Fun* – but, then, they were in America, weren't they? As I read and reread the comics, I wondered what it was like to live over there. No war. No rationing. No evacuation. And no Mrs Hunter.

The holidays ended and, back in the playground, I sought out the boys with the latest issues to swap. Gerald had some *Beano*s. 'Swap you two *Dandy*s for them,' I said, and we did.

Just then Sammy sidled over. 'I've got this week's *Hotspur*,' he said. 'Easily worth your mouldy old *Wizard*.' But I knew he wanted it.

'Let's see,' I said, tucking mine under my sweater. I really wanted that *Hotspur*. It had the next instalment of that POW camp serial, but I didn't trust Sammy.

'Here,' he hissed. 'Wan' it or not? Bernie's got a *Rover* to swap me if you don't hurry.'

'Let me see yours first.' He showed me the cover and I knew it was genuinely this week's. 'Okay,' I whispered. 'Let's swap.'

Just then the second bell sounded and we trooped into the hall but neither of us noticed the headmistress by the doorway. She saw the coloured covers being waved about and, with three short steps, confronted us and snatched the comics.

'You know you're not to open comics in the line or in class,' she snapped. 'Wait here, both of you.'

We stood to one side, sullen and dejected, ignoring the smirking boys as they filed past.

'Your fault, David,' scowled Sammy. 'If you hadn't been so bloody suspicious, we'd never had 'em copped. I'll thump you if I lose that *Hotspur*.' I looked at the wood-block floor, choked, wondering which would be worse: a thumping from Sammy or losing my cherished comic. But the headmistress wouldn't destroy them, surely.

Just then she came back. 'You know the rules. No comics in class!'

'Yes, Miss Pizer. But we weren't in class, Miss. We were puttin' them away. And my mum only sent it yesterday,' I added mournfully, laying on the anguish. The headmistress didn't seem impressed but she must have known how much those small things from home meant to us.

'Well, I'll give you both one more chance. They stay in my desk for today. If you are well behaved in lessons, you can have them back when you go home.' It was the longest day I ever had to endure.

After classes, we hung around the doorway but Miss Pizer was in no hurry. Eventually she called us over.

'This will be the last warning.' She wagged a finger at us, then lifted the lid of her desk. 'Off you go, then.' We grabbed our respective comics and scampered out of the hall – probably leaving her with a faint smile on her lips.

Sammy and I made the swap, then I dawdled down the lane in the fine drizzle that had followed the thaw. Droplets of water hung from the brow of my balaclava, but I was so engrossed in the *Hotspur* that I was unaware I had passed the gateway until I turned the page.

'Crikey!' I gasped, and spun around to run back to the house.

Mrs Hunter must have seen me through the front-room window. The front door flew open as I ran down the yard. 'Never you mind about dawdlin' down t'lane reading silly comics,' she called. 'You get home late again and there'll be no tea for thee, m'lad. That's for sure.'

'Sorry, Mrs Hunter. The teacher kept us in today. That's why I'm late.'

'Well, no doubt you deserved it. Just hurry up and get yer tea. Then you can finish them dishes.'

I kicked off my wellingtons and slipped into the kitchen. Jennifer had already eaten and was in her room. I sat down at the table and spread a thick layer of dripping on a slice of bread and continued reading my story. Suddenly I heard Mrs Hunter coming. Hurriedly, I stuffed the comic up my sweater and grabbed the slice with both hands just as she entered.

'And you can sweep out yer room. It's like a pigsty,' she nagged. I must have left a sock on the floor. Even when the room needed tidying, half the mess was Donald's but she never said anything to him.

The next day after school I hid in the cow stall with a slice of bread and dripping from tea. Mrs Hunter wouldn't come out to look for me here and I would have peace until suppertime. Daisy stood by the manger chewing hay but Joanna lay on the straw, her chest heaving, her breathing irregular, her hip bones poking through the taut skin. Did animals fall ill? Could you give them medicines to make them better? I was stricken by the cow's plight, her misery seeming to mirror my own.

Chapter 22

Song of the Nightingale

Whenever it was not absolutely freezing, Mrs Hunter didn't need to throw me out of the house: I took every opportunity to make myself scarce in the hope that someone else would do the washing-up. Sometimes it worked but usually it was there for me to do when I got back. That was how the second plate got broken.

I had progressed now to wiping three plates at once – the more you held in one hand, the quicker it went – and for a time it worked. But that day it didn't. Two plates fell out and smashed on the Hunters' quarry-tiled floor. This time, I didn't have time to hide the pieces before Mrs Hunter stormed in as I stood with the wet cloth in one hand and four broken pieces of plate in the other.

'Them's not the first you've smashed!' she screamed. 'I been wondering where t'others were. Now I know, you clumsy dolt!'

I cowered back against the sink and folded my skinny arms over my head, fearing she would hit me. I waited like that for what seemed ages, my mind whirling. If she hit me, I was thinking, it would leave a mark and I could show the teachers. Then they'd believe everything else I'd been saying about her.

She'd be sent to prison and they would have to find a new billet for me.

Opening my eyes, I saw her hands clench and unclench. Then, without a word, she turned and stalked out into the passage. I continued with the washing-up. Perhaps if I broke a few more, she wouldn't make me do it again – but her screams and wagging hand had terrified me. The next time I broke one, I put the halves carefully between two other plates and set them at the bottom of a pile on the dresser. She was bound to notice one day, but at least it would put off the evil moment.

The washing-up was like a recurring nightmare. If I washed up, I could stay indoors. If I didn't, I was outside. On frosty days, it was best to be warm but I began to grow more careless with the drying-up. Mrs Hunter had a complete dinner and tea service – white with brown and blue rings around the rim and four sets of blue and brown dots – but they were becoming fewer as the plates slipped through my small soapy hands. Looking back, I reckon there could not have been more than half a tea service left by the time I went home.

That night in bed, the rings and dots of the plates' pattern swam in front of my eyes. She had deliberately switched off the light early. I slid under the covers and curled up to keep warm. January had been a rotten month: bitterly cold, Mum hadn't come and, worst of all, I'd nearly lost a new comic. I wished I could be like the squirrels and stay curled up for months, only waking in the spring.

February came in rainy, miserable and still very cold. The first snowdrops peeped through the bare black soil around the chicken run and I wondered how the fragile white bells withstood the fierce winds and frosts. I waited impatiently for spring, to be able to wander through the woods and fields without getting frozen stiff. February was a hungry month, too. The cheese-rind lorry hadn't come for weeks so the bin was empty and hunger gnawed at me.

Occasionally when hungry, I went round to Rita's billet. She always managed to bring me a slice of bread and dripping or margarine to the back door. When Mrs Roebuck asked what I was doing there, Rita made excuses. She couldn't tell her why I really came round. Although her billet lady was quite kind, we thought she might snitch to Mrs Hunter. When we were both older we used to joke about her secret 'back-door' offerings. At the time, she didn't know how much they meant to me. They showed that she cared. Although from my teens I grew much taller than her, for Rita I always remained 'her little brother'.

At other times, I went to the teachers' house. Miss Pizer still welcomed me but I knew now that I wasn't special to her. Now there was just the quiet room, the flickering fire and occasionally something to nosh. The magic had gone. But at least it was warm. Much later, I learned that she and her sister had had quite a hard time managing disputes with the village school and foster-parents, and eking out their rations while striving to remain *kosher*.

Once or twice I went to see Granddad Ziyder. The old man seemed too concerned about Grandma to talk much. And all the time I was with him, there was the rustling in the passage as that huge bulk listened outside the door.

All that winter, raw-kneed and shivering in my shorts, I felt terribly alone. I wondered what I had done wrong and why God didn't help. Day after day, making sure that no one was near, I walked down the winding lane back to the billet, cap or hand on head, and prayed. But it brought neither response nor respite from the bitter north wind – or from Mrs Hunter's scolding tongue.

The evenings gradually lengthened into March and I noticed yellow crocuses under the front window in the yard. On the first really sunny day, I wandered up to the lake and sat on a grassy rabbit hill. Around the water, new bulrushes were sprouting amid the tattered brown stalks, and bright green grass shoots were pushing up through last year's withered stems.

After the previous week's storms, it was strangely quiet – only the shrill *keewit, keewit* of the returning green plovers flying over the nearby meadow. They quickly settled, then probed the sodden turf, their cheeky black crests bobbing over white necks. I wondered where they had been all winter.

On the lake, three mallard drakes circled a dowdy brown female, the sun glinting on their iridescent green heads while rings of water spread to the far side. I looked across the still water and beyond, up to the hills and the camouflaged monument, and into the pale spring sky. 'I will lift up mine eyes unto the hills, whence cometh my help,' ran the psalm we'd learned at school. But no help had come for me that terrible winter, despite all my praying. I had got through it – but by myself. And from that moment, I began to doubt whether God was there at all. And if He wasn't, there was no point in praying.

At night, I continued to look for the telltale orange glow over the skyline from my bedroom window. In the past few weeks, I'd seen it less often – perhaps the air raids were petering out. And if they did, we could all go back to London. But in the watery sunshine, as I watched the plovers wheeling and settling, and smelt the freshness of the new grass, the feeling I'd had the previous summer came back: I wanted to stay in the countryside.

I pulled some dried grass and twisted it into a plait. Going home would mean getting away from Mrs Hunter, but would return me to the old rules – dreary Saturdays cooped up in long services at synagogue while outside the sun shone and there was a world to explore.

A wood-pigeon called from the charcoal branches of an alder tree. I looked up towards the hills again. The distant monument pointed, like a huge finger, into the sky, to heaven. If God really was there, He would be watching me, wouldn't He? I looked down to the silvery waters of the lake but they, too, reflected the sky. Ziyder said God was everywhere, that He knew even your secret thoughts.

I once imagined God to be like Granddad, only bigger: a kind old face with a white beard and soft, forgiving eyes. But He hadn't helped, no matter how many times I'd prayed. No, God must be more like my strict father: a florid, angry face but with a dense beard, forever demanding more and never forgetting when you did wrong.

A light, crisp breeze ruffled the still waters and blew over the reed beds. I stood up and stamped my feet, then broke off a thin branch from the alder and swish-swished it against the bare hedgerows as I walked back to the billet. At the top of the lane I stopped. Every day I used to pause there to start my prayers – and every day it had done me no good. Again, I felt that if He'd allowed me to suffer like that there really couldn't be a God at all.

So, at that tender age, God and I were parting company. I didn't leave Him – He'd left me. Whether the disenchantment had started with the taste of bacon and my defiance of Hebrew laws or my growing attachment to the countryside and a different way of life, I shall never know.

Now, as I stood there, the breeze freshened and tossed the tops of the elms. I shivered – but it wasn't from the chill: as I started to walk down the lane towards Mrs Hunter, I decided that I wouldn't pray any more. Ever. Yet I was so used to mumbling my prayers along this stretch of the lane, I found I had to say something else. Words became tangled in my mind and I played with the prayer 'Hear, O Israel', which I usually muttered. Instead of 'The Lord is God, the Lord is One', I said, 'There is no God, the Lord is None.' I glanced around as the words echoed in my head: 'There is no God. There is no God.' And, as I walked on, I whispered the words to the rhythm of my footsteps: 'There is no God. The Lord is None . . .'

At that moment the strengthening wind brought the sound of distant thunder. Was God answering? To cover the blasphemy, I recited, 'March winds and April showers bring forth May flowers,' in time to my feet tip-tapping on tarmac as the first raindrops fell on my face. I broke into a run down the lane and charged in through the gateway, straight around the house and in through the back door.

The next day, the rain had cleared and it seemed like real spring. As the days passed, I stroked the pussy-willow buds by the brook and watched the moorhen add extra branches to its nest on the pond. Bright yellow hazel catkins shed pollen at every touch and the woods would soon be full of bluebells.

After the rain, everything smelt clean and fresh. Now that I could stay out and away from the house, I hankered less and less for London.

I knew that spring had truly arrived when I woke very early one April Sunday morning. It was still silent in the house and pitch dark outside. I could hardly make out the window frame, but through it came the clear notes of birdsong. I guessed it must be a nightingale.

I'd heard it last summer in the late evening. With the last twitterings of the starlings on the telegraph wires and the cows lowing, I'd had to strain to pick out the song that Frank Baker had pointed out. Now, in the silence of the inky morning, the song was as clear as if the bird were in my room. I swung out of bed and silently twisted the cockspur catch so that Donald wouldn't wake, then opened the window.

With the rush of cool air came the smell of dew-damp grass as I rested my chin on the sill and gazed into the blackness, listening. The joyful song came from the direction of the willow thicket by the brook.

As I listened, a wood-pigeon cooed, then other birds joined in. The dawn chorus drowned my lovely nightingale, and she was gone. A faint grey light glimmered over the end of the garden and, as dawn broke, I quietly closed the window and dived back into bed.

After tea that day, I went out along the brook. I thought that if I walked very slowly and softly perhaps I would see the nightingale. Of course I didn't, but there were other signs of spring: the three-toed footprints of the coot in the mud where she had been probing for food, yellow marsh marigolds and pussy-willow buds. I was so absorbed that I lost all sense of the hour – and not for the first time. As the sun sank, I realized how long I had been out and ran home, only to find Mrs Hunter standing in the yard, hands on hips and scowling. Beside her stood Rita.

'So, there y'are,' she barked. 'Yer sister's been lookin' everywhere for you. Where y'bin?'

'Nowhere, Mrs Hunter. Just in the spinney along the brook.'

Rita was angry too. 'Didn't I tell you I'd call for you today? We're going to the grandparents, for *Pesakh*, aren't we?'

'Sorry,' I stammered. 'Just forgot, Rita.' I knew she had arranged for us to spend the first night of Passover, *Seder*, with them but it wasn't the first thing on my mind. What boy of nine remembers appointments? That's what mums and older sisters are for.

''Bout time y'learned to remember summat, lad.' Mrs Hunter snorted.

Rita suddenly seemed to realize that her own anger would get me into trouble and softened her tone. 'Well, no harm done, Mrs Hunter. We've got time.' She had on her new green velvet dress, a hair ribbon and gleaming white socks. As usual, she made me look such a scruff. 'Come, David,' she said, 'get changed and we'll go.'

I ran up to my room where Mrs Hunter had laid out a clean shirt, pressed shorts and my navy pullover. She always made such a show to Rita, my parents or the teachers. Through the window I saw the sun was just setting, but it wouldn't be too late. Ziyder never started the *Seder* night until the first star had come out.

* * *

Pesakh – Passover – was when the Angel of Death had passed over the Israelite houses during the Ten Plagues in Pharaoh's Egypt. In our house in the East End, as in many others in the neighbourhood, there were weeks of preparation beforehand: buying matzos and jars and packets of food labelled 'Kosher for Pesakh' by the court of the chief rabbi. From the top of the kitchen cupboard, Mum would take down crockery and cutlery that had been wrapped in brown paper and was used only once a year in Passover week. The cutlery would be washed in salt water to make it *kosher*.

Before the start of the festival, every household would get rid of its bread, often to the non-Jewish children from Cable Street. They would come round carrying small metal pots and shouting, '*Hometz! Hometz!*', the Hebrew word for leavened bread. Our mothers would give most of them a stick of firewood and a piece of coal, a strange custom that was repeated every year. I often wondered how those kids knew when it was *Pesakh* and where they had learned the Hebrew word.

I enjoyed *Pesakh*, not only for the feast and sweet wine on the first night but because I loved matzos – thin, crispy flatbread made with flour and water, no yeast, in remembrance of the Israelites' hurried flight from slavery in Egypt. Mum wasn't keen on them because she felt they didn't give me enough nourishment. So, early on the first morning of *Pesakh*, she would wake me to give me a huge bowl of cereal and bread and butter before the eight o'clock deadline – while I was eagerly waiting to crunch the matzos.

Now, this evening, as we walked up the slope to the close, I was a bit anxious, wondering whether Ziyder would notice that I had forgotten some of the *Seder* prayers and, worse, whether he would ask me if I still prayed at night. What would I say? He was wise and sure to know. I loved him so much that I had resolved to tell him one day how I felt, how the prayers to God had never helped me through that terrible winter with Mrs Hunter and hope he would understand. But not just yet.

Rita knocked at the faded green door just as the sky darkened. I stood close to her as a rustling came from the other side, expecting to be confronted by Mrs Suffolk. Instead it was Ziyder, dressed smartly in a grey waistcoat, white shirt and striped trousers, with a white *couple* – skullcap – on his head. He smiled and put one finger to his lips.

'*Gut yomtov*,' happy festival. 'Come in, *kinderlekh*,' my children. 'The Suffolks have gone to the pictures in Aylesbury,' he said.

Rita kissed his cheek and wished him good *yomtov* and, as he bent down and kissed the top of my head, I also greeted him. When we turned into their tiny room, I was surprised to see Booba – I'd got used to her being ill in bed most of the time. In a long maroon dress and white headscarf, she was standing by the small stove and stirring a pot.

Rita went to help lay the small table and I sat on a stool in the corner, hands under my thighs, staring at the starched white tablecloth on which lay plates of chopped almonds, a burned egg and other small dishes of *Seder* specialities. There were also red boxes of Rakusen's matzos and a bottle of deep red Bozwin wine, all 'Kosher for Pesakh'.

Ziyder saw me wondering where all the necessities had come from. 'Your father brought it all a little while ago.' He smiled. '*Shlepped* it all the way from London.'

He went out to the front door and checked that a few stars

were out. Then Booba lit the candles and the four of us sat down at the table, each with a small *Hagodoh* prayer book. It told of how we were slaves in Egypt but that, after God sent the Ten Plagues, we were set free to leave; when Pharaoh's army chased after us, they were drowned in the Red Sea.

Ziyder read and we joined in from time to time, sipping from the four glasses of wine. A traditional fifth glass stood full at one side, ready for the prophet Elijah who would bring the Messiah. I looked around in the flickering candlelight at the dingy yellow distempered walls, the heavy blackout curtains. There were just the four of us in that miserable little room in the midst of a country village and I recalled *Seder* nights from before the war at Ziyder's house with all the family, the extended table, the noise, the heat, the singing and jokes, and felt homesick.

I followed the service in my *Hagodoh*, which had an English translation alongside the Hebrew on each page, interspersed with medieval woodcuts – Egyptian soldiers in armour and helmets, Israelites in long robes and strange hats. I could see my turn coming, when, as the youngest, I would ask the traditional four *Mah Nishtoneh* questions. At the appointed moment, I started reciting the: 'Why is this night different from all other nights, that we eat only matzo, that we lean at ease, that we eat bitter herbs?' and so on, halting now and again, having forgotten much of it. But Ziyder prompted and encouraged, and at the end he patted my head, saying how well I'd read it.

Then came the long second half of the service, Ziyder reading out the answers at length: matzo recalled that our ancestors had had no time to leaven the bread, that we relax as a sign that we are no longer slaves but free men.

But the old man wasn't free. He and Booba were at the mercy of those vicious Suffolks and cooped up in this grim room.

Ziyder continued the service in a long singsong. This was the time at home when, having sipped too much wine, I usually fell asleep, only to be wakened when the meal was served at the end. Tonight, though, Ziyder read through it quickly, halting only to stand and recite the traditional curse: 'Remember what Amalek did to you!' Calling for God to strike those who had persecuted us, the old man's voice quivered with anger, the wine glass shaking in his hand. He must have been thinking of his brothers and their families in Poland. The full horror of the Holocaust was yet to be revealed but we knew something of how the Nazis treated Jews.

At home, just before eating the meal, it was time to open the street door and recite the traditional prayer for 'all who are needy to come in and eat'. And if the prophet Elijah was out-side, he, too, was welcome.

Ziyder nodded to me to go to the door. I sat up, surprised. Here? In the village? To open the front door? He smiled and nodded, his small, pointed beard glowing in the candlelight. Dutifully I went out, opened it and stood there as an owl hooted from behind the house. What if the villagers opposite noticed? But Ziyder was insistent so I waited there for some minutes, staring up into the star-studded sky. But there was no Elijah, no needy strangers, only a meteor streaking across the vault then vanishing.

Rita came and called me in. Relieved, I shut the door and we sat down to the meal of chicken soup, matzos, potatoes and chicken, which Booba had cooked and now bustled around, serving from the pot on the stove.

After the meal, Ziyder read from the Song of Songs and I tried to follow the translation: 'For lo, the winter has passed, the rains have gone . . . the time of the nightingale has come and the song of the turtle-dove is heard in the land . . .' Yes, spring had come and the biting cold of the Hunters' yard was over. And, as we sang and prayed, we heard the drone of heavy bombers overhead. Wellingtons, I guessed, getting our own back on Berlin.

It was after nine when we finished and got up to go. Kisses all round. Ziyder pressed a new threepenny bit into my hand.

'You shouldn't,' Rita said to him. 'You need it.'

He just smiled. 'I should need it? It's *Pesakh*. And David looks such a *mensch*. Why not? Buy yourself some sweets after *Pesakh*, my *yingeleh*,' he said, and patted my head.

We went out and the door closed behind us. As we walked down the slope, arguing voices came up the other side of the road: the Suffolks. The thought of them going back into the house almost spoiled the whole evening.

As it was so late, Rita came with me to explain to the Hunters, but only Mr Hunter answered the knock.

'Sorry it's so late, Mr Hunter,' she said. 'We've been with the grandparents.'

'Oh, that's no trouble,' he said, then grinned at me. 'Well, you certainly look a bit smart tonight, little 'un.' He added, 'Didn't know you had such a young lady for a sister either, did I?' Rita blushed as she said goodnight.

He went in and I stood alone in the darkness. There was hardly a breeze. Just then, from the thicket by the stream, came the soft, trilling notes of the nightingale: 'For lo, the winter hath passed . . .'

Chapter 23

A Song from Home

The following Sunday, Mum came on the coach. She brought a few comics and lots of nosh. I hugged her close, but now that it was no longer freezing cold, I didn't want to trouble her about Mrs Hunter or the washing-up: with the warmer days, my misery had faded into the past. I could get away from the house to wander the fields and woods, which took the sting out of my domestic chores.

As we walked up the lane to Rita's billet, I plucked yellow primroses from the roadside banks and presented Mum with a posy – my gift from the country, I said. She kissed me and laughed. She said there were fewer air raids, so perhaps I could come home after *Pesakh*.

Spring had indeed come but fierce winds roared through April, almost as though winter had returned. I mooched around the yard in my wellies and long brown overcoat and again took shelter in the cow stall, watching the breath steaming from the animals' huge nostrils. Over the door, rainwater dripped from the overflowing gutters.

Now Donald spent much of his time with Jennifer so I was alone again. Once, I had thought that the divide was between the evacuees and villagers. Now I felt differently. She was inside the house because her father was paying the Hunters extra. Another thought occurred to me: perhaps she was inside the house because she wasn't Jewish and I was out in the rain because I was. Granddad said we were God's chosen people. Chosen? I remembered Issy's comments on that Southend beach just before the war: 'Chosen people. Huh. Chosen for trouble, that's what.' Everyone had laughed but now I decided it wasn't funny in the least.

With the returning cold came the hunger again. The cheese bin was still empty and there were no Brussels sprouts in the back garden either. On the last day of the month, knowing I would be starving later that evening, I went round to see Rita straight after school.

'Good you're here, David. I heard from Mum today. Dad's coming this Sunday.' She handed me the letter, which I stuffed into my coat pocket to read later. 'And Mum sent some sweets.' She tried to straighten my hair, then went back into the house. When she returned, she had Mum's presents and, in a small paper bag, a surreptitious slice of bread and margarine. In her white blouse and navy-blue gymslip, she looked so neat and tidy – and so much older than me. 'I've added my sweet ration, David,' she added. 'I don't need it, really.'

I didn't refuse, grateful that she believed my tales of woe. 'If you're sure?' I touched her arm and stepped back. 'Thanks, Rita. See you on Sunday.'

Rita was with the gentle Mrs Roebuck and went to the high school in Aylesbury so I felt a bit envious of her – she was having a much easier time than me. After the war, she told me about Mrs Roebuck's own strict rules and about having to take the bus each day to a school where she was the only Londoner and had no friends. She hadn't had it easy at all.

I waved goodbye and ran home down the lane. The rain had stopped, but heavy clouds still scudded across the sky. On the verges the grass lay flattened and silvery wet from the storms. Dad was coming on Sunday and I wondered whether he would take me home, now the raids had eased. He hadn't been to the village for ages. Why now? And if he asked whether I was praying, what would I say? I couldn't tell him I'd stopped – I daren't.

Sunday dawned still and grey but the sun was trying to break through. Mrs Hunter made me put on a clean shirt and pressed shorts, and gave me Cherry Blossom polish to clean my shoes.

'An' jest keep out them puddles till yer sister comes,' she ordered. I knew she would be as nice as pie to Rita.

At midday, Rita hurried through the gateway while I was kicking at the dead bracken by the forge door. 'Sorry I'm late. Dad had to come by train – there weren't enough people for a coach.'

Mrs Hunter came into the yard, wiping her hands on her apron. 'An' how are you, m'dear?' She smiled.

I felt sick.

'Fine, Mrs Hunter, thank you.' Rita smiled back. 'Can David come now?'

'Of course.' The woman nodded at me. 'Tried to keep 'im a bit tidy.' As we walked away, she called, 'You'll bring your father round, won't you?'

'Yes, Mrs Hunter. Later on.' I scowled as we went out onto the road. Two-faced witch! 'Where's Dad?' I asked, as we walked up the lane.

'He's gone to see Booba and Ziyder first, but he left a parcel. It's salt beef sandwiches for you and me.'

My mouth watered all the way up the road.

When we got to a grass bank opposite Rita's billet, Rita disappeared into the house. I sat down and glanced behind me. There, through the bare hedgerow, was the cottage with the leaded-lights window! That was where we had heard on the wireless that Chamberlain had declared war. It seemed such a very long time ago.

Rita came out, clutching a sewn-up brown-paper bag – Dad made them in the workshop from old paper patterns. We sat and munched the thick red meat between slices of soft white *khollah* bread. It was a real feast.

'Pity we ain't got no mustard,' I said.

'Don't moan, David. Dad's *shlepped* them all the way on the train.'

'Did he bring any comics?' I asked.

'Yes. They're inside. We can collect them on the way back.' She wiped my mouth with her handkerchief – just like Mum did. 'Come, let's go round to Ziyder first.'

We didn't stay long. Booba wasn't well and my father had already been there a while. I kissed Booba's cheek as she sat in her chair. Ziyder kissed my head and gave me a penny. I prepared to refuse but Dad didn't say a word, just shook the old man's hand and kissed his cheek. We waved goodbye, and left. As we went down the path, a podgy hand twitched the grubby lace curtain at the adjacent window. I imagined those mean eyes watching, always watching, and shivered.

None of us was in any hurry to get to my billet. Rita didn't know the Hunters well and Dad didn't want non-*kosher* food

325

pressed upon him and, for me, the longer we could stay out the better. Luckily, the sun had broken through and it was quite mild.

'A quick cup of tea will do,' said my father, and I was surprised by his leisurely pace as he strolled along the lanes. At home, he always walked so fast – like he was still in the army. I lagged a step or two behind and let Rita do the talking, hoping to avoid awkward questions.

As we stopped opposite the stile, Dad pointed across the field. 'Isn't that where you first lived?' I hopped up onto the board. Yes, there was the Clarks' red-brick house and I could see my old bedroom window. Already it seemed like another world. The meadow had been 'Dug for Victory' into neat allotments.

I jumped back down and stepped into the road. Dad leaned back against the bleached timbers – short, stocky and ruddy-faced, dressed in a dark suit, white silk scarf and brown homburg – while Rita sat on the top rail. They chatted about the family, Auntie this and Uncle that. Cousin Pearl was in the WAAFs, Uncle Manny in the army in Iceland . . . Family talk reminded me of those dull, never-ending Sunday afternoons, with cups of tea and honey cake.

I walked across the road and sat on the grass verge. Sorrel grew by the hedge and I picked two leaves to chew. They'd been frostbitten and were red, but I liked the tangy acid flavour – though they were much tastier in the summer. A blackbird hopped down and picked up a twig in its sunlight-yellow beak. From the hawthorn hedge, where tiny green buds were bursting out along the dry branches, its mate sang with liquid notes.

Rita and Dad were singing – songs they had sung around the glowing candles of our Friday-night supper. This time

Dad, who used to sing in the Yiddish Theatre at the People's Palace in Whitechapel, was teaching her a new one in his rich bass voice. Line by line, verse by verse, he went over it and she repeated it, hesitantly at first, then again, before they both sang together – in Yiddish:

> *Oy, Freitig oif der nacht*
> *Er zits a Yiddesheh maideleh . . .*

A dutiful Jewish wife preparing the Sabbath meal . . .

> *Oy lokshen und yoich*
> *A bisseleh fleisch iss oi sehr git . . .*

Some tasty soup and a little meat . . .

Rita had picked up quite a lot of the language but I hardly knew any and didn't want to. It was old-fashioned and foreign, like Dad. On and on they continued, the doleful Russian-Jewish melody echoing between the shadowy hawthorn hedges and drifting up through the young oak leaves into the spring sky.

Sitting on the grass verge across the road, I was with them, yet trying to distance myself from them and the East End world they represented. At each cadence, I shrank back lest a villager come round the bend, mistake the Yiddish for German, hear my father's heavy accent, and rush to call out the Home Guard.

They sang on, engrossed, while I continued to glance up and down the lane, desperate to be free of my father's world, which was rapidly becoming alien to me. I sat and willed them to finish but they carried on, verse after verse, my sister eagerly learning the words, my father correcting her from time to time and she following lovingly. Their singing reminded me of the tedious rituals of our faith, and after just a year of evacuation, I was so in love with the countryside, the open space and the relative freedom that I wanted to forget everything associated with Dad's ways, to become completely and utterly English.

The afternoon was getting on. High above, hidden by the clouds, an aeroplane droned. In the treetops, rooks were calling. Rita jumped down and took Dad's arm and I walked alongside him, still wary, but he didn't ask any awkward questions.

Later, I guessed that he didn't question me because the Blitz had shaken everyone and now he was glad we were out of London. After Ypres, he'd never expected to see shattered bodies again but, as an air-raid warden, he'd helped the rescue teams to drag lifeless forms from the rubble. On top of that, his siblings and their families were trapped in Poland and now my brother, his elder son, was away in the navy. Perhaps he was thanking God that at least these two children were safe.

Mrs Hunter had laid on a high tea. I was amazed. I'd never seen such a spread there, except perhaps at Christmas. She'd even got out the large white starched tablecloth.

Dad had mellowed. He even took a cucumber sandwich and a piece of Mrs Hunter's fruit cake. He was probably praying for forgiveness but ate it all the same. I looked at the brown and blue tea service. There weren't enough small plates to go round, so she'd had to use some dinner ones. I'd probably have to wash this lot up after Dad had gone – the thought dulled the taste of her fairy cakes.

Mrs Hunter was doing most of the talking. Such a nice

boy, your son . . . What a healthy appetite . . . I choked on a sandwich. No wonder some might believe that my tales of woe were exaggerated.

Mr Hunter and Dad had found common ground over the war news.

'Well, the old Eyeties are runnin' for it in Abyssinia,' said Mr Hunter. 'Never could fight, them lot.' I had seen the first Italian POW farm workers that month. A telltale square green patch was sewn into the backsides of their brown trousers. 'Won't want their arse 'angin' out if they try to rip it off an' escape,' laughed Mr Hunter.

His wife frowned.

Dad took out his pocket watch and glanced at the time. He'd missed the train he wanted to catch. There was another two hours later but it would get him to London after dark.

'You'll catch the five o'clock bus, easy,' said Mr Hunter. 'Get you to town in half an hour.'

'I think I could get the train before, if I walk to the main road,' said Dad, then laughed. 'We old soldiers don't mind a short walk.' Over tea, they had discovered that in the last war they had been less than a mile from one another in Flanders.

Eventually, outside in the courtyard, the two men shook hands, my father short and stocky in his brown hat, and the blacksmith, tall, brawny and bareheaded, in an open-necked blue shirt and brown waistcoat. Town and country.

As we walked up the lane, Dad drew three deep breaths. 'Ah. A *mekhayeh* – such a blessing. Fresh air.' He looked down at me, then at Rita. 'Lucky you were out here all the time,' he said softly. 'Yes. Better you two were out of all that.' And didn't say any more.

We walked in silence to the green. Dad had decided to wait for the bus. Suddenly he bent down and kissed my head. 'Here,' he said, taking out a roll of Maynard's wine gums – my favourite sweet. 'Look after yourself, Dovidle, and visit Ziyder more. He needs company now that Booba is so ill.' I felt strange, being asked to look after my granddad. It had always been the other way round.

'I will, Dad. And thanks for the comics and the sweets. Kiss Mum for me.' I reached up and planted a kiss on his stubbly cheek.

The bus throbbed down the hill to the green.

In the grey evening, Rita kissed and hugged Dad and he patted her straight brown hair. 'Bye, Dad. Take care.' She wiped the corner of her eye. 'Tell Mum I'll write.'

Dad hugged us both again, then jumped onto the running board. A short wave, and he was gone. I felt a huge wave of relief. He hadn't asked me once. Not once. The bus drew away, chugged round the bend and we were alone. I walked with Rita to her billet. She went in, then brought out the bundle of comics and Mum's biscuits. 'Bye, David,' she said. 'Be good. See you soon.'

I noticed her eyes were moist. 'Ta-ra, Rita. See ya.' I turned and ran away.

The rooks had fallen silent and the clouds hung lower. Donald crossed the yard as I raced in. I waved the bundle of comics and he grinned. Perhaps he would be my friend again, like before Jennifer came. Dad's visit hadn't been awkward, and I felt relieved and warm inside. If only he was always like that . . .

My father's experiences that day didn't end there. Mum later told me the story.

330

Having caught a train later than intended, he arrived at Liverpool Street station well after dark. As he came out, the sirens sounded. Air raids were now sporadic but no less heavy when they happened.

With the sirens blaring, the buses had stopped and he began to walk up Kingsland Road just as the first bombs were falling. I suppose he should have looked for a shelter but he was so concerned Mum would worry – we had no telephone – that he just kept on walking to get home as soon as he could. It was a particularly heavy raid, so he dodged from doorway to archway after each bomb blast, trying to get ever further away from the docks and the City, hoping it would soon be over.

Finding a street-side shelter, he rested for an hour or so until there was a lull when he carried on – but it was only a lull. He lost any idea of the time until, just before dawn, the all-clear sounded.

He was resting in a shop doorway when he heard the clip-clop of hoofs and saw a milkman's cart coming along. Dusty, sweating and tired, he asked if he could cadge a lift. After such a night, the milkman must have been glad of his company and agreed immediately. Dad hopped on and went the rounds with him through the backstreets of Stoke Newington delivering milk until daylight, eventually jumping off at the police station to walk down the road to our house.

Mum said afterwards that he came in covered with dust and soot, his eyes red and his face virtually green. She said she wanted to tell him off for not staying in a shelter, but he looked such a *nebekh* – so destitute – she couldn't. Later 'Jack's night-time walk through the Blitz' became a family joke – but at the time, for him, it must have been truly terrifying.

331

Chapter 24

Facts of Life

In the school holidays, Donald, Jennifer and I had breakfast together, and one morning we found a hot cross bun each next to our plates.

'Not till after breakfast, mind you,' Mrs Hunter instructed – she couldn't give us anything without a condition.

The year before I'd had my first hot cross bun at Mrs Baker's and loved the taste of the sweet, spicy bread. I'd had no idea of its religious significance: Easter came immediately after *Pesakh*, both religious festivals having usurped the pagan spring festival. A year later I learned the truth – painfully. I was back in London when I spotted some buns in the bakery and I asked Mum to buy me one. The response was a light slap round the ear: 'Don't you know it's a *Yoysel* cake?' she snapped. The cross gave the bun its significance.

After breakfast, the three of us wandered up to the rabbit hutches together and I helped to pull grass and dandelion leaves for the rabbits. There was a new litter, said Donald, but all I could see was the ball of grey fur the doe had plucked from her chest to make the nest. Then the two went out of the yard together. I didn't follow. They didn't really want me with them, did they?

It was a fine morning, so I wandered out of the back gate and along the brook. Yellow flag irises waved in the soft breeze and sunlight rippled on the water. With the warmth and the burbling water, I soon forgot them. I was alone but, now that the weather was good, never lonely. In the country, there was always so much to see, hear and smell.

The next day was even warmer. After lunch, I wandered up the old Roman road, shooting arrows until I lost them all. When I came back to the yard, a flat-backed lorry with a sloping ramp stood by the cowshed door. Donald had said that Joanna the cow had been sick so I ran across and my heart began to pound. Had something happened to her?

A short, dark-haired man in a grubby flat cap was pulling a cable from a winch on the lorry and dragging it into the stall. I pressed myself against the wall outside as he reappeared.

'Right'yo,' he called. 'Make sure the loop's tight.'

'Okay.' Mr Hunter's voice echoed from inside. 'Take up the slack!'

The man jumped into the cab, engaged the winch gear and revved up the engine. I watched the cable grow taut.

'Right then,' came the voice from inside, 'take her away.'

The cable began to wind on the drum and, with a horrible scraping sound, the brown and white hind legs of the cow slid through the doorway, followed by her manure-spattered carcass. She had died then, poor Joanna. I'd spent so much time in her warm straw during that rotten winter and now she was gone. Yet, despite my sadness, I couldn't stop myself gawping at the blackened tongue hanging from the mouth and the glassy eyes as, slowly, she was dragged up the ramp onto the back of the lorry. The eyes seemed to stare at me, helpless, accusing. My stomach clenched and I had to turn away as Mr Hunter came out, wiping his face with a large red handkerchief. Unable to look any more, I hurried out of the front gate, across the road and up the track to the hay meadow.

April ended with more showers, so it was still quite cool and I was often still hungry after tea. One evening when I went round to Rita's back door to scrounge something to eat, she had on her coat and was about to visit the grandparents. Did I want to come? I hadn't been for some time so I walked with her to Rye Close.

She tapped on the side window and Ziyder's face appeared, then went away. A few moments later, the front door opened.

'Booba's not well,' he said softly. 'She's upstairs.'

As we walked into his little room, I wondered where the Suffolks were. The house was deathly quiet. Perhaps Rita knew they were out and had deliberately timed the visit.

'Just making something for Booba,' said Ziyder, stirring a small pot on the stove.

'I'll take it up,' said Rita, 'and say hello at the same time.'

Just then, however, the front door banged and heavy foot-steps sounded from the passage. The Suffolks were back. The stove flame flickered as the door was thrown open to reveal the scraggy figure of Mr Suffolk. Behind him, in the shadows, loomed his wife.

He stalked into the room, leaned over the old man and flung an arm towards Rita. 'Who let them in, without us knowing?'

'I'm sorry, Mr Suffolk, but you weren't here . . . and the children came past. That's all.'

The man glanced at his wife, then turned back to Ziyder.

'We said before, ain't we? Anyone comes in, we want to know before. Right?' He wagged a finger in the old man's face. 'It's our house and don't you forget it.'

The old man spread his hands. 'Of course, Mr Suffolk. But it was just the children.' He waved his arms weakly at Rita and me, trying to apologize. I sat on my hands, trembling, hoping that that was the end of it. Suddenly the woman pushed past her husband. The room seemed to shrink to half its size. She bent over the table and picked up a white enamel jug, her enormous backside pushing into my face.

'What's this doin' down 'ere?' she snarled, and held it in front of my grandfather's face.

'I've just brought it down to get hot water for my wife. She's not well, in bed. I'll take it up in a minute.'

The woman raised her voice. 'No, you won't. You'll take it up right now. I've told you before, things upstairs stays upstairs and are not carted all over the bloody 'ouse.' She pushed the jug into his hands. 'It's not the first time neither – but it'd better be the last!'

Not to be outdone, the husband sprang across the room to the oil lamp, his jerky movements those of a ventriloquist's dummy, his wife pulling his strings.

'An' jest look 'ow 'igh that wick is! You'll smoke the 'ole 'ouse out for us.'

How could they shout at an old man? Everyone in the village liked Ziyder.

Meanwhile, Rita had turned to the woman. 'It's all right, Mrs Suffolk,' she said. 'I'll take it up straight away.' Her voice was firm as she took the jug from the old man. She seemed to have grown suddenly and didn't seem scared like I was. 'My grandmother's very ill. We didn't want to disturb her. That's all.'

The man snatched the jug back from her. 'You keep out of it,' he ordered. 'She's talkin' to 'im, not you.'

Rita spun round, her face flushed and her eyes wide. I could see that she was losing her temper and I squeezed deeper into the corner.

'Leave him alone!' she shouted. 'He's old and Grandma's sick.' She put her arms around Ziyder's shoulders and started to cry. 'Just leave him alone.' She turned to Mrs Suffolk and said, 'You want their money, but you won't let them live in peace.' The old man's lips were moving as if in prayer, his eyes closed.

Mrs Suffolk leaned towards Rita, her face even redder. 'This is my house. Don't tell me how to run it.' She straightened up, shaking her solid fist at Rita. 'Just clear out. The both of you!'

I sprang out of my corner. Scared as I was, if she hit Rita, I would kick her shins. Rita wiped her eyes on her coat sleeve and glared at her.

'I'm not leaving him alone with you two bullies. It's his room. He pays you the rent, doesn't he?' She stamped her foot, her hair falling over her forehead. 'You're wicked, both of you,' she screamed.

Mrs Suffolk's wobbling cheeks turned crimson, her lips twisting into a sneer, showing her discoloured teeth. I stared at her hands, her fingers clenching and unclenching, and I trembled as I tried to hold back my tears. Poor Ziyder.

Suddenly Mr Suffolk stiffened and looked towards the door, his eyes staring as though he'd seen a ghost. In the doorway, huddled in a white blanket, stood my grandmother, her eyes puffed and swollen, her face deathly white.

'*Voos vils deir?*' she mumbled in Yiddish. 'What do they want from us?' Her eyes flitted from one to the other.

Ziyder went towards her. 'Leah. Go back to bed. Please. You shouldn't be down here.'

'No, no. I'll take her up, Ziyder.' Rita crossed to the door. 'Come, Booba.'

As she reached the doorway, Mrs Suffolk threw out one arm and barred the way. 'Oh no you don't. I'm not 'avin' the 'ole family traipsin' all over my 'ouse.'

'But she can't get back up on her own,' Rita insisted. 'She's very sick. Can't you see?'

At that moment, Mr Suffolk took his chance to become 'the man of the house'. Leaning towards her, he growled, 'Don't you shout at my wife like that!'

I looked from one to the other and, as the shouting and crying began again, Booba flopped down on a rickety chair by the door. I thought she would fall off and ran to her, but Mrs Suffolk shot out her hand. 'You just get out,' she growled at me.

I raised my hands over my head, thinking she might hit me.

'Don't you raise your fists to me!' she screamed.

Rita gasped and stepped across as if to protect me, but the husband scurried after her and stood between us and Ziyder. 'Right,' he whinnied. 'Now you can clear out. Both of you.'

He and his wife came together and, with their combined bulk, edged Rita and me out of the room and down the passage. I caught a last glimpse of Ziyder's white, drawn face and the helpless look in his eyes. I flailed at Mr Suffolk's legs and waist but, scraggy as he looked, he was wiry. Lifting me by the waist, he opened the front door and pushed me out onto the path. A second later, the woman bulldozed Rita outside and the door slammed shut.

Rita and I hammered and kicked at it, leaving big black marks.

'Leave them alone!' I shouted. 'Leave them alone.'

Rita was hysterical. 'You'll kill them!' she shrieked. 'Murderers. She's sick. You'll kill her!'

I kicked again, yelling, 'Let me in. Let me in!' But my voice grew weaker as tears filled my eyes.

In the houses opposite, blackout curtains twitched. One door opened a tiny chink, but no one came to see; no one came to help. Gradually we tired. Our hammering grew weaker and eventually we stopped. Rita's hair hung wet and matted over her face. My head burned as though it would burst as I sat on the path and rubbed my bruised hands.

It was now pitch black; no moon, no stars. Within, the house was deathly silent. Around us, everything was silent too, apart from Rita's quiet sobbing and my sniffling. Then, without warning, the door opened and the man threw my coat and Rita's gloves onto the pathway.

'Take them with you and clear off,' Mr Suffolk snarled. Then it was quiet again, the silence of the country night, as though nothing had happened. An owl called from the meadow. Another answered in the distance. We stood by the gate and listened. The upstairs room showed a tiny crack of light, then that, too, went out.

Rita put a hand on my shoulder. 'Come, David,' she said. 'There's nothing we can do. They must have gone to bed.' I wiped my eyes on my cuff as we hurried away down the slope, feeling helpless – helpless to defend Ziyder and Booba from those animals. When I was big, like my brother, I'd come back and show them, the bullies.

The owl hooted again, its cry following us down the road, growing fainter and fainter as we walked back to Rita's billet.

'Wait a minute,' she said, and disappeared into the house. I gazed up into the shadowy, clouded skies. How could there be a God and that happen to Ziyder?

Rita came out holding a slice of bread and dripping. 'Here, David. You'd better hurry home.' She kissed the top of my head. She'd never done that before and I felt awkward but also, after the trauma, comforted.

'Thanks, Rita,' I murmured. Her eyes were hidden in the darkness but I knew she'd been crying. 'Bye.' I nibbled at the bread on my way down the lane, making it last.

A faint light glinted from a puddle. A thin crescent moon shone down through a gap in the clouds and in its arms the ghostly shadow of the old one. Staring at it, I seemed to see Ziyder's pale face. 'God helps if you pray to Him,' he always told me. But God hadn't helped, had He? Maybe if I prayed again for Ziyder, He would. Someone had to help.

I glanced up and down the lane. It was deserted. Placing my hand on my head, I began to pray: '*Shema Yisroel* . . . Hear, O Israel . . .' Just this once I would pray. 'Please, God, please help Ziyder and Booba – and protect them from the Suffolks . . .'

To this day, the image of those two heartless, bullying people looming over my granddad in the dingy room is as sharp as ever.

At the Hunters' gateway I wiped my eyes and blew my nose. It was very late and I would now face the other witch. Mrs

Hunter was hanging washing on a clothes horse in the kitchen when I came in at the back door.

'Sorry I'm late, Mrs Hunter.' I panted, as though I had run all the way home, my socks round my ankles.

I was about to tell her that I'd come from Ziyder when she said, 'It's pretty near your bedtime, so you may as well go up.'

I went to the foot of the stairs, dumbfounded. No scolding? Then I saw my green cap hanging on the newel post. She must have thought I'd come home from Cubs. What a stroke of luck.

I undressed and jumped into bed, still thinking about what had happened. Mum had written that the air raids had almost stopped, so perhaps my grandparents could soon go back to London, away from the Suffolks. Again I prayed for Booba and Ziyder, knowing that no one but God could help them.

Chapter 25

The Black Car

Throughout May, after school and at weekends, I was able to stay away from the house and roam through the fields. With the changing of the season, though, came memories of the year before and Mrs Baker teaching me flower names.

I often went to the lake and sat chewing a stalk of grass or sorrel and gazing out over the still water. I sometimes walked along the canal near the aerodrome and launched little boats made of twigs on the murky, still water, with sails of large, dried leaves. I wonder what the parents and teachers of today would make of a nine-year-old spending hours alone by such deep water with not a soul around. As far as I can remember, none of my schoolmates ever came to grief during our time there. Perhaps, left alone, we learn to take care of ourselves.

As for Donald and Jennifer, I didn't see much of them as she went to the village school and the two of them continued to go off on their own. I don't know whether Jennifer would have stayed with us for longer but when I came home from Cubs one evening, Jennifer's parents' sleek, grey car was parked in the yard and the Hunters' front door was wide open. Hearing raised voices from inside, I slipped behind a cart on the far side of the yard, wanting to know what it was all about. Mr Black's voice grew louder: he sounded furious. I heard Donald's name, then silence. A moment later, Jennifer came out with her mother, head down and gripping a crumpled handkerchief, her eyes puffy. They slipped into the back seat, where Jennifer slumped against her mother. A moment later her father came out, red-faced. He turned and glared back through the doorway, then marched around the car and jumped into the driving seat, started the engine and accelerated out of the yard and up the road in a shower of gravel.

At the time I imagined there had been an argument over money. Looking back, I remember that Donald and Jennifer had been spending quite a lot of time together, always giving me the slip, so perhaps things had got out of hand, Donald taking advantage of her. I never did find out. Either way, Donald looked quite sheepish for a week or two, after which we became more friendly again. He never mentioned her again and neither did I, as we wandered together again up the Roman road with our bows and arrows.

June came in, sultry and sunny, with fierce thunderstorms. Sometimes they caught me out in the fields and I ran home soaked to the skin. Mrs Hunter always let me in to change and dry out. I didn't thank her – I thought she was scared I'd get sick and she would be blamed. Yes, many times I really hated her for being thrown out in the cold, the scolding and the washing-up, yet I had to concede that the meals were always there, as were clean clothes and bedding.

The weeks passed: school in the mornings, Cubs now once a week, and, at every free moment, I was out in the fields and along the brook. Every so often Mum would come with the coach, though now she spent more and more time with the grandparents. I'd been scared to go back ever since that horrific scene with the Suffolks and met Ziyder occasionally, with Rita, when he was out for a walk. At night, the sky towards London was no longer tinted red over the hills: perhaps he and Booba would soon go home.

And me?

Ever since Easter, Miss Pizer had been preparing Gerald, myself and one other boy for the Junior County scholarship (now the 11-plus), giving us homework books with questions to answer. The problem was that, after school, I had nowhere to sit and write. I wasn't allowed to stay in the house after tea and was out in the fields or in the yard until nearly bedtime, when I was too tired to tackle homework. And if I hung about the yard, Mrs Hunter would always find a plate not washed well enough, coal to fetch, geese to feed or some other chore.

On fine evenings, I would take the book and a pencil and sit on the flat-topped stone wall around the churchyard filling in the answers. When it rained and I couldn't find anywhere dry, I sometimes went to the teachers' cottage and worked in their front room or kitchen. Even though they knew about Mrs Hunter and didn't doubt my tales, I didn't feel at home there. Perhaps they didn't want the other children to think I was getting special treatment.

Meanwhile the war news sounded better. The Italians had surrendered in Abyssinia and General Wavell was fighting them in the desert somewhere. Like last summer, though, and despite rationing and local Home Guard manoeuvres, the war hardly intruded into village life.

One night when Mrs Hunter was out at a neighbour's, Donald and I played Ludo in the back room until very late. Mr Hunter was listening to the wireless and we did, too. At the end of all the programmes, the wireless played the national anthems of all the countries fighting the Germans: France – I recognised 'La Marseillaise' – then Poland, Russia, Denmark, Norway, Holland, Czechoslovakia and the others. I liked the Dutch one best. It was so rousing, much better than 'God Save the King'. Then came the Victory sign – morse code for V – bom, bom, bom, boom. Bom, bom, bom, boom. Donald said it was for resistance fighters listening to that signal on secret radios in occupied Europe. There followed 'Goodnight' in all those languages. Later, after they joined the war, the Russian *Dobro notz* stuck in my memory.

On another evening, when we were alone, Donald twiddled the wireless knobs until we heard a strange, slimy voice in English: 'Jairmany calling. Jairmany calling . . .' It was the traitor 'Lord Haw-Haw' broadcasting his propaganda from Germany, telling of German victories, England's shortages – and 'Jewish profiteers making money from the war'. The two of us laughed, wondering how anyone English could really be on the German side. At the end of the war, he was captured, stood trial and hanged for treason – though it later transpired that he was Irish.

The next day, though, the wireless was less encouraging. Although Greece had been occupied, much had been made of the Royal Navy being able to prevent any seaborne attack on Crete. But suddenly Crete had fallen too.

'Bloody Jerry parachutists,' muttered the blacksmith. 'Thousands of 'em. Caught us nappin' again.' I looked at the map in the newspaper and tried to picture the sky full of white parachutes coming down over the village, German soldiers firing from above. You wouldn't be able to hide anywhere, would you? And German parachutists could easily be flown across the Channel! Suddenly the war seemed so close again. For the first time, I felt a bit scared.

By chance, the following Saturday, I was walking up the lane when Gerald ran past, eyes wide with fright, his mop of brown hair standing out in all directions. 'Just seen a parachutist comin' down over the aerodrome. I'm gettin' 'ome,' he gasped, and hared off up the lane. I looked over the trees. If there was an invasion, they would ring the church bells. But what if the Germans captured the church first to stop 'em doing that? I threw myself down under the hedge and lay still, staring towards the aerodrome, imagining more and more parachutes dropping and grim-faced men in field grey creeping through the orchards towards the village. They stuck bayonets in kids, didn't they?

A plane droned overhead. Then there was silence again, only bird calls and the skylark trilling out of sight overhead. Gradually I calmed down. Gerald was a right panic-monger. As I clambered out and dusted myself down, my sleeve caught in the hawthorn hedge and ripped off a button. I cursed. That would give Mrs Hunter another excuse to complain.

The following Sunday, Mum came down with the coach. I walked round to call for Rita and we went to the Suffolks' house.

'You won't want to come in, David,' said Rita. I was glad: I was afraid of what Booba might look like. I knew that whatever was making her ill was only getting worse. While Rita and Mum were inside, I sat on the grass verge on the far side of the close, outside Mrs Atkins's house. Her garden was a riot of flowers and her apple tree was covered with pink blossom. In the Suffolks' garden, yellow groundsel and dandelions poked up through the couch-grass and ashes. I picked a sorrel leaf – it was sharp and juicy. Just then a shadow fell across my legs. Ziyder had come out so silently I hadn't noticed.

I jumped up and kissed his rough cheek. He looked so frail and bent. The white stubble crept down his neck and up his cheeks. Usually he was so well groomed.

'Hello, Ziyder. Didn't hear you coming.'

'*Nu*, my angel.' He half smiled. 'We old people don't make much noise.' He stroked my head. 'And you have such a good colour in your cheeks today.'

'Must be the sunshine.' I smiled briefly and brushed back my hair. 'How's Booba?'

The old man sighed and spread his hands. '*Nu*. Not so good. Your mother says she should go to hospital for a while. They're arranging an ambulance tomorrow.' I looked into his eyes. They were red-rimmed and sorrowful. 'She will get better there,' he said. 'With God's help, she will get better soon.'

'Will she be there long, Ziyder?'

'*Nu*. As long as she needs.' He smiled. 'But don't you worry. You are young. You have your whole life yet. We are old. We'll manage.'

In the glorious sunlight, the old man's peaked cap cast a

deep shadow across his face. He laid a hand on my shoulder. 'Rita tells me you are taking your scholarship soon?'

'Oh. Yes. Next Tuesday.' I smiled up at him.

'Well. I'm sure you will do well. You're a clever boy.' He wagged a finger in my face. 'Don't waste your chance, my angel. We didn't have one. You can be something when you grow up – a doctor, a lawyer, a chemist. Your mother and father should be proud of you. They've worked hard all their lives. Worked hard . . .' He fell silent.

'Well, I do all my homework, Ziyder.'

'Good. It's the most important thing, learning. That, and good health.' He glanced in through the doorway. He looked tired, with sunken eyes. 'With health, and learning, my angel, you can do anything, please God.'

Ziyder always talked to me like a grown-up. Perhaps when I plucked up courage, I would ask him about God, prayers and religion. Yes, after the scholarship exam.

Mum and Rita came out of the Suffolks' house and, as the old man turned, he pressed a warm coin into my hand so that they could not see. I was relieved. I didn't want my mum lecturing me about taking money from him.

'*Nu?*' the old man asked, as they came down the path.

'So-so,' said Mum, but Rita's eyes were red and she looked away as the two of them talked softly in Yiddish. I knew they didn't want me to understand – Mum and Dad spoke Yiddish when they wanted to keep a secret. When they stopped whispering, Ziyder patted my head again.

'A real *mensch*, your son,' he said to Mum. 'A clever boy.'

'Bye, Ziyder.' Rita kissed him and I kissed him as well, before he shuffled back into the doorway.

'*Zay gezundt*,' he said, as he turned back with a thin smile. 'Goodbye, my children.'

I waved and he disappeared into the Suffolks' dim hallway. It seemed to swallow him.

Examination day dawned bright and cloudless.

'Looks like it's flamin' June for you, m'lad,' said Mr Hunter at breakfast.

I was surprised – astonished, even – that the Hunters knew about the exam, and even more so that Mrs Hunter was friendly. I'd put on the pressed grey shirt she had laid on my chair. 'An' y'ought t'wash that face properly for today,' she said, in a normal voice instead of her usual brusque tone, and bustled me to the kitchen sink. The scrubbing she gave me stung but I glowed afterwards. She also made me wet my hair and combed it.

Two other boys and I were the only ones taking the exam and I felt important as we were sectioned off on one side of the partition. Everyone else had to read or draw for the whole morning and they were cautioned to keep quiet.

The headmistress gave out the papers, then looked at her watch. 'Remember, don't waste time on the questions you can't answer. Go on to the next.' She paused. 'Right. You can start now.'

The first page had lots of little boxes and diagrams to compare and tick off where they matched or didn't, now known as IQ tests, I suppose. I'd practised these in Miss Pizer's home-work book and didn't find them difficult, but struggled with some of the arithmetic. For my composition I chose 'A Naval Scene'. With all the war news, photographs in the papers and my cigarette cards, it was easy. I soon filled two pages and could have done more. Then time was up.

'Didn't have time to finish, Miss.' I smiled as she collected the papers.

'Don't worry, David.' Her teeth flashed in the sunlight from the tall window as she smiled.

The three of us ran outside.

'Crikey,' said Gerald. 'Didn't know what to write about.'

'Couldn't finish those long divisions,' I said. 'Tough, weren't they?'

We swapped notes until the others came out, wanting to know what it had been like.

'You'll find out next year,' I said, feeling really grown-up.

I felt elated as I sauntered down the lane. In the clear sky, a few tiny cotton-wool clouds had appeared, reminding me of the shellbursts I'd seen over London; here, everything was so peaceful. A charm of goldfinches twittered in the hedgerow, balancing on purple thistle heads, so colourful with their flaming heads and golden wing flashes – just like the caged birds I'd seen down Petticoat Lane.

Post-exam excitement soon blotted out anything else, though. If only I'd had more time! I wouldn't know how I'd done until the results came out the following month. If I passed, I'd go to a grammar school, Miss Pizer said. Would Dad be able to afford it? Brushing the white cow-parsley heads along the verge, sending a cloud of seeds into the ditch, I ran into the yard. Mr Hunter was shoeing a large grey horse. Smelling the acrid scent of burned hoof, I forgot about the exam and ran over to work the bellows. Perhaps today he would let me help make the nail sockets on the spike he set in the anvil.

Luckily for the horseshoe, he didn't, and I had to be content with watching as he made the holes, then fitted the shoe.

The next day, white cirrus horsetails whipped a clear blue sky. It was warm and I ran to school without my jacket. I was a big boy – a scholarship boy. Green propeller seeds floated down from the high elms to the notes of a song thrush. I ran past the vicarage, excited. Although the papers were sent away for marking, perhaps my teacher would know how I had done.

At the first break, Miss Pizer called to me as we all ran out to play. 'David. Just a minute.' Her voice was hardly more than a whisper. 'Now, David, I'm not allowed to say anything definite, but the headmistress and I glanced at all the exam papers before we sent them off yesterday.' She smiled briefly. 'We think you did very well.'

My heart thumped. 'Can I tell my granddad, Miss? It'll make him really happy, Miss.'

'Well.' She paused. 'I suppose he can keep a secret . . .'

I smiled up at her. 'I'll go and see him straight after school, Miss. Thanks, Miss.'

It transpired that as I was a few weeks short of my tenth birthday, the result didn't count. I had to take the exam again the following year in London, but the experience served me well.

Miss Pizer didn't take my class in the afternoon and the headmistress had both classes together in a general-knowledge quiz. I was still excited about the exam and raised my hand to every question whether I was sure or not about the answer and laughed with everyone when I got one wrong.

Just before it was time to go home, Rita's billet lady Mrs

Roebuck popped her head round the door. The headmistress walked across to her and the two women had a brief muttered conversation. Miss Pizer turned and came towards me.

'David, could you come here a moment?' she said.

I tensed. Was it something to do with Rita? Had I done something wrong? All the children looked at me as I shuffled out to the front, head bent.

'I'll leave you with Mrs Roebuck,' said the headmistress. 'She has something to tell you in private, David.'

Puzzled, I followed the woman through the porch and out into the yard. Rita's billet lady looked a bit like the headmistress, with her brown tweed outfit and tight, grey hair. I hardly knew her. Why had she come for me?

'What's up?' I asked, impatient, as we walked onto the road. 'Is Rita all right, Mrs Roebuck?'

'She's fine.' The woman smiled. 'She's in Aylesbury with your mother.'

Then her face grew serious and immediately I thought that Booba must have died. She stopped halfway along the lane and turned to face me so I stopped, too.

'Now, David. Don't be too upset.' She put one hand on my shoulder. 'Last night – or early this morning – your grandfather passed away.'

'Grandfather? You mean Grandma,' I said, not wanting to believe what she'd said and thinking – hoping – she'd got it mixed up.

'No, David. Your grandfather, I'm afraid. Such a dear man.'

My stomach churned. Granddad Ziyder? It was Booba who was ill – she'd been taken to hospital. And I'd talked to him just a few days ago. My head whirled and I felt sick. 'Granddad?'

I said again. I shut my eyes tight. It couldn't be true. And just when I was going round to tell him about the exam, like Miss Pizer had agreed. I could never tell him now.

Tears were forming in my eyes but instead of real tears came anger – anger at the Suffolks. They'd made him die, hadn't they? They'd killed him. I'd run and shout it outside their door. I'd let the whole village know how cruel they'd been. I hated the Suffolks. Hated them. If only I were big enough to hit that horrible fat woman until she cried and begged forgiveness. I wanted to kill them both – murderers.

Shocked and angry, I caught only snippets of Mrs Roebuck's words: '. . . died in his sleep. Peacefully. The ambulance took him last night . . . no pain, the doctor said. And your grandma is still in hospital. They're taking her home to London . . .' Her voice continued as though from a distance, but I was hardly listening and we started walking again, up the road towards the close.

A long black car stood outside the Suffolks'. I hesitated. It might be a funeral car and I didn't want to see a dead body. I was truly terrified and a shiver ran up my spine. My aunt Fanny came out of the house carrying a large bundle of bedding. A tall driver in a peaked cap pulled up the boot and she dumped it in, then returned to the house. Booba's white blanket trailed on the ground and I breathed out. It wasn't a hearse, just an ordinary car.

Mrs Roebuck nudged my arm. 'It's all right, lad. Come.'

Auntie Esther came over from the car and hugged me, her black coat smelling of mothballs. The driver started polishing the windscreen and Auntie Fanny appeared again, this time with a box of cooking pots and utensils.

'Booba won't need all those,' said Auntie Esther.

Auntie Fanny humphed. 'I wouldn't leave that woman the drippings of my nose,' she said, stuffing the box into the back of the car.

I hung back with Mrs Roebuck until they'd finished. Then Auntie Fanny came over and hugged me. 'Oh, David. Poor Ziyder.' She kissed me. 'But we have to go now. Your mum's waiting for us at the hospital with Rita – they've been to see Booba. She'll be down here next week. Here.' She reached back into the car and handed me some comics with a packet of sweets.

In the house, towards the back of the passage, I saw the scraggy figure of Mr Suffolk. His wife was nowhere to be seen. Too bloody scared, I bet, too ashamed of what she'd done. Again the anger held back my tears but still I couldn't believe Ziyder was gone, that I'd never speak to him again, never be able to ask him all the questions that troubled me.

With the packing finished, both aunts kissed me and climbed into the huge black car. It rumbled away down the close and turned right at the road. Clutching the sweets and comics, I walked down the slope with Mrs Roebuck, hating everything and everyone – especially Him, who was supposed to be up there. He had done nothing for me at the Hunters' and now he had allowed poor Ziyder to be hounded to his death. Despite Ziyder being so *frum*, always praying – and all my special prayers – God hadn't helped him at all.

Mrs Roebuck walked with me as far as her house, then reached out her hand to shake mine and wished me well. Rita said she could be quite strict at times, but she had been so kind to me.

I walked away down the lane, not wanting to go back to school or to the billet but, as I passed the vicarage, kicking at the loose gravel, my teacher happened to come out of the gateway. I stopped and we looked at each other. Then she came over to me.

'Hello, David.' She smiled but her eyes were dull. 'Why so sad on such a sunny afternoon?'

At first I couldn't understand why she asked. Then I remembered that she hadn't been in school that afternoon. 'Just come from my granddad's, Miss.' Tears came to my eyes again. 'He died, Miss. He's dead.'

Her hand flew to her throat. 'Oh! I'm so sorry, David. I didn't know. When?'

'Last night, Miss. They came to fetch me from school.' Tears trickled down my cheeks. 'I just come from there, Miss.'

She put an arm around my shoulders. 'I'll take you home, if you like.'

'Don't want to go back there, Miss, not yet.' I sniffed. 'The Suffolks killed him, Miss. They did.'

She reached down and tucked in my shirt tails, then turned down my collar. 'Would you like to tell me about it, David? Let's find somewhere quiet, eh?'

We walked across the road and through the kissing gate into the meadow. 'Here,' she said. 'We'll sit on this bank by the hedge.'

I sat beside her. 'I was going to tell my granddad what you said about my scholarship, Miss. I wouldn't tell anyone else but he would have been really happy, Miss.' I sniffed. 'He was so miserable at the Suffolks'. They were rotten to him, Miss. Cruel, they were. No one knows. You ask Rita, Miss.' I told her everything that had happened that terrible evening. Miss Pizer's face paled. 'An' I wanted to talk to him, Miss. He was so kind. I had so many things to ask him, Miss. An' I never will now.'

A blackbird flew out of the nearby hedge, clucking its warning cry. The teacher looked up at it, then back at me. 'Well, you might find someone else to ask, David. You can talk to me, if you like.'

'P'r'aps I could, Miss, but . . .' the tears started again, '. . . but it don't matter any more, Miss. It don't matter no more.' The tears now flowed unchecked. I dropped my head on to her lap and the pent-up misery and anger burst out.

'That is very sad, David. So very sad.' She laid a hand on my back.

High in the elms, like black sextons, the rooks cawed, and a cow lowed from a nearby field. The sun was bright, but the air felt close and oppressive. Her lap was soft and warm, reminding me of the times I'd rested on my mum's lap when we rode home late on the tram. As a horse and cart clattered by on the road behind the hedge, I wiped my eyes with my cuff and sat up. She wasn't smiling as she usually was.

'Are you sad for my granddad too, Miss?'

She nodded and brushed back my hair. 'Yes, I am, David. But also because the vicar has just learned that someone he knew has been killed in action. And that's very sad, too.' As we both sat silently, I wondered whether that was why she hadn't been in school that afternoon.

The sun dipped towards a bank of heavy cloud that had formed and the air grew close and humid. My teacher looked down at me. 'Come,' she said, 'we'd both better be getting home, eh?' She stood up and smoothed down her skirt.

'Yes, Miss.' I pulled up my socks. 'Thanks, Miss.'

'Oh. Don't thank me, David. I was so glad to help.'

As she stepped over the ditch, I saw tiny green cleavers clinging to her light-blue cardigan. We used to throw them at the girls' hair.

'Half a mo', Miss. You got sticky-balls on your sweater.' She tried to look over her shoulder. 'Wait, I'll pick 'em off.'

She stood in the middle of the road while I reached up and pulled them off. 'That was very kind of you, David. Thank you.'

''S okay, Miss. 'S nuffin', Miss.'

Miss Pizer walked me to the gateway of the Hunters' yard. 'Will you be okay, David?'

'Yes, Miss. Fine, Miss.'

'Well, see you in school tomorrow.' As she walked away up the lane, she turned and raised her hand, smiling.

Clutching my comics, I walked into the yard and as I did Mrs Hunter appeared at the front door. She came towards me and I flinched, wondering what I had done wrong. But her eyes looked different. 'Sorry to hear about yer granddad,' she said. News travelled fast in the small village. 'Here. Come and have some tea, lad.'

I couldn't say anything. I was in shock as she touched my arm and led me in through the front door. The front door! I couldn't believe it – or the huge plate of sausage and mash she set on the table.

She sat opposite me as I ate.

'He was a nice old man was your granddad,' she said. 'An'

I know you must be real sad, lad. But it'll pass.' She gazed out of the window at the old cart by the smithy. 'You're young, lad. It'll soon pass.' Her voice sounded so strange – distant. I wondered whether I was dreaming, but the touch of her hand on my arm still burned. I looked at her sharp face and black eyes with a mixture of puzzlement and gratitude. She must have a heart, after all, Mrs Hunter.

The thick cloud brought darkness early that night. I went up to my room with the new comics, but I didn't feel much like reading them. I stood by the window in the gloom and opened it on one side. It was hot and close. I gazed up into the dark sky. God hadn't helped Granddad. Now I was sure He wasn't really there.

A raindrop fell on the sill, then another. From the distance came the low rumble of thunder. More drops fell, huge ones. I put out my hand. They were warm. I looked up at the dense sky again. Even the heavens were crying – weeping for Granddad Ziyder.

The next morning, Hitler marched into Russia.

Chapter 26

Goodbye, Skylark

The summer term was almost over; it was the last week of July. Stephen and Gerald had already left and the rest of the school was going home the following week. Mum wrote that the siren hadn't sounded for ages because all the German planes were over Russia. On Friday, a special bus would take us to Aylesbury railway station.

With the warm weather, after school and at weekends, I was often away from the house, alone and wandering the fields and woods, along the canal and around the lake, occasionally with Donald but mostly alone.

Despite the war, I felt content and that summer period has probably coloured my perception of the bucolic green English countryside ever since. I was doing what I liked and liking what I was doing, being at one with the natural world, with no grown-ups telling me what to do or where to go. It was a formative period that put the final seal on my love of the countryside and was instrumental in forming my character – a dreamer, thirsting to know everything about the world and, above all, a resourceful loner.

* * *

The last week of that term was the last week of my evacuation. Rita wrote a final letter to our parents, to which I added a few sentences and a small cartoon. School finished on a half-day on Thursday, but I didn't go straight home. Mrs Hunter had returned to her old nagging ways, although she didn't make me wash up any more – perhaps because of the empty spaces on her dresser.

It was a balmy day with high, hazy cloud and I wandered up to the lake for a last look. Yellow and blue dragonflies darted among the bulrushes. They looked so fierce. I whipped my head aside as one sped past, still not believing they couldn't sting. I rubbed the back of my neck; my hair reached down to my collar. 'You look like Lloyd George,' my father – who always had a close-cropped Russian haircut – would say disparagingly.

In flight, two mallard ducks glided over the alders and splashed into the water, feet first. It was the only sound in the vast green silence. I looked across the water and felt a twinge in my stomach. In a day or two, I would be beyond those hills with the camouflaged monument, back in smoky London.

At first I'd been so excited when Miss Pizer announced the departure date. Going home! Away from Mrs Hunter and home to Mum. Eating *choulent* and bread pudding and spending money at the corner shop. I'd be a secondary-school boy next term, I still thought, not knowing that I'd been just too young for the exam. Perhaps I'd have to go to school on a trolleybus. I'd find out where Ronnie lived and, cor, would we swap stories! I still had no idea that we would never meet again.

But as the day drew near, I began to think about the things I would leave behind: the smithy with its blazing forge, Donald's rabbits in their hutches, Daisy, my bow and arrows, the conkers and the hazelnuts. Above all, I would miss the greenness – and the silence where I could be alone with myself, yet never really lonely.

A cloud of gnats rose from the damp water's edge and hovered around my face. I stood up and waved my arms until they dispersed. Home. But when I got home, there would be the synagogue every Saturday with Dad, no wireless on Friday night – and the long prayers to someone I no longer believed was there. The gnats gathered again. I took one last look at the mallards with their glossy green heads, bobbing on the still water, then climbed down the bank to the road.

I went into those half-finished houses with their graffiti. Stumbling over the rough ground and half-bricks, and through the tall weeds that had grown right up through the joists, I climbed the rough-sawn stairs and stared at the pink plaster, now stained black with mildew, wondering what Ronnie was doing at that moment. Two sycamore saplings had grown up high by the walls but the pictures were still there – and the rude words. And I was still no wiser.

A plane droned overhead and, looking up, I recognized the high tail fin of a Wellington bomber. On the road outside a car purred by. I tensed. Someone might catch me gawping at those things. I hurried down the stairs and ran out.

I took the long way home, past the aerodrome. Airmen in bright blue uniforms, white shirts and red ties wandered up and down the road, some with bandaged heads, others with arms in slings – so many more than last year, when I had sat there with Ronnie.

360

* * *

After tea, Mr Hunter was still working in the forge. I watched him match some new horseshoes to an old one. The sweat glistened on his huge biceps.

'Dunno who I'll get to work the bellows now!' He winked at me. 'Shouldn't think you'll get much call for working bellows in Lunnon neither.' He laughed.

I grinned, then stepped forward, my face glowing in the fire's heat. 'Could I use the hammer a bit, Mr Hunter?'

The smith rested the hammer head on the anvil. 'Well, I reckon so. You ain't got time enough to do much damage.' He pulled a glowing yellow shoe from the furnace and held it on a spike set in the anvil socket. 'Right. When I nods my 'ead – you 'it it. The shoe, mind you, not my 'ead!'

I raised the hammer and let it fall on the shoe with a dull clink, my hand gripping the shaft near the head.

'Here,' smiled the smith. 'Don't strangle th'ammer, lad. Hold it down the handle – and 'it it like you mean it!'

I struck again. The clink was sharp and loud. The spike point poked up through the now red-hot shoe. He turned it over and nodded. I struck another blow and a small hole appeared in the centre of the square countersink. I'd made my first nail hole. The smith took the hammer, thrust the shoe back in the furnace and, smiling, nodded to the bellows. I jumped across, grabbed the handle and, with all my might, pulled it up and down, raising a roaring flame, while Mr Hunter finished off the shoe.

'Right,' he said, 'that'll do for tonight. Tomorrow is also a day.'

Yes, I was thinking, tomorrow is another day, but I won't be here.

That night I reread my old comics. The gallant Finns were still fighting the cruel Russian invaders but, on the wireless, the announcer told us how the brave Russians were putting up a great fight against the Germans. It was all a bit puzzling. How could a country change sides overnight?

Later, as I was going to bed, I looked out of my window for the last time to watch the sunlit tree-line darken to merge with the night sky and the stars come out.

The next morning, Rita called to help with my case. As usual, she looked so neat in her red dress, ribbon and white cardigan. I looked quite smart for a change, too, in an air force-blue lumber-jacket Dad had made for me and pressed shorts, with my hair wet and flattened on my head.

The Hunters stood by the gateway, said goodbye, shook our hands, then watched us walk away up the lane. I thought she seemed a bit miserable and wondered why. She'd be glad to get rid of me, wouldn't she? Or perhaps she was unhappy because she'd have to wash the dishes herself. But I was truly sorry to leave the blacksmith – Mr Hunter had been really friendly. So, just once, I turned and waved.

At Aylesbury station, there was the usual mad scramble for window seats but I managed to nab one. Smoke from the engine obscured the town until we were well on our way and soon we were rattling through the high chalk cutting in the hills. It felt as though we were crossing a border. Behind us lay a lush country landscape I'd come to love; ahead, the other world, black and smoky, where I was born but which I felt I now knew less.

At Harrow, we waited on the platform to change to the Metropolitan Line train. Children and teachers from other schools were there, while soldiers wandered up and down humping kitbags, rifles slung over their shoulders. By the waiting room, Fougasse propaganda posters looked down from the walls. On one, a man held a finger to his lips: 'Be Like Dad,' the caption read. 'Keep Mum.' Alongside, an orange poster showed two women chatting in a restaurant while, at a nearby table, a man in a raincoat and Hitler moustache was growing a huge ear: 'Careless Talk Costs Lives!'

A special red Metropolitan Line train came in. We scrambled for places, then tunkety-tunked along the rails, the telegraph wires swooping up and down, faster and faster, speeding through stations without stopping. Red-brick houses with snaking back gardens now hid the trees and fields, and the railway tracks grew from two to four, then six. Grey-backed, terraced houses closed in, and red and green lights winked from black gantries overhead.

On the left, wisps of steam rose from three gigantic concrete cooling towers. In the carriage, Miss Pizer sat across the aisle in a navy-blue dress and maroon jacket. She caught my eye and smiled, then turned to look out over the grey slate roofs. I wondered what she was thinking.

I began to feel drowsy and leaned against Rita's arm. My eyes closed and, from high above, the skylark's song floated down, rooks cawed in the elms over the vicarage red-brick wall and blue forget-me-nots bobbed in the ripples of the brook, as I dozed off.

The train began to slow down. I opened my eyes. High black walls closed in on either side. The huge boot of the 'Dig for Victory' poster flashed by. I would make an allotment in the back garden when I got home. I could grow fresh vegetables for Mum – I'd show 'em all how to do it. Perhaps I could make a hutch and keep my own pet rabbits.

The jolt of brakes shook me from my daydreams. Cases and coats banged around my ears. Rita nudged me onto the platform and we filed along and up the steps to the barrier, through a forest of waving arms and everyone shouting.

Mum waited in her black astrakhan coat and matching hat, her face freshly powdered. 'David, my love, my love. Dad couldn't come. He had to stay at work.' She clutched me to her, then leaned back. 'How tired you look – and your hair! We must get a haircut before *Shobbos*.' She hugged me again, then kissed Rita. As we clung to each other, Miss Pizer walked through the barrier ahead with the headmistress. I hadn't managed to say goodbye.

Mum stepped forward and touched her elbow. 'Thank you for looking after the children, Miss Pizer,' Mum said. 'And you too, Headmistress. Thank you, and God bless you both.'

As they shook hands, my teacher looked down at us. 'Oh, they were very good, really.' She tweaked my nose. 'Weren't you? So be good, David, and enjoy your new school.'

Only then did it hit me that Miss Pizer wouldn't be my teacher any more and I might never see her again. I wanted to say something, to ask her to write, to ask if I could visit her. Instead, I just blushed and mumbled. 'Bye, Miss Pizer. Thanks for everything, Miss.'

My mother tugged at my hand and we walked away, my socks round my ankles again. A few yards on, I turned to wave. Miss Pizer waved back. As my mother hurried me out through the archway, I glanced over my shoulder for one final look at her. At the escalator, she was with that soldier and he was carrying her case. She was smiling – a flash of white in the gloomy tunnel. Then she was gone. My eyes misted. I would never see that lovely smile again.

During my evacuation, so many things had changed and not only for me. Bombed out in the Blitz, like the school, the traditional East End community with its specific way of life revolving around the synagogue and the close family would disperse; many of the old ways would vanish for ever.

As for me, by the end of the war I'd become so used to being moved around that, later in life, I never felt rooted anywhere. Each move must have been traumatic and left its mark but, on the plus side, it enabled me as an adult to fit in wherever I happened to find myself, geographically or socially.

All we evacuees were probably deeply affected in one way or another. A famous psychologist once remarked that even as adults, he could distinguish an ex-evacuee from just a short conversation, as though we had been marked for ever.

We left the platform and, after taking the Circle Line, came up the steps at Liverpool Street station and out onto the pavement. As we waited for a 649 trolleybus, the excitement of meeting Mum and the homecoming began to fade. I was losing my lovely teacher and I was not going back to the country. I stared at the red blur of the approaching bus then half closed my eyes. From high above, beyond the dull grey buildings, the black roofs, and over the thunder of the traffic, it seemed to float down: the song of the skylark.